Ueda's NETSUKE HANDBOOK

1. TOBACCO POUCH AND NETSUKE. (Netsuke: ebony. 1 $^1/_4''$ long. Signed: Yokoya Somin. B 1107.) The pouch is made of gold brocade. The clasp, a gold peony in full bloom, is signed Shomin (B 1016) and has a kakihan (written or carved seal). The ojime is of solid gold in the shape of a shishi or lion-dog, which is sometimes called kara-shishi (Chinese lion) or koma-inu (Korean dog). The netsuke simulates the fushi and kashira used as sword furnishings (Fig. 8). It is made of ebony and decorated with representations of shishi. Both ojime and netsuke are signed with the name of Yokoya Somin and have kakihan. This is a good example of a netsuke carved by a master metal artist. See text, pages 113–14. *(See overleaf.)*

THE NETSUKE

HANDBOOK

OF UEDA REIKICHI

adapted from the Japanese
by RAYMOND BUSHELL

RUTLAND·VERMONT : Charles E. Tuttle Company : TOKYO·JAPAN

Representatives
For Continental Europe:
BOXERBOOKS, INC., *Zurich*
For the British Isles:
PRENTICE-HALL INTERNATIONAL, INC., *London*
For Australasia:
PAUL FLESCH & CO., PTY. LTD., *Melbourne*
For Canada:
M. G. HURTIG LTD., *Edmonton*

Published by the Charles E. Tuttle Company, Inc.
of Rutland, Vermont & Tokyo, Japan
with editorial offices at
Suido 1-chome, 2–6, Bunkyo-ku, Tokyo

Copyright in Japan, 1961
by Charles E. Tuttle Company, Inc.

Library of Congress Catalog Card No. 61–8739

International Standard Book No. 0-8048-0424-9

First printing, 1961
Seventh printing, 1971

Book design and typography
by F. Sakade & M. Weatherby
Layout of plates by M. Kuwata

PRINTED IN JAPAN

Table of Contents

List of Illustrations

Adaptor's Preface

UEDA's *Netsuke no Kenkyu* is the only comprehensive work on the subject of netsuke written by a Japanese, with the possible exception of the small Japan Travel Bureau Tourist Library volume by Yuzuru Okada. The fact is quite remarkable in view of both the exclusively Japanese origin of the art form and the growing literature on the subject from the pens of citizens of Germany, England, Holland, Sweden, France, and America. Herein lies my justification for "doing" Ueda's *Netsuke*. It is high time that the Western collector and student have an opportunity to see and appreciate netsuke through the eyes of a Japanese who was himself an enthusiast and collector and who did a considerable amount of original research into the subject.

By necessity, my work has been that of adaptor and not of translator. It is extremely difficult, if not impossible, to understand easily an English version from the Japanese of a book on art unless it is substantially rewritten. A mere literal translation of many parts of Ueda's book would be riddled with lost meanings. The rewriting consists principally of transforming that which sounds vague to the Western mind into clear and tangible phrases. To a lesser extent it consists of minor reorganizations of material and the elimination of some repetitions and irrelevancies. I hope that I have not done violence to Ueda but that I have, on the contrary, clarified his meanings for the Western reader.

A number of the netsuke illustrated in this book are unsigned. At least half of all those produced were not signed by their makers. The custom of carving the artist's signature is found much more frequently among the later netsuke artists than the earlier. Another group of the netsuke illustrated are signed by carvers whose names are not listed in the biographies that follow the text. The omissions, however, should occasion no surprise, since the number of artists who carved netsuke either as a profession or as an avocation probably approached ten thousand during the Tokugawa and the Meiji eras.

In the text of this book, Japanese personal names are usually given in the Japanese order: family name first, followed by the given name. In the case of artists, however, I have made an exception: the name by which the artist is generally known is printed first and followed by the family name; for example, Mitsuhiro Ohara. Textual references to the biographies are indicated by the letter B followed by the number of the biography. Thus B 779 is Biography No. 779: Nonoguchi Ryuho. This procedure has also been followed in the captions for the illustrations. The names of legendary and historical Chinese figures who served as subjects for the netsuke carvers are given in their Japanese versions.

A note on the spelling of certain Japanese names is also in order. In the old-style romanization, the sounds of *ka* and *e,* depending upon the characters they represented, were sometimes rendered as *kwa* and *ye,* with the result that names like Kaigyokusai and Ekisei were spelled Kwaigyokusai and Yekisei. Since such renderings are neither accurate nor any longer approved by the Japanese themselves, this book uses the modern spelling. To obviate any inconvenience to the reader who may be accustomed to the old-style spellings, the names of netsuke carvers involved in the change are cross-referenced in the biographies and the index.

The illustrations are those of netsuke from my own collection; none are reproduced from Ueda. Textual references to illustrations are also my own, as are notes and comments regarding the illustrations. Measurements of netsuke are given in inches and, unless otherwise indicated, refer to the height of the netsuke. Other explanatory notes will be found at the beginning of the biographical section.

Finally, I must acknowledge my indebtedness to those who aided me in the preparation of the manuscript for the book. My greatest debt is to my secretary, Mr. Yanagihara Katsuya, whose unstinting assistance made possible my work but deprived him of all normal hours of freedom. My previous secretary, Miss Inoue Toshiko, now happily married, was the ground-breaker and pioneer.

I also owe deep gratitude to Mr. Uchino Shoei, a calligraphist of scholarly level; to Mr. Ouchi Yasushi, who helped unravel many a puzzling point; and, last but not least, to Mr. Imai Kenzo of Kyoto, whose practiced eye and innate judgment are the marks of the true connoisseur.

Mr. Ouchi Jiro and Mr. Nakamura Tokisada, whose respective *noms d'artiste* are Sosui and Masatoshi, are almost the last two carvers in the old tradition whose technical information is always reliable.

I am sure that multitudinous errors will be discovered. I welcome all communications, whether they are for the purpose of criticizing or of exchanging information on any aspect of netsuke. Letters to the publisher will always reach me.

RAYMOND BUSHELL

Tokyo, Japan

Author's Preface

MY FATHER loved painting, calligraphy, and curios. He placed them in alcoves, on walls, and on bookshelves and ended by regarding his rooms as too small. He always said that to own the works of great craftsmen and artists, to sit before them, and to appreciate them is akin to travel in strange lands; one is transported and refreshed. His words were engraved on my mind.

While studying in Kyoto I happened on some tiny carvings in an old shop. I bought them somewhat aimlessly, but as I examined them I realized that although these were sculptures in miniature, their designs were superb, their carving remarkable, and their technical craftsmanship extraordinary. It was the beginning of my initiation into a fairyland.

This was the moment that I became interested in netsuke, and since that moment I have collected them for thirty odd years. I have traveled from Tohoku (northeast Japan) to Kyushu (southwest Japan) in my avid search for the works of fine carvers. I also devoted considerable time to a search of all the literature pertaining to netsuke. I succeeded in discovering only a small number of volumes devoted to an appreciation of swords but including brief sections about netsuke. To say the least, much superior accounts were available in countries of the West. It is most regrettable that the netsuke, a unique product of the arts of Japan with a history of several hundred years, lacks a single comprehensive record in Japanese.

One of the differences between sculpture and painting is that sculpture is much more time-consuming. Nevertheless the financial reward for sculpture is even less than for painting. It is no surprise then that the sculptor frequently leads a life of poverty, but it is a surprise that poverty does not discourage him from a constant striving for the perfection of his skills. Hence the finest of the netsuke, those that have been handed down from generation to generation, captivate one and cause one "to drool three inches."

I have had the collecting habit since childhood. I collected in turn paintings, calligraphy, curios, old coins, gold *menuki* (small metal plaques attached to the sword hilt as decorations; see Fig. 9), clocks, and other things. Nevertheless, I have a special love for netsuke, and I shall never be able to stop collecting them even should I want to stop. The beauty of sculpturing seen in some netsuke almost transcends belief. The fascinating subjects portrayed in netsuke come alive in a panorama of the life and customs of the times represented. I can conscientiously recommend netsuke as a rich mine of historical material.

My friend Namioka Sonoö strongly urged me to write this book. In April, 1934, in complete disregard of my lack of proper qualifications, I brought out *Shumi no Netsuke* (Netsuke as a Hobby), but the supply was quickly exhausted, and the book has been unobtainable for a long time. People with whom I enjoyed no prior acquaintance urged me to republish the book. I have therefore added the knowledge I have gained in my study of netsuke since the publication of my previous book, and I have written *Netsuke no Kenkyu* (Study of Netsuke).

I am sure that many omissions and errors will be found, since most of my time for study was saved at odd moments from my regular work. I hope my readers will be understanding and will call my numerous errors to my attention.

UEDA REIKICHI

December 8, 1942

Part One: NETSUKE

1: Netsuke
as Related to the
History of Sculpture

OUR DEITIES, since ancient times the symbols of the religious beliefs of the Japanese, are utterly ethereal. We Japanese adore and worship our deities as celestial beings. The level of our veneration is uniquely spiritual. Our worship is of the intangible, being entirely dissociated from the physical. Nevertheless, according to some traditions, the divine essence of our gods is embodied in the sacred Mirror, the Sword, and the Seal and Pendant. It is also said that certain trees and stones are deified and that occasionally particular mountains or rivers are venerated as divine. But this is only surmise. However it may be, the veneration of our deities, being purely spiritual, furnishes no tangible subject matter for the artist.

By contrast, Buddhism, which was imported into Japan from abroad, developed on terms of intimacy and even equality between the divine and man. The saints of Buddhism are commonly represented in statues which are familiar to their followers. They are regarded as neighbors although worshipped.

Each of the various representations of Buddha has its individual characteristics. For example, the Buddhas of Love and Grace bear an expression to reassure even timid women and little children, while the Buddhas of Wrath and Vengeance inspire fear and dread. The representation of various expressions requires careful study and a perfection of techniques. These various expressions have been accomplished in different ways at different times and places.

Of course Buddhist art was introduced into Japan along with Buddhism. Not only was excellent Buddhist sculpture imported, but prominent sculptors from abroad sojourned in our country. In this way, Buddhist art gradually developed and eventually attained its full flourishing.

In the Nara era (710–793), especially during the Tempyo period

(729–748), Buddhist sculpture reached the zenith of its development, a perfection of which we can be proud in the eyes of the world. Many of the Nara statues are marvels of a rich, rounded refinement and spirituality. In this period most of the statues represent Kannon (goddess of mercy), Yakushi (deity of healing), Miroku (deity of reincarnation), Shaka (Buddha), Amida (deity of endless life), Nikko (sun god), Gekko (moon god), and others. These have gentle, soulful countenances of an unusually high standard.

As time passed, Buddhist sculpture of later periods became overstylized and suffered a deterioration. However, in the Kamakura era (1186–1334) a remarkable renaissance in sculpture took place. This renaissance had two aspects. One was a new form resulting from intercourse with China and was marked by a strong Chinese influence; the other was a revival of the style of the Asuka era (552–645) and the Tempyo period. The Kamakura era was the time of knighthood, with the military in complete control of the government. No wonder that violent figures such as the Nio—Deva kings or temple guardians (see Fig. 3)—at the Nara Todai-ji, and Tentoki and Ryutoki (lantern-holding ogres) at the Kofuku-ji were in style.

After reaching a high level of achievement during the Kamakura period, sculpture declined until the Momoyama era (1574–1602), when a remarkable innovation occurred. In this period architects promoted a new use for sculpture: the decoration of their edifices. Other uses for carvings were found in Noh masks (Figs. 4, 41, 85, 87, and 222) and in sword ornaments and furnishings (Figs. 6–9), which were required to meet a growing demand.* On the other hand, the carving of Buddhist images stagnated in reproduction and repetition. The Tokugawa era (1603–1867, also known as the Edo era) continued the trends of the Momoyama era with even greater emphasis. For example, the entire Nikko Byo Shrine is a mass of carved figures and decorations.

* In the Noh drama, the principal characters usually wear masks. Since there are well over one hundred masks for the various characters in the plays, identification is often extremely difficult. There is also some confusion among the masks intended for the Noh and those used in Gigaku and Bugaku, which are other more ancient forms of music and dance dramas. Add to the already existing uncertainties the variations and quirks of the individual netsuke carver, and it is no wonder that only the more common and distinctive mask netsuke such as Hannya (female demon) and Okina (good old man) can be readily identified.

Figs. 4, 41, 85, 87, and 222 represent Noh masks. Figs. 5 and 88 show netsuke

Wood predominates in our country as the favored material for sculpture, and more of it is used than of all other materials combined. This preference for wood is peculiar to Japan. The reason may be that our country produces a variety and quantity of woods of superb quality. An analogy is found in Italy, whose quarries furnish an abundance of fine marble and whose artists have created stirring sculpture in marble since ancient times.

We can be proud of the perfection to which sculpture was brought in the Nara and Kamakura eras. However, the carvings produced in those periods were for the most part made by foreigners (Chinese), and even those made by Japanese usually imitated the techniques of China and the Chinese. During the Tokugawa era, as is well known, the shoguns excluded foreigners and prohibited foreign influences, including Christianity. Under this enforced isolation the artcrafts of Japan, freed of foreign influences, developed strong national characteristics. By the term artcrafts, I mean delicate miniature art work. From ancient times, the Japanese have been blessed with a nimbleness of finger, and their artcrafts are characterized by an exceptional delicacy, preciseness, and exquisiteness.

Our country is surrounded by the sea; we are an insular people. Our absorption in the production of miniature objects has been relatively free from continental influences. The skill of the Japanese in the production of delicate and exquisite handwork is attributed to their partiality for the diminutive and to the digital skill that they acquire from infancy in the manipulation of chopsticks.

Spurred by national preferences and abilities, the development of miniature works of art such as sword furnishings, woodblock prints, netsuke, and *inro* (Fig. 2) took place naturally. Such works of art are the essence of Japanese taste. They not only represent the great art of the Tokugawa era, but it is no exaggeration to say that they represent the native artistic tradition of Japan.

imitating masks for the Kyogen, the comical interludes of the standard Noh performance. Figs. 65 and 84 represent Gigaku masks.

Many netsuke carvers simply sought to amuse. Their masks are merely funny faces that do not represent characters from any of the classic dramas or dances (Fig. 43.) The comment for Fig. 154 includes an explanation of the amusement netsuke. Chapter 7 also contains information on netsuke of this type.

The fashioning of metal sword ornaments is one of the miniature art forms for which —along with netsuke, lacquer, prints, and others—Japan is famous. Figs. 6–9 illustrate the principal sword decorations mentioned in the text.

Although we occasionally find handicrafts vaguely similar to our netsuke in other countries, we practically never find the delicate and precise carving characteristic of netsuke. In Western countries we do find coins and paper currency of minute design, but this is a most limited application of the miniature art form.

It is quite evident that no other country has so fostered the development of miniature carving as has Japan. Hence netsuke represent the pure, the absolute, the characteristic, the traditional, and the unique in Japanese art. The true value of the netsuke is grasped when it is regarded as a representation of pure Japanese taste.

To understand the Nara and Kamakura eras under the flourishing of Buddhism, we study the Buddhist art of those periods, and to understand the rich tastes of the warrior class of the Momoyama era, we study the sumptuous architectural carvings of that period. In the same way, to understand the character of the Edo era, when Japan enjoyed a time of serene development free of outside influences, we should study the popular growth of the netsuke.

In the history of sculpture in Japan, the netsuke represents a most important aspect. Nevertheless, the Japanese tend to ignore the study and appreciation of netsuke. They should consider the fact that foreigners alone value netsuke highly. Many foreigners are making studies of them and are assembling fine collections. By means of netsuke, foreigners learn about Japan and introduce Japan abroad.

2. INRO AND NETSUKE. (Lacquer. Diameter of netsuke: 1 3/8″. Unsigned.) Inro, ojime, and netsuke of fine tsuishu (cinnabar) lacquer. Tsuishu is a uniform red lacquer which is built up of many successive layers to a thickness sufficient for relief carving. The design on the inro is that of a mounted archer starting off on a hunt. The reverse side (not illustrated) shows a mounted hunter smoking and relaxing after the chase. The ojime (sliding bead for loosening or tightening the cords) is decorated with a plum-blossom design. The netsuke is a manju comprising two equal fitted sections and has a design of karako (happy Chinese boys) spinning tops.

▼

3. TEMPLE GUARDIAN: NIO. (Cherry wood. 2 $\frac{5}{16}$". Signed: Miwa yearns for Aoyama in Kofu Province. B 710.) The Nio stand guard in pairs at either side of the
entrance at the outer gate of Buddhist temples. They are massive, fierce, and awe-
inspiring. Their function is to ward off demons and evil spirits. The pair represent
the dual principle of nature: male and female, material and spiritual, right and left,
etc. Thus the mouth of one Nio is open, the mouth of his companion closed. In
sequence they utter the sacred Sanscrit word "a-um."

4. Noh Mask: Okina. (Boxwood. 1 $^{13}/_{16}$".
Signed: Shugetsu. Kakihan. B 1042.) The netsuke represents a mask of Okina, a good old
man. Simulated mask strings are carved on the
reverse side for attachment of the inro cord.
This touch of realism is an instance of the carver's conscientious attention to detail. For a representation of the dance of Okina, see Fig. 212.

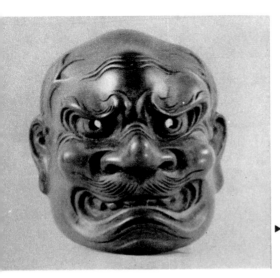

5. Kyogen Mask: Buaku. (Wood.
1 $^{1}/_{2}$". Signed: Hozan saku. B 290.)
The mask of Buaku, a courageous but
evil man, or sometimes a devil, is used
in the Kyogen, the comic interludes
in the Noh theater.

▼

6. TSUBA. (Silver bronze. Signed: Mitsu-hiro. Kakihan.) The tsuba is the sword hilt or guard that protects the wielder's hands from the sharp edge of the blade. The design shows Kanshin, the Chinese statesman, crawling between the legs of a ruffian rather than demean himself by engaging in a brawl.

7. KOZUKA. (Gold bronze. Signed: Ki-kuoka Mitsumasa. B 694.) The kozuka is the dagger carried in the scabbard of the two-handed sword. The design pictures goats in gold on a nanako (simulated fish roe) ground.

▲

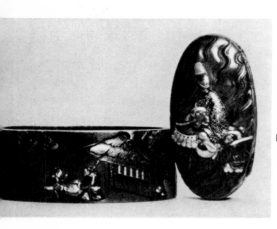

8. FUCHI AND KASHIRA. (Silver bronze with designs inlaid in various metals. Signed: Made by Katsumori at Atago-shita in the eastern capital [Tokyo].) The fuchi and the kashira (collectively called fuchigashira) are used for attachment to the top and the bottom of the sword handle. The kashira shown here portrays Narihira, one of the six great poets of 9th-century Japan, on his way to exile as punishment for an intrigue with the empress. The design on the fu-chi is a rural scene that Narihira might have observed along his route: the pounding of mulberry bark with a wooden mallet to make cloth.

9. MENUKI. (Various metals. Signed: Tomonao and Kosetsu.) Menuki are paired decorations for attachment to the handle of the long sword. Represented here are Kan-u (with a long beard) and Chohi (with a parted beard), two famous Chinese military strategists of the Han dynasty. For individual illustrations of Kan-u and Chohi mounted, see Figs. 201 and 52 respectively.

10. KAGAMIBUTA NETSUKE. (Wood and metal. Diameter: 1 $^{7}/_{16}$". Signed: Natsuo. B 757.) The bowl section is in wood, the metal lid in gold. The design of a ◄ moth in flight is achieved by delicately raised gold lines simulating the lacy veins of the semitransparent wings.

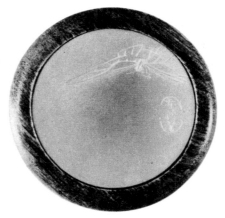

11. KAGAMIBUTA NETSUKE. (Ivory and metal. Diameter: 1 $^{7}/_{16}$". Unsigned.) An unusual form of kagamibuta. The "bowl" is a simple ivory base with a shallow excavation to conform with the shape of the metal "lid." The subject portrayed is the story of Moso, one of the Twenty-four Paragons of Filial Piety, known in Japanese as the Nijushiko. Moso dug bamboo shoots in the dead of winter to satisfy a craving of his mother. The metal part of the netsuke is decorated in gold, copper, silver bronze, and gold bronze. See text, page 56.

▼

12. KAGAMIBUTA NETSUKE. (Wood and metal. Diameter:
1 ¹/₂″. Signed: Mitsunaga *to*.) The bowl part is wood. The
metal plaque or lid fits into the bowl. The outlines of the
design, which portrays the chivalrous hero of the Kabuki
drama *Shibaraku*, are gouged or incised in the metal. The
actor's face, hairdress, and kimono are decorated in gold,
silver, silver bronze, and gold bronze, which are inlaid flat.

13. KAGAMIBUTA NETSUKE.
(Ivory and metal. Diameter:
1 ⁷/₈″. Signed: Eisai. Kakihan.) The netsuke comprises an
ivory bowl and a metal lid ap-
pliquéd in gold, silver, copper,
silver bronze, and gold bronze.
The design is that of a demon
collecting alms in the name of ◄
Buddha and entering the
names of the donors in the sub-
scription lists. This is a representation of the Japanese saying, "Oni no nembutsu" (a
demon's prayers to Buddha),
which refers to pretended vir-
tue and hypocritical conduct.

32

14. MANJU NETSUKE. (Ivory. Diameter: 2 $^7/_{16}$″. Unsigned.) A solid ivory manju fitted on the reverse side with a metal ring for attachment of the cord. The design, in relief, portrays Sasaki Takatsuna racing his fellow officer, Kajiwara Kagesue, across the Uji River in the face of a storm of arrows in order to be the first to meet the enemy. This large and heavy netsuke was probably used by a sumo wrestler. See text, page 56.

15. MANJU NETSUKE. (Ivory inlaid with gold and other materials. Diameter: 1 1/2". Signed: Ryumin. B 861.) An ivory manju comprising equal halves inlaid with gold, copper, silver bronze, malachite, opal, and tortoise shell. The design portrays the famous Taoist, Sha-en, as a young student too poor to buy oil for a lamp. He gathered glowworms into a bag which he suspended from a pole and studied by their faint glow.

16. RYUSA NETSUKE. (Ivory. Diameter: 1 5/8". Unsigned.) A ryusa netsuke completely perforated to create an all-over design of famous family crests (mon). See text, page 56.

17. KIRIN. (Rhinoceros horn. 1 13/16" long. Unsigned.) A rare rhinoceros-horn netsuke in the form of a smiling recumbent kirin. For another example and comment on the kirin see Fig. 194.

▼

18. MANJU NETSUKE. (Ivory. Diameter: 1 ¹³/₁₆″. Signed: Ono no Ryomin. Kakihan. B 837.) An ivory manju comprising two equal fitted sections. On the inside of the top section is an eyelet to which the cord is attached and passed through a hole in the bottom section. The raised design represents Tokiwa Gozen fleeing from the Taira soldiers with her three sons, the youngest of whom became the famous Yoshitsune.

▼

19. KAGAMIBUTA BOWL. (Ivory. Diameter: 1 ¹⁵/₁₆″. Signed: *Oju* Gyokuzan saku. B 164.) An excellent example of the superbly carved ivory bowl referred to on page 56 of the text. The design is a conglomerate of symbols and signs of good fortune, happiness, and long life (takarazukushi). Among them are Hotei's bag of toys, Daikoku's hammer, Jurojin's fan, happy Chinese boys, a scroll of wisdom, a sea bream, a dragon, a crane, and a turtle. Hotei, Daikoku, and Jurojin are three of the Seven Happy Gods of China and Japan. Hotei represents happiness; Daikoku, wealth; and Jurojin, longevity.

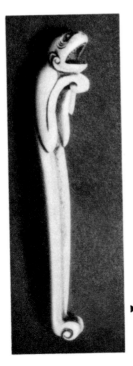

20. SASHI NETSUKE. (Staghorn. 4 ³/₈″ long. Signed: Koku, in a characteristic seal form standing for Kokusai. B 527.) An elongated monkey designed to be worn thrust into the ▶ obi, the cord being attached to the hole pierced between the paws and under the monkey's chin. See text, page 56. For another type of sashi netsuke, see Fig. 26.

35

27. TEAPOT. (Cane. 1 1/8''. Unsigned.) A finely woven cane teapot
▶ with loose ring handles and lid. The cord is atta hed through an eyelet on the inside of the lid.

28. BASKET. (Wisteria
vine. 1 1/2''. Signed:
Ryuryusai saku.) A netsuke woven of wisteria
vine into a miniature replica of the huge baskets
used foɪ hauling rocks
and for damming rivers. ◀

29. NARA NINGYO. (Painted wood. 2 1/4″. Signed: Toen. B 1177.) The design of this painted wood netsuke is that of a Noh actor. The carving was ▶executed with a single knife (itto-bori), and this accounts for the rough, angular surface. See text, pages 114 and 123, for Nara ningyo and page 74 for ittobori.

30. LEAF-CLAD SENNIN. (Bone. 4 3/8″. Unsigned.) A powerful carving of a sennin (a class of Chinese "immortals" who live as hermits) wearing a coat of mugwort leaves. The coat of leaves is a ◀ common attribute of the sennin. The figure balances on one foot and thus passes one of the tests of a good netsuke.

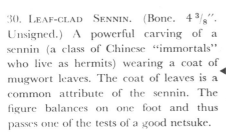

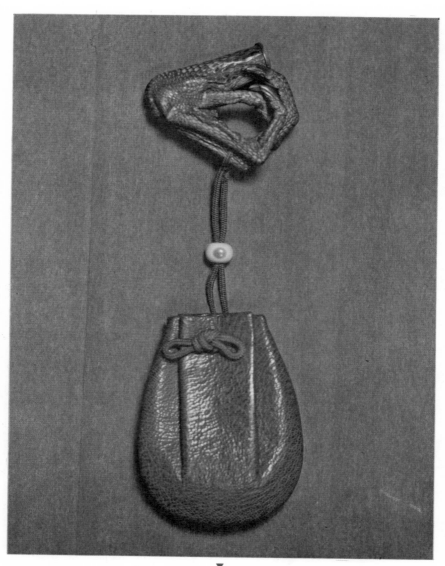

31. KINCHAKU AND NETSUKE. (Netsuke: bone. 2 ½″ long. Signed: Chinai.) The kinchaku (purse) is made of undecorated leather. The netsuke is the natural foot of a crane upon which has been lacquered in raised gold characters the following legend: "Made by Chinai in Tempo 12 on the 19th day of autumn [November 19, 1841] from the leg of a crane which was captured." The ojime is made of the ivory-like casque (hōten) of the hornbill, which has a characteristic bright orange and yellow coloration. Compare Fig. 170.

▼

32. TOBACCO POUCH AND NETSUKE. (Netsuke: ivory. 2″ long. Signed: Kaigyokusai Masatsugu. B 430.) The pouch is made of soft woven bamboo strands. The clasp, in ivory, is an octopus with eyes inlaid in yellow mother-of-pearl and black coral. It is signed on the back section: Kaigyokusai Masatsugu. The netsuke, also in ivory and likewise signed, represents an oyster encrusted with a few barnacles. The two halves of the oyster open to reveal a minute carving of temples, gates, and trees under floating clouds. The ojime is colored glass.

33. CRAB AND LOTUS LEAF. (Tortoise shell. 2 3/4″ long. Unsigned.) A tortoise-shell netsuke representing a lotus leaf supporting a crab. It is carved of one piece. The cord hole is fashioned at the natural separation of the tortoise's upper and lower shells.

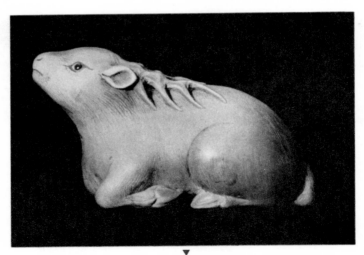

34. DEER. (Stone. 2 1/2″ long. Unsigned.) A recumbent deer made of a "soft" stone of light grayish buff color. Inlaid eyes. Stone netsuke are extremely rare and are for use only with leather or cloth tobacco pouches, purses, or other unbreakable sagemono.

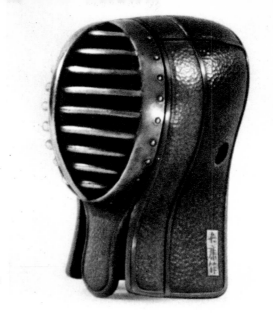

35. KENDO MASK. (Silver and silver bronze. 1 ½". Signed: Masayasu saku.) A finely wrought metal netsuke in the form of a kendo (Japanese fencing) mask.

36. HOTEI, GOD OF HAPPINESS. (Porcelain. 2 ⅛". Signed with the brand of Ninsei. B 761.) Hotei, wearing a kimono decorated with a design of Chinese characters, carries his treasure bag on his back. See text, pages 76 and 115.

43

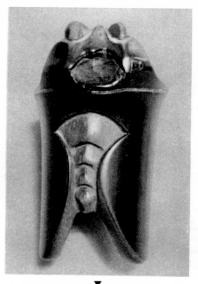

▼
37. Gourd Netsuke. (Natural gourd. 2 ³/₈″. Unsigned.) A natural gourd cleverly selected and fitted with a stopper in the form of a bird beak to imitate a young bird. The infinite variations of the gourd shape are the basis for its enduring appeal as a netsuke. See text, page 60. The cord is attached by tying it to the narrow waist of the gourd.

▼
38. Cicada. (Bamboo. 1 ³/₁₆″ long. Signed: Hoshin. B 274.) A stylized cicada made of bamboo that has been treated and preserved by smoking. See text, page 77.

▶ 39. Snake and Frog. (Ivory. 1 ¹/₄″ long. Signed: Masatsugu. B 633.) In this representation of a snake crushing a frog, the frog is almost entirely concealed in the snake's coils.

40. DARUMA. Wood. 2⁵/₈″.
Signed with a kakihan
widely established as the
written seal of Toen.
B 1177.) The netsuke rep-
resents Daruma (Bodhi-
dharma) and is carved in
angular surfaces in the
ittobori style. See Fig. 29
for another example of a
netsuke by Toen.

▼
41. NOH MASK: KUMASAKA (?). (Wood. 1⁵/₈″.
Signed: Deme Joman. B 69.) This Noh mask, probably that of Kumasaka, was presented as a gift to F. M.
Jonas, the author of the first book in English on the
subject of netsuke, originally published in 1928 and
reissued in 1960. Mr. Jonas wrote as follows when he
in turn gave the netsuke to the adaptor of this book in
Kobe, Japan, during the early months of 1946: "The
netsuke (wooden mask bearing the name of Deme
Joman) had been the property of the Taira Inaba
Mono no Kami Masanori, the lord of the feudal castle
of Odawara in Sagami County, who died on the 13th
day of the 9th month, 13th year of Genroku (1700) and
a part of whose remains were buried at the cemetery
within the compound of the temple Kofuku-ji, Gyo-
to-san, Mukojima, Edo (Tokyo). In July, 2nd year
of Showa (1927), the cemetery was removed due to
a town planning extension scheme and the grave
opened. Several articles of interest were recovered
and among them was found the above netsuke, which
was presented to F. M. Jonas through the courtesy of
Viscount Inaba, his [Masanori's] direct descendant.
The authenticity of the article and the date of the
period of the carver can thus be verified."

▼

43. FUNNY-FACE NETSUKE. (Natural walnut. 1 5/8″. Unsigned.) A walnut carved in relief on both sides in designs of humorous faces. The side illustrated (the back) represents no standard theatrical mask. It was carved for amusement. The nostrils of the face form the himotoshi. See footnote, pages 24–25, for a few comments on mask netsuke.

▼

42. STONE NETSUKE. (Natural stone. 3 13/16″ long, with chain. Unsigned.) An unusual netsuke: a natural black stone to which is attached a wooden link chain fashioned from a single block. The manner by which the chain is attached to the stone is artfully disguised. See Fig. 34 for comments on the use of stone netsuke.

44. CHRYSANTHEMUM. (Leather. Diameter: 1 1/2″. Unsigned.) A leather netsuke in the form of a stylized chrysanthemum of sixteen petals, the petals variously colored. The cord is attached by a metal ring. ◀

45. FUJIMAME. (Natural wisteria bean. 2 1/2″ long. Signed: Carved by Shunyo.) The netsuke is made of a dried fujimame or wisteria bean. The etched designs of ◀ turtle, crane, and pine trees are all symbols of longevity.

46

46. BAKEMONO. (Black coral. 2 5/8". Signed: Chomin.) A bakemono with pendulous tongue and bulging eyes terrifies the child cowering at its feet. Bakemono are demons and fiends of fantasy. They are distinguished from ghosts in that they have legs and are not the spirits of ▶ deceased human beings. As with Noh masks, the distinguishing characteristics of various bakemono have been lost with time and through artistic license. The bakemono represented here is probably the giant Mikoshi. The subject of the hyakki (one hundred demons) has been used by many artists.

47. MALACHITE NETSUKE (Malachite and silver. 1 7/16". Unsigned.) A rare netsuke of polished malachite to which are attached silver fittings in the design ◀ of cherry blossoms. The cord is attached by means of a silver ring.

47

▼

48. GONG. (Wood. 3″. Unsigned.) The netsuke represents a gong of Chinese origin decorated with Buddhist and Taoist symbols. According to Chinese lore, the dragon and the shishi portrayed here are animals of good omen. Similar designs of Chinese gongs are sometimes found in jade.

49. GOURD NETSUKE. (Wood. 1 3/4″. Unsigned.) A gourd-shaped netsuke, artfully fash-
▶ ioned from wood to simulate leather and fitted with a metal stopper and a ring for cord attachment.

▼
50. SAKÈ GOURD. (Wood; various inlays. 2 1/16″ long. Signed: Tokoku. B 1184.) A gourd-shaped netsuke realistically simulating a sakè container in a knotted-cord carrying net. The netsuke is inlaid with various materials, including ebony, ivory, glass, and boxwood.

51. SEAL NETSUKE. (Wood. 2 3/4". Unsigned.) The shishi sits on a human-headed snake. The seal itself is carved with a Chinese character meaning pleasure. ◄ The design is of Chinese origin but was made by a Japanese carver in imitation of the Chinese style. See text, pages 61–62.

52. CHOHI. (Ivory. 1 7/8". Signed: Shogetsu. Kaki-han. B 988.) Chohi, one of the three famous Chinese military strategists of the Han period, mounted with a bared halberd. The other two of the trio are Kan-u and Gentoku. See Figs. 9 and 201 for other illustrations of Chohi and Kan-u.

53. FILIAL PIETY. (Ivory. 1 ¹³/₁₆″. Signed: Doraku. B 85.) In this portrayal of filial devotion, a dutiful son happily guides the steps of his old blind father. The subject is a Chinese one adopted by the Japanese, ◄ although it is probably not included among the Nijushiko (Twenty-four Paragons of Filial Piety). For other portrayals of filial piety, see Figs. 11 and 200.

▼
54. SEAL NETSUKE. (Wood. 1 ³/₄″ long. Signed: Kyusai. B 576.) A seal netsuke in the shape of an arm and a three-fingered hand—an allusion to the heroic exploit of Watanabe no Tsuna, who cut off a demon's arm at the Rashomon gate in Kyoto. The seal impression reads "Gansho," which is most probably an art name.

55. KARAKO. (Ivory. 1 1/2″.
Signed: Anraku Shukosai. B 2.)
A happy Chinese boy (karako)
▶ astride a water buffalo. As with
many nationalities, the easiest
way to distinguish Chinese
subjects from Japanese is by an
examination of their dress.

56. GOKI. (Ivory. 2 3/16″.
Signed: Shokyokuken.) This
netsuke represents Goki, the
Chinese militarist who slew his
wife to demonstrate his loyalty
to his country when it was at ◀
war with hers. Her ghost
haunted Goki to his death.
Here he attempts to force the
ghost back into her grave.

52

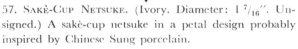

57. SAKÈ-CUP NETSUKE. (Ivory. Diameter: 1 $^7/_{16}$''. Unsigned.) A sakè-cup netsuke in a petal design probably inspired by Chinese Sung porcelain.

58. DAGGER NETSUKE. (Lacquered wood. 5 $^1/_2$'' long when closed. Signed: Keiraku.) This netsuke is shaped like an elongated dolphin (shachihoko), the mythical animal whose figure often decorates the roofs of castles—notably Nagoya Castle, where two immense golden shachihoko surmount the gables. The netsuke is made of wood cleverly lacquered to simulate iron and bears the artist's signature in red lacquer.

53

59. BUKAN ZENSHI AND TIGER. (Boxwood. 2 $^1/_2$". Signed: Shumemaru Unjudo. B 1058.) The subject is Bukan Zenshi, a famous priest of 7th-century China, who is portrayed, as usual, accompanied by a tiger. Note the fraternal resemblance of the tiger to the priest, an example of the humor with which the Japanese frequently treat their holy men. The netsuke itself is not signed, but it has an original box signed Shumemaru Unjudo.

▲

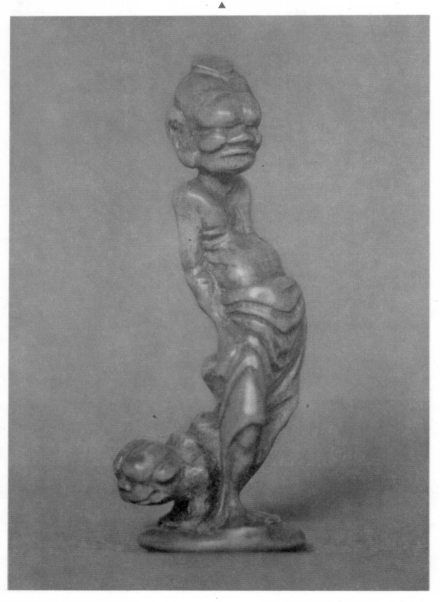

2: The Netsuke and Its Types

THE ARTICLE called netsuke originated in the old days from the custom of attaching a toggle to one end of a cord that passed between the obi and the hip and that had at its other end a *sagemono* (suspended object) such as a bunch of keys, a *kinchaku* or purse (Fig. 31), an inro (Fig. 2), a tobacco pouch (Figs. 1 and 32), or some other type of single hanging object to which the general name of *hitotsusage* was given. In the *Wakun no Shiori* (Dictionary of Classical Japanese) the netsuke is defined as "a small hanging object." In the *Soken Kisho* (Appreciation of Superior Sword Furnishings) it is explained that the word netsuke was used in ancient books to designate objects attached to the cord that suspended the sagemono. In other references, netsuke are called *obihasami* (the clip or clasp illustrated in Fig. 26), or sometimes the Japanese syllables "ne-tsu-ke" are given as the reading for the Chinese characters 佩子 (small object for adornment) or 墜子 (small hanging object). In the *Meibutsu Rokujo* (Six Volumes of Noteworthy Objects) the characters 懸錘 (suspended weight) are used. In China, netsuke are not commonly used in the same manner as in Japan. The Chinese, however, use objects similar to netsuke and write the names of these with the characters 懸錘 (suspended weight) or 佩陲 (wear suspended) or sometimes the characters 佩垂 (wear hanging) or 佩墜 (wear dropped). Netsuke are also called *obiguruma* (disk) or *obiguruwa* (link).

Should the word netsuke be written 根付 or 根附? It is understood that 付 means "to suspend" and 附 means "to attach." Accordingly the word netsuke should more properly be written 根附. In most cases in the old books, however, it is written 根付. In this book I use the characters 根付 to accord with the weight of precedent and custom.

Netsuke are generally classified into such types as *katabori, kagamibuta, manju,* and *ryusa.* Katabori are netsuke carved in the form of human beings, animals, or groups of these. Kagamibuta (called *kana-buta* in the Kyoto and Osaka areas) are bowl-shaped netsuke, usually of ivory, bone, or horn, with a second part consisting of a metal lid or cover made of various alloys. On the reverse side of the metal disk there is an eyelet for attaching the cord, which is passed through a hole in the bowl-shaped part. The design of the metal disk is achieved by various techniques: etching, inlay, and relief (Figs. 10–13). The merit of the kagamibuta lies more in the working of the metal disk than in the carving of the bowl. Occasionally, however, one finds a superbly carved ivory bowl (Fig. 19). The carving of the disk was usually done by metal artists, some of whom are famous.

Manju netsuke are made of ivory, horn, wood, bamboo, and other materials and are usually round and flat in the shape of the cake called manju. One type of manju netsuke is solid, and the decoration is applied to the surface of the material by etching or relief carving (Fig. 14). Another kind of manju consists of two equal sections fitted together (Figs. 15 and 18). Manju netsuke are also sometimes square or oval in shape. For the attachment of the cord, a metal ring is sometimes affixed, or holes are made in the material itself.

Ryusa netsuke are actually a variety of manju. Flower and bird designs or arabesques were fashioned by cutting and perforating the material (Figs. 16 and 25). When it was made of two sections, the ryusa netsuke was frequently hollowed out by use of a lathe. This technique was used particularly in Edo, where a man named Ryusa (B. 870) was the first to make this type of manju. His name has now been adopted to designate the entire category.

Sashi netsuke are elongated netsuke with cord holes at one end. This type of netsuke is worn thrust inside the sash (Figs. 20 and 26). It is usually considered to be a variety of netsuke, but there is an adverse opinion which regards it as a form of dagger handle for use with a bag in which flint and steel were carried.

Ichiraku netsuke are gourd or other shapes made of braided or woven bamboo, cane, or wire (Figs. 22, 23, 27, and 28). *Kurawa* or ash-tray netsuke are named for their use, and this type of netsuke actually serves as an ash tray (Figs. 21 and 24).

Many categories of netsuke are named according to their particular designs or characteristics. Typical of these are the *ningyo* or dolls (Figs. 29, 61, 68, and 114) and the *men* or masks (Figs. 4, 5, 41, 65, etc.).

Netsuke are often classified according to the material used: wood, ivory, bone (Fig. 30), horn (Fig. 17), tortoise shell (Fig. 33), porcelain (Figs. 36, 89, and 91), metal (Fig. 35), stone (Figs. 34 and 42), peach-stone, nut (Figs. 43 and 45), lacquer (Figs. 119, 169, 172, etc.), bamboo (Figs. 38 and 157), coral (Figs. 46 and 117), amber (Fig. 146), and others (Figs. 44 and 47). They are also classified according to artist or school, date or period, subject matter, and other features.

3: The Origin and Development of Netsuke

THE INDIVIDUAL in Western clothing has more than ten pockets convenient for carrying things, but the individual in Japanese kimono has no pockets, nor is there any provision for carrying a tobacco pouch, a purse, an inro, or any similar article. It therefore became the custom to carry such articles between the hip and the sash, and even swords were worn in this manner. One may say with assurance that the absence of pockets was the necessity that mothered the invention of netsuke.

The netsuke is not used independently but together with a pouch or sagemono. It is therefore advisable to study the sagemono prior to discussing the origin and development of the netsuke. The oldest sagemono mentioned in the ancient chronicles is the flint bag *(hiuchi-bukuro)*. It is recorded that Prince Yamato Takeru, on the occasion of his departure to subjugate the "eastern barbarians" (Ainu), visited his aunt, Princess Yamato Hime, who was serving at the Ise Shrine. She presented him with a sword to which was attached a flint bag which the prince put to good use on the battlefield.

During the Fujiwara era (889–1185) a flint bag was generally carried by the traveler in order to build fires through the night for protection against the attacks of wild animals both in deep mountain recesses and open plains. Yoshiie Hachiman Taro, a famed general of the Genji clan, in a picture scroll of the War of Gosannen, is depicted carrying a flint bag. The flint bag was usually carried suspended from the handle of a small sword.

In the Kamakura era the purpose of the flint bag was extended to the holding of money and medicine in addition to flints. The *Taihei-ki* (Chronicle of the Wars of Bumpo [1317–1318] and Shohei [1346–1369]) relates that Fujitsuna Aoto inadvertently dropped some small coins in the Nameri River, that the amount was ten coppers, and that it was lost from a flint bag. Rosaries, known as *juzu* (Fig. 182), were also carried in flint bags. Despite the designation "flint bag" its actual use was substantially the same as that of the pouch.

There is a series of picture scrolls of the Mongol invasion that preserves for posterity the great exploits of this battle. On February 9, 1293, Suenaga Takezaki Goro Hyoe-no-jo, who defended Japan against the Mongol invasion, commissioned Nagataka Tosa, a famous artist of the period, to portray the stages of the battle. In one of the pictures constituting the scroll, a scene in which Suenaga reports to Akita Yasumori at Kamakura, an attendant is depicted wearing a flint bag attached to the handle of a short sword. This custom continued into the Tokugawa period, when small bags similar in style to the flint bags and decorated with grass patterns were frequently worn solely as adornments. They were usually carried empty.

As time passed, several variations of the flint bag developed; for example, the kinchaku (purse), the *doran* (leather wallet), and the inro. The flint bag carried by the Himeji clan was described as belonging to the Yoritomo style. Since the Yoritomo style is understood to comprise a diamond-shape netsuke attached to an open bamboo pouch, detailed historical research by scientific methods is necessary in order to determine whether netsuke were in use in the time of Yoritomo (1148–1199) and, if so, whether they were in existence prior to that time.

It may be that the name kinchaku originated in the Momoyama period. A detailed description found in the *Jiseki Goko* (Historical Commentaries) reveals that during his retirement Tokugawa Ieyasu went hawking wearing a silk garment with pongee padding, a coat made of woven Kokura cloth, a leather purse, and a black Nagato inro with a gourd netsuke. (Nagato was a technique of weaving and lacquering paper string.) Obviously since the names kinchaku, inro, and netsuke were current in the Tokugawa period, the use of netsuke must have antedated the period. One gathers that in the early stages of its history the netsuke was often in the form of a gourd (Figs. 37, 49, and 50).

The *Kabuki Zoshi* owned by Marquis Tokugawa Yoshichika is a horizontal scroll that illustrates and describes scenes from the Kabuki theater of Keicho (1596–1614). Its gorgeous coloring is characteristic of the Momoyama style. In the last scene of this scroll two actors occupy the center of the stage, one leaning on his sword, the other strutting at his right; both wear purse, inro, and gourd, which are attached to the obi by means of links (obiguruwa). The accuracy of this picture is corroborated by indications in the *Kabuki Koto Hajime* (Roots of Kabuki) that in Bunroku (1592–1595) Okuni wore a pouch when she danced for Hideyoshi at a command performance, and by indications in the *Razan Bunshu* (a book written by Hayashi Razan, a scholar of the Tokugawa period) that Kabuki actors wore pouches. From these facts one infers that in the Bunroku period people were already wearing pouches attached by links. It is quite possible that Okuni, who was extremely popular, set the fashion by sporting a pouch at her performances. In the picture referred to above, only the two actors, and none of the spectators, wear links. It is noteworthy that both the sagemono and the sash were passed through the link and worn at the hip.

Although other natural objects were sometimes used as netsuke, the gourd was by far the most popular toggle (Fig. 37). Even in later days when more sophisticated netsuke found favor, the custom continued of wearing a gourd in addition to the second netsuke attached to the purse or the inro. The reason for its enduring popularity may be that the gourd can be used in its natural state; besides, it has a lovely and infinitely varied form. Natural gourds and sea shells often made the most popular netsuke.

In the *Kotto Shu* (Collection of Curios) published about 250 years ago, there is an illustration of a woodblock print in which a purse is suspended by a shell netsuke and a gourd. During Kanei (1624–1643) and Shoho (1644–1647) and in fact until the end of Genroku (1703) it was the style to wear the inro and pouch together attached to the one netsuke. It does not seem that the *ojime* (sliding bead through which the cord was passed) was in use at that time. In the *Honcho Seiji Dangi* (Discourses on Worldly Affairs) it is stated that the pouch represents a survival of the flint bag.

Inro were already popular in Tensho (1573–1591). At that time they were decorated in simple black lacquer. However, by the end of Kanei (1643) inro were artistically and beautifully decorated as gold and silver lacquering became popular. A painted screen of the Momoyama period owned by the Daigo Temple portrays the training of horses. The equestrian wears an inro, but unfortunately his clothes hide the place where the netsuke might otherwise be visible. A netsuke, however, was necessary to support the inro, and since the inro was already in use, one may safely assume that the netsuke was also. In later days the preference for luxurious pouches and inro grew. For example, quality leather from China and India was imported for the working of fine pouches.

As already indicated, there are no records definitely establishing the date of the first use of netsuke. Opinions differ, and the eras assigned are variously the Tokugawa, the Toyotomi (1574–1602), the Ashikaga (1335–1573), and the Kamakura. The late Mr. Kyuichi Takeuchi (B 575) stated that "netsuke were already in use in the Ashikaga era to suspend keys at the hip. Netsuke were then generally carved ivory seals called *tobutsu* (Chinese articles), and even the designs of the seals were in the Chinese style." While I do not know the source of Mr. Takeuchi's information, it does seem that the practice of attaching a netsuke to a bunch of keys has been in existence since quite early times.

Since the netsuke was an article of utility, people made use of such natural materials as shells, wood, bamboo, and gourds for service as netsuke. It is for this reason that we do not know precisely when netsuke were first used. During the vague periods when they originated, the Chinese used ivory, wood, and various stones to make seals and similar articles which were exported to Japan. It is clearly stated in the *Soken Kisho* that the Japanese adapted these articles for use as netsuke. (See Fig. 51.) For this reason the opinion is held by some scholars that netsuke originated in China. However, it is more accurate to hold that netsuke *as such* originated in our country.

The first netsuke, then, were natural materials such as gourds, shells, wood, and stones (Fig. 42). Even after the start of an artistic treatment of netsuke, signatures do not appear on the very early ones. The first netsuke artists are therefore unknown, as are the dates when they carved their works. Moreover, it is not possible to determine the precise period when Chinese carvings adapted as netsuke were first imported from China. It is also impossible to fix accurately the age of a netsuke from an examination of the piece itself. The only sure way to know its age is by studying the life of the artist who carved it. One can sometimes guess at the age of netsuke by studying old picture scrolls, old picture books, and old paintings.

In Kanei, Koetsu Honami (a lacquer artist) and Nonoguchi Ryu-ho (B 779) were already producing artistic netsuke, and I believe that a quite large number of artistic netsuke had been made before that time. In Kambun (1661–1672) and Tenna (1681–1683) the number of persons who wore inro and purses increased, and the result was a greater demand for netsuke.

In those days not only students of the Chinese classics but also educated and literary people revered China as the fountainhead of culture and wisdom. Chinese *objets d'art* were much in vogue. Various objects from China such as *ito-in* (copper or bronze seals affixed to shipping cases), seals, sword handles, cane heads, and ornaments for cap and obi were quickly made into netsuke by the insertion of holes and a cord. Pursuing the vogue, the Japanese made a great number of netsuke for which Chinese subjects were adopted (Figs. 52, 53, 55, 56, etc.). This imitation of Chinese subject matter explains the enormous output of *shishi* (temple dog) netsuke, since the shishi was a frequent subject on the seals imported from China (Fig. 51). In the *Soken Kisho* many of the netsuke illustrated reveal carving that is Chinese in subject matter and feeling (Fig. 221).

From Genroku through Shotoku (1688–1715) the demand for netsuke increased still further. Both maker and wearer gave more attention to the quality of the carving and were no longer satisfied with natural form or childish design. This growing popularity required the production of netsuke in large quantities. Industrial artists, including painters, carvers of Buddhist images, lacquerers, mask carvers, metalworkers, architectural carvers, and metal casters produced netsuke as an avocation or amusement. Some of these artists gradually devoted themselves exclusively to netsuke as their life work. In this way netsuke of superb artistry made their appearance.

From Kyoho until after Horeki (1716–1763) the wearing of tobacco pouches was the style. Businessmen particularly, almost without exception, wore them. The tobacco pouch was as much the mark of the successful businessman as his stock in trade. Thus the demand for netsuke increased apace, and great numbers of them were made to meet the demand. Businessmen spared no expense in acquiring fine tobacco pouches as vanities, and they took as much pride in sporting them as samurai did in their swords. This trend was not limited to men of commerce but extended to the rich, the artists, the workmen, and the playboys. A large production of fine tobacco pouches, and of fine netsuke to go with them, was required. In Bunka and Bunsei (1804–1829) the netsuke reached the summit of its popularity. This was the golden age of the tobacco pouch and of the netsuke.

4: Netsuke
with
Secondary Functions

NETSUKE WERE USED for the purpose of suspending inro, tobacco pouches, keys, purses, amulet cases, leather wallets, money bags, chopstick kits, sakè cups (Fig. 57), and other objects. Of these, the inro was the particular mark of the samurai. It was his custom to place medicines in it and to carry it with him on all ceremonial occasions. Inro were already in use during the Temmon period (1532–1554) and increased in popularity thereafter until the Meiji period (1868–1911), when they declined as knighthood's adornment. Even today, however, an inro is occasionally seen in use.

The inro required an accompanying netsuke, and great care was taken to produce netsuke suitable for this use. Inro netsuke were generally smaller and lighter in weight than others in order to reduce the danger of damage to the inro. Occasionally, the tusk of the narwhal (sometimes known as the sea unicorn) or the horn of the rhinoceros is used for making netsuke. Both these animal products were known as *ikkaku*, meaning single-horn. The narwhal is a kind of whale found in arctic waters. The tusk is similar to, but distinguishable from, elephant ivory.

In the *Wakan Sansai Zue,* an illustrated encyclopedia published in the early 18th century, *ikkaku* is described as follows: "In common usage *ikkaku* includes the horn of a kind of rhinoceros as well as the tusk of the narwhal. Dutch merchant ships occasionally bring narwhal to Japan, but it is usually very difficult to obtain. Narwhal tusk is about six or seven feet in length and about three to five inches in circumference. It resembles elephant ivory but is more yellowish in color. Its surface is sinewy and spirally grooved or fluted. The grooves tend to diminish near the tip, which is curved. The center core is often hollow. As the cost of narwhal is extremely high, off-white rhinoceros horn from Cochin China is imported as a substitute, but this also is lately becoming rare. The surface of rhinoceros horn is fibrous and lacks a gloss or luster. It has a distinct grain and cuts like bamboo. The longer horns measure more than one foot."

At a quick inspection it is difficult to distinguish narwhal from ivory. Because of its great value and in order to identify the material as narwhal in the completed netsuke, the carver usually left portions of the characteristic grooved skin of the tusk exposed, particularly at the cord holes and at other parts of the netsuke that did not mar the design.

Persons attacked by fever were given medicinal concoctions to drink, the essential ingredient of which was chips from the cord holes of the narwhal netsuke. Thus narwhal netsuke served a secondary purpose as a medicament. Even today narwhal tusk and rhinoceros horn are used as curatives for fever. Netsuke of narwhal are designed so that a small amount of chipping around the cord holes does no harm to the overall design.

In the *Shui Tomi Roku,* a collection of stories from Kyoho to Horeki, there appears the following tale: "As a youth the young Lord Chikara, the third son of Matsusada of Kii, often hawked and fished in the mountains on the way to his villa beside the Urushi River in Wakayama. One day on his way home he passed through Shinnai Street and stopped at a curio shop selling old sword guards, small swords, tobacco pouches, and books hung on bamboo poles. A netsuke made of horn aroused his interest, and Chikara ordered that it be delivered to his villa. Since the curio shop was operated only by a widow and her young daughter, the mother sent the girl to deliver the netsuke. She received in payment a few farthings, the price she asked. Later an expert informed Chikara that the netsuke was made of narwhal tusk. The young lord felt sorry for the widow and her daughter, who obviously did not understand their business. The next time he passed the shop, Chikara gave them two hundred copper coins. The two women were extremely grateful, and the widow sent her daughter to the lord's villa to express thanks. The daughter's modest manner and attractive appearance excited the young lord, and he 'placed his hands upon her' in secret. Thereafter he visited the curio shop often on his way home from hawk-hunting, and occasionally the comely daughter visited him at his villa. One day she reluctantly disclosed that she was with child. The matter was kept secret, since the young lord was still dependent upon his father. He gave her as solatium things of value, including ten gold coins, a sword forged by Kunimune, and the narwhal netsuke that had started their liaison. Months passed and a child was born. . . ."

The inference is clear from this account that the narwhal netsuke was most highly valued. In addition to narwhal tusk, there are other examples of netsuke materials reputedly possessed of great medicinal value. Ivory shavings were used for extracting thorns and splinters, and staghorn shavings as an antidote to viper poisoning.

The ash-tray netsuke, designed for use with the tobacco pouch, was a popular form, particularly with farmers. It was usually of metal, especially cast metal. As its name implies, it was intended for use as an ash tray (Figs. 21 and 24). The cast-metal netsuke made by Kyubei (B 574) of Sakai (a city near Osaka) are good examples of this type (Fig. 21). Kyubei's designs include pots, pots with lids, turtle shells, and others—usually decorated with geometric or arabesque motifs. There are also ash-tray netsuke made of cloisonné.

Another type of netsuke that was popular for use with the tobacco pouch was one designed as a lighter. It was made of brass, iron, copper, or wood. The inside of the lighter-netsuke contained flint and a tiny hammer activated by a spring release. When a small button on the outside of the netsuke was pressed, the spring released the hammer, which struck against the flint and produced a flame in a small depression that contained inflammable material. The flint-lighter netsuke was used for lighting both pipes and cigarettes. In the Meiji period, a matchbox netsuke for holding wax matches came into use.

The sundial netsuke was another type with a secondary use (Fig. 63). It was made in two sections—usually two hemispheres—one of which contained a compass and the other a sundial marked with the animals of the zodiac to indicate the hours. Thus the netsuke indicated both direction and time and served a most useful purpose in former days when mechanical watches were expensive and difficult to obtain.

Hunters used small folding knives or daggers as netsuke (Fig. 58). Tea-ceremony masters employed tea-whisk netsuke to suspend sets of utensils used in the preparation of the beverage, and merchants used abacus netsuke for their calculations. Most of these last were of wood, although ivory ones appeared at a later period. Abacus netsuke of metal are rare. Other netsuke that combined their primary function with a secondary one included candlesticks, spyglasses, *yatate* or writing-brush containers (Fig. 62), cases for the solid ink used with personal seals, magnifying glasses, and many others (Fig. 132). It appears that ideas for secondary functions of netsuke were practically exhausted.

As the above outline shows, many netsuke were produced that combined their basic use with an additional function. This practical trend, dictated in part by a desire for economy, was paralleled by a trend toward very luxurious netsuke that were preferred by persons of ample means. It is most interesting that the trend toward the practical, inexpensive netsuke and the trend toward the luxurious, expensive netsuke coexisted and developed concurrently.

5: Netsuke and the Tobacco Pouch

BEFORE DISCUSSING the netsuke and its use with the tobacco pouch, I should like to outline briefly the history of tobacco. Although it has been said that the word "tobacco" came from Tobago, the West Indian island where tobacco supposedly originated, this was actually the name of the pipe in which the natives smoked it. The Spanish explorers assumed it to be the name of the weed itself, and the word thus came into universal use. Tobacco was introduced into Europe following the discovery of the new continent by Columbus, who had observed the natives smoking and returned to Europe with samples of tobacco obtained from them. It was during the Ashikaga era, in 1525, that the Spaniards brought tobacco plants to Europe. In 1560, Jacques Nicot, a Frenchman, began importing tobacco seeds into Europe, and the smoking habit has been prevalent among Europeans ever since.

As for the importation of tobacco into Japan, it is assumed that the Portuguese carried tobacco with them when they came to this country in 1543. While there exists no actual record to corroborate this date, the fact remains that smoking was in vogue in our country in the early days of Tensho. At that time, since it was an imported product, tobacco was extremely expensive. In 1605, tobacco seeds were introduced. Farmers sowed the seeds at Sakurababa in Nagasaki and learned the art of cultivating and curing tobacco. After this, the cultivation and smoking of tobacco spread by rapid stages. One can gauge how rapid from the fact that in 1609 the second Tokugawa shogun issued an edict prohibiting the planting and selling of tobacco. Despite this prohibition, a large number of cultivators and tradesmen continued to deal in tobacco in violation of the shogunate's ban. By the era of Jokyo (1684–1687) tobacco was already the stock in trade of importers as well as shopkeepers.

In our country the tobacco craze, initiated in the Kyushu area, spread to the Kyoto-Osaka area and a little later to Edo (Tokyo). In the old days smokers did not carry tobacco pouches. The social amenities of the day required the host to furnish the tobacco to be smoked by his guests. As is only natural, time produced a change in this custom. Smokers began to carry their own tobacco with them. Thus arose the necessity for the tobacco pouch. At first smokers carried tobacco in purses or wallets, the wallet being preferred. Later, but prior to the general adoption of the tobacco pouch, smokers often carried paper pouches or paper bags containing tobacco which were attached to long pipes *(kiseru)*.

In Genroku (1688–1703) and Gembun (1736–1740) the hanging tobacco pouch was already in general use, as may be seen in the *Kotto Shu* (Collection of Curios) written by Seisai Edo in 1813 and in the *Ehon Makuzugahara* (Picture Book of Makuzugahara) by Nishikawa Sukenobu. In Anei (1772–1780) a large number of standard hanging tobacco pouches were to be seen decorated with fine metal ornaments *en suite* with ojime and netsuke. Note the pictures drawn by the painter Shimokobe Jusui in the book bearing his name.

During Anei a tradesman in Osaka named Yodoya Seibei created a particular tobacco pouch known as the Yodoya tobacco pouch. Since then, even including the present day, there are shops specializing in tobacco pouches; for example, the shop of Kagiya Gohei. Needless to say, tobacco pouches are also made and sold in the Tokyo area. Those produced at Ise enjoy an honorable fame as souvenirs of a pilgrimage to the Ise Shrine. Pouches made of a special material similar to leather popularly known as *kappa* enjoy a wide distribution. The trademark for kappa, "Watch out for Fire," is known everywhere.

So we see that as smoking grew in popularity, carrying tobacco became the accepted custom. The samurai, however, did not adopt the new custom but adhered to the old one requiring the host to offer tobacco to his guests. At the samurai home it was common etiquette to serve the guest with a tobacco tray and two pipes. It is also recorded in the *Saji Kiroku* (Records of the Tea Ceremony) that the tobacco tray furnished to tea-ceremony devotees was prepared with two pipes. Although the warrior class did not usually carry a tobacco pouch, in later periods an occasional samurai carried one in the sleeve pocket of his kimono. But the samurai never carried a tobacco pouch of the hanging or suspended kind.

Contrary to the old custom maintained among the samurai, carrying tobacco pouches was a most popular practice among the tradespeople. Businessmen considered smoking not only an aspect of good manners but also an essential concomitant of business negotiations. Most farmers, artisans, and merchants carried tobacco pouches hanging at their hips. Usually these pouches were opened and displayed as men smoked and talked. It was only natural for businessmen meeting in daily competition to spend a good deal of money on their tobacco pouches as the hallmark of success, just as the samurai splurged his wealth on his sword, the essence of the warrior spirit, even to the point of impoverishment. In those days commercial houses did not permit clerks and apprentices to smoke. Only those in managerial positions, however low, were permitted to do so. What a proud day when some young *banto* (executive) celebrated his promotion by sporting a tobacco pouch!

Among the tradesmen there were quite a few sports and dandies who squandered sums utterly beyond their means for luxurious tobacco pouches of which they were inordinately proud and vain, and they disputed with one another over the relative superiorities of these pouches. Usually they succeeded only in making themselves wretched from the strain of financing their costly purchases. Their preferences were often for cynical designs—snakes and skulls and such—of which these dandies were extremely fond (Figs. 39 and 64).

To sum up, then, among people other than the samurai, to carry a tobacco pouch and netsuke was the fashion. The trend went to the luxurious and expensive ensemble. People vied with one another in securing fine tobacco pouches and netsuke.

Spurred by their desires to express their individuality, these enthusiasts, sparing no expense, demanded new ideas in the leather pouch, the metal ornaments, the ojime, the netsuke, the pipe, and even the cord. The man whose sexagenary cycle was the Year of the Rat would utilize the rat and related subjects as decorations for the pouch; or he would for variety utilize the animal at the opposite side of the zodiac. In the case of a mask motif for decoration there might be, for example, a *tengu* (demon) mask (Fig. 65) for the metal part, an Ofuku (goddess of good nature) mask for the netsuke, and another mask for the ojime. Smokers gave expression to their own ideas about subject matter, design, and composition, and they owned not one but many tobacco pouches from which they selected the appropriate one for the particular season or occasion; for example, pine, bamboo, and plum blossom for the New Year; the animals of the zodiacal year, an appropriate subject for the *chugen* or summer lantern festival; and fitting subjects on the occasion of marriages or funerals. These ideas were applied not only to the tobacco pouch but also to the purse and other sagemono.

There were various kinds of leather *(kawa)* used in the manufacture of tobacco pouches: sprinkled-gold leather *(kinkara)*, soft deer leather, calfskin, Persian, Indian, Moorish, dyed, painted, tooled, and others. The metal parts of the tobacco pouches were wrought by such noted craftsmen as Somin (B 1107; Figs. 1 and 62), Yasuchika (B 1244), Shuraku (B 1075), and others. Semiprecious stones and valuable materials such as coral, amber, agate, and ancient Egyptian glass *(tombodama)* were made into ojime. The pipe also was made of various materials and in a variety of shapes to suit individual tastes. Needless to say, netsuke used in conjunction with the tobacco pouches were also very luxurious. Preferences in netsuke subjects varied widely and covered the entire range of individual predilection. Farmers often preferred ash-tray netsuke; businessmen were partial to such subjects as Daikoku (Fig. 60), rats, frogs, and Ofuku (Figs. 91 and 196); and others selected still other suitable subjects almost without limit.

In view of the great popularity of the smoking habit, the total number of netsuke produced in Japan must have been enormous. Before the advent of the tobacco pouch, the number in existence was small. But once the tobacco pouch came into general use, the netsuke became indispensable. In Tokyo, Kazusaya Kihei, Omiya Gorobei, and others were old and reputable wholesale dealers in pouches of all kinds. An association of pouch dealers that included 128 members was formed in 1904. The Maruchu, owned by Saito Chushichi, and the Maruka, owned by Saito Kasuke, were rated as first-class shops. In Osaka, Yawataya Sakubei, Mizuochi Shobei, Kawai Rihei, Tanaka Zembei, and others were well known wholesale dealers. It is easy to picture the wholesale dealers gathering together netsuke produced locally in the various provinces and buying and selling great quantities of them. The industrial artist who carved as a hobby grew into the netsuke specialist. The carvers made two classes of netsuke: one quickly produced for the wholesaler, the other finely designed and carefully executed for special order. Thus we see that the universal use of tobacco and the huge production of tobacco pouches assured the swift popularity of the netsuke.

6: Netsuke Materials

THE CARVERS of netsuke employed an almost endless variety of materials in creating their products. Although wood, because of its ready availability and its historical use for carving Buddhist images, was the most common medium, ivory ran it a close second in popularity in the later periods. Horn, metal, porcelain, and lacquer were also frequently used. Other materials included bamboo, gourds, shells, stones, coral, tortoise shell, agate, glass, and amber.

WOOD

There are many fine woods produced in our country. In fact, they stand unique among the woods of the world. Cypress *(hinoki)* is one of the best. It has a delightful fragrance and a subdued luster. It was prized in ancient times for the construction of shrines and temples and for the sculpturing of Buddhist images. It was a natural choice among materials when the carving of netsuke reached an artistic stage. Because Shuzan Yoshimura (B 1092), the first great netsuke artist (Figs. 143–145), generally used cypress, his followers tended to use it also. It is a soft wood, and the constant use of cypress netsuke leads to the effacement of the carving and sometimes to breakage, particularly of the part through which the attached cord passes. Since details are prone to be obliterated, cypress is not ideally suited to netsuke carving.

The most suitable material for netsuke is boxwood *(tsuge)*. Because of its strength, it has often been used for the manufacture of women's combs and for the carving of seals. It is well adapted to the netsuke's primary function of supporting the tobacco pouch or the inro. It is the first choice of the netsuke carver, not because of a random preference but because of its characteristic toughness, its fine and even grain, its smoothness, and its lustrous patina that improves with use and age. Boxwood is the ideal material for minute and delicate carving. It is therefore preferred above all other woods for the carving of netsuke.

The quality of boxwood varies to some extent with the area in which it is grown. That produced at Mt. Asakuma, near Ise, is the hardest and most lustrous and is used for carving *objets d'art* for the tokonoma *(okimono)*, and Japanese chessmen *(shogi no koma)*, as well as netsuke. The netsuke from the Ise and the Nagoya areas are generally made of boxwood. Ebony *(kokutan)* and cherry *(sakura)* are next in the order of preference.

Miwa (B 710), the renowned netsuke carver of Tokyo (Figs. 3, 68, and 71), was greatly concerned about the damage and defacement to which cypress netsuke were prone. As a result, he became the first prominent netsuke artist to use cherry, although he also used ebony and boxwood. He was also the first to line the cord holes of the netsuke with stained ivory.

Other woods frequently found in netsuke include black persimmon *(kurokaki)*, yew *(ichii)*, tea bush *(cha—*Fig. 61), camphor *(kusunoki)*, Zelkova *(tsuki)*, camellia *(tsubaki)*, jujube *(natsume)*, and pine *(kusabi)*. Netsuke were also occasionally carved from fragrant woods such as sandalwood *(byakudan)*. Even certain nuts (Figs. 43 and 45), as well as peach and apricot stones, were used, sometimes quite cleverly.

Some wooden netsuke are colored with paint or lacquer (Figs. 60, 61, 143, 144, and 145). Most are simply carved, sometimes in a series of angular planes—a style called *ittobori* or single-knife carving (Figs. 29, 40, and 126). Occasionally ivory as well as wooden netsuke are inlaid in the Shibayama style with coral, malachite, tortoise shell, shell, mother-of-pearl, jade, and other materials. There are still other types of mosaic or inlaid netsuke representing the human form. In fact, the technique of inlaying ebony for clothing and ivory for faces and hands was practiced from very early times (Figs. 66 and 72).

IVORY AND HORN

Except for boxwood, ivory was the most popular material for netsuke. During the three hundred odd years of the Tokugawa period, the people were blessed with peace. Music and dancing were popular pastimes for the humbler classes as well as the samurai. The samisen, with its strings and its ivory plectrum—the *sine qua non* of song and dance—was as much in vogue in the home as in the gay quarters. The demand for ivory plectrums was heavy. Shrewd businessmen collected the triangular-shaped pieces of waste ivory left in the places where plectrums were manufactured and sold them to the netsuke makers.

Most of the netsuke made from such waste material conformed to the shape of the material, with the result that they were triangular in shape. These were sold to people of ordinary taste. The size of such netsuke was larger than usual, and the carving did not appreciably reduce the weight of the material. Although they were sometimes signed, they were usually of little quality and were only occasionally worthy of great appreciation. Nevertheless, such netsuke reveal the subjects and designs that appealed to average people.

In contrast with this practice, the master netsuke carvers were conscious of their reputations and their prestige as artists, and they shunned the use of the triangular ivory remnants from factories. They used only the choicest of materials for their efforts. Kaigyokusai (B 430), for example, used *tokata*, the finest quality of ivory—usually found in Siamese and Annamese tusk—for his netsuke in this medium (Figs. 32, 70, 74, and 75.) Tokata is a very delicate-textured and beautiful ivory. Although it was exorbitantly priced, Kaigyokusai selected only the supreme material from among the best tokata.

After elephant ivory, the tusks of the boar, the narwhal, the walrus, and the hippopotamus were preferred. The Seiyodo school of netsuke carvers frequently used boar tusk (Fig. 67), and Issai Ogasawara (B 352; Fig. 80) and his followers used whale tooth in many cases. In the old days the ivory used for netsuke was imported through China and Korea. There seem to be two types of ivory: one that changes to an amber tint after long use and another that does not. I suppose the difference is due to variations of habitat and environment.

The next material in order of frequency of use was horn. Of this class, staghorn was the most popular (Figs. 20, 26, and 78.). The most famous netsuke carver in horn was Kokusai Takeda (B 527; Figs. 20 and 26). His style was unique and highly popular. Water-buffalo horn was next to deer horn in frequency of use. Rhinoceros horn (Fig. 17) and narwhal netsuke are found only infrequently.

The carving characteristics of wood and bamboo on the one hand

and of tusk and horn on the other are quite different. Wood has knots that must be cut away, and for this purpose a comparatively thin-bladed knife is used. Tusk and horn are shaped by shaving and consequently require a thick-bladed knife. The knives required for various types of wood and bamboo also differ.

METAL AND PORCELAIN

Metal netsuke are usually kagamibuta (Figs. 10–12) and ash-tray types (Figs. 21 and 24). The materials used in kagamibuta were mainly alloys of copper such as *shakudo* (copper and gold) and *shibuichi* (copper and silver), gold, silver, and others. Many kagamibuta netsuke were produced by noted metal artists (Fig. 10). A typical ash-tray netsuke is the one made by Kyubei of Sakai (Fig. 21), a dealer in Chinese metal articles of the Ming dynasty. His technique and designs were exceptional and won him wide acclaim. Kyubei's metal netsuke were cast from wax, and only one of a kind was made. Metal netsuke made by other artisans were usually cast in a mold that was used over and over again. Such netsuke were heavy and solid, and the price was cheap. They were recommended for reasons of economy, and the demand was great.

In addition to the above, there were netsuke made of brass or copper wire skillfully woven into various designs (Fig. 22). Occasionally one finds metal netsuke that are embellished with allover designs, as well as wooden netsuke to which metal sword furnishings like *fuchi-gashira* (pommels) or large *menuki* (hilt ornaments) have been affixed.

Porcelain netsuke were made from comparatively old times. Raku-yaki, Kyoyaki, Hiradoyaki (Fig. 89), Ibeyaki, Kiyomizuyaki, Kutani, Bando, Onko, and Kaseyama are some of the wares found in netsuke, and many of these are quite artistic (Fig. 91). Porcelain, although not so amenable to the delicate treatment possible in wood and ivory, is nevertheless capable of great artistry (Fig. 36). Some porcelain netsuke, however, were produced on the potter's wheel in great quantity.

LACQUER AND OTHER MATERIALS

Lacquer netsuke were also made from the old days, many of them by famous lacquerers. Since netsuke were used in combination with inro, it was natural for the inro maker to design the netsuke as well, harmonizing the design of both or complementing the design of one with that of the other (Figs. 119, 196, and 197). Ritsuo (B 826) made original designs for both inro and netsuke by applying lacquer to porcelain. Netsuke in *tsuishu* or red lacquer (Fig. 169), *tsuikoku* or black lacquer (Fig. 197), *mage* or twisted wood or paper, *kanshitsu* or carved dry lacquer, *negoro* or red and black lacquer polished to form a blotched pattern (Fig. 172), and *Kamakura-bori* (wood carved in various designs to which red or green lacquer is applied) have been known since early times.

There are three kinds of bamboo netsuke: *chikkon* or bamboo root (Fig. 225), carved bamboo stem (Fig. 38), and woven split bamboo. In most cases the bamboo is smoked. It is sometimes carved with a cutting edge. Most bamboo netsuke are in good taste. Some are light in color and done in ordinary style, while others are of darker tone and show a refined style. The bamboo artists Shogen (B 986) of Kyoto and Gyokkin (B 133) of Osaka also made netsuke as a hobby. The special bamboo from Matsushima called *midake* was used for making a considerable number of seals that also served as netsuke. Other unusual types of bamboo were also used for making netsuke.

Natural and carved gourds or shells are among the oldest of netsuke (Fig. 37). Many were also fashioned of rattan or the cane called *to* (Fig. 27). Ichiraku (B 311) was the originator of the technique of weaving netsuke out of split bamboo, and netsuke of this type are named for him.

Among novelty netsuke, we find such natural objects as a boar's jaw with the teeth, tusk, skin, and flesh removed; segments of the jaws of wolves, foxes, badgers, dogs, or bears; and leopard and tiger claws. Hunters were particularly proud to preserve some natural part of their kill for use as netsuke trophies (Fig. 31).

Stones (Figs. 34 and 42), *umimatsu* or black coral, also known as sea pine (Fig. 46), *bekko* or tortoise shell (Fig. 33), *umoregi* or fossil woods, *sumi* ink sticks, glass, agate, *sango* or coral (Fig. 117), and other materials were used as netsuke. Some were made of *kohaku* or amber (Fig. 146), or of silicified coal *(tamaishi)*, but such items were generally imported from abroad and have less interest as netsuke.

In netsuke depicting human beings or animals, black coral, black persimmon wood, ebony, and water-buffalo horn were used to represent the eyes. Unfortunately, however, buffalo horn and tortoise shell are likely to become worm-eaten. Master carvers like Kaigyokusai and Soko (B 1101) used inlaid yellow pearl *(kigai)* for animal eyeballs and black coral for the pupils. They used *hoten* (Fig. 170) secured from India for rabbit and monkey eyes in ivory netsuke.

▼

60. DAIKOKU. (Boxwood. 1 7/8″. Signed: Shuzan.
B 1093.) A painted netsuke representing Daikoku
carrying his bag of treasures. Shuzan was more
particularly known as Nagamachi, after the slum
section of Osaka, where he lived. Shuzan Nagamachi, who always signed his work, should be distinguished from Shuzan Yoshimura, his teacher,
who never signed. It is said that Shuzan Nagamachi
showed his profound respect for his teacher by using
hard woods instead of soft and by signing his netsuke, so that there could never be any uncertainty
between his creations and those of his teacher.

61. TEA PICKER. (Tea wood. 2″. Unsigned.) A
painted netsuke made from the branch of a tea bush.
It represents a typical tea picker of the Uji area in
her working costume. Netsuke of this type are known ◄
as Uji ningyo or Uji dolls and are sold as souvenirs
of the Uji district, which is famous for its green tea.
See Gyuka, Biography 167.

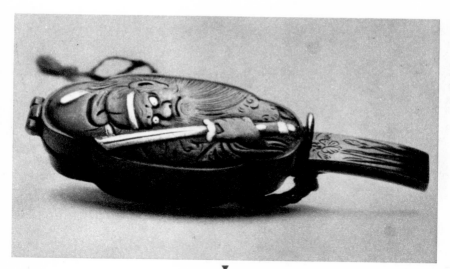

62. YATATE NETSUKE. (Metal. 2 ⅛″ long. Signed: Yokoya saku. B 1107.) A yatate (case for writing brush and inkpot) netsuke in metal decorated with an etched and inlaid design of Shoki the Demon Queller, sword unsheathed. See text, page 66. See Fig. 143 for another illustration of Shoki.

63. SUNDIAL NETSUKE. (Silver-bronze decorated with cloisonné. 1 ⁷⁄₁₆″ long. Unsigned.) An unusual type of sundial netsuke. One section contains a compass, the other a sundial. See text, page 66. The basic material, silver bronze, is decorated with cloisonné in floral and butterfly designs.

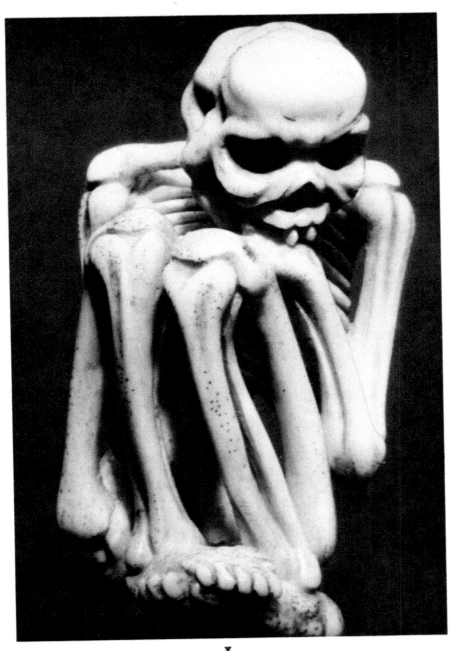

▼

64. SKELETON. (Ivory. 1 ¹³/₁₆″. Unsigned.) The artist has cleverly handled the problem of carving a complete skeleton so that its shape and compactness serve its function as a netsuke. See text, pages 107 and 159.

▼
65. GIGAKU MASK: TENGU. (Wood. 2 1/8".
Signed: Ittokusai.) The masks of the no longer
extant Gigaku dance-drama are the first
historic masks to survive in Japan. Among
the characters that figured prominently in
the Gigaku were the long-nosed demons called
tengu, of which there are two classes: the
konoha tengu, which are in human form but
have extended noses like that of Pinocchio,
and the karasu (crow) tengu, which have
bird beaks. The netsuke pictured here portrays the latter type.

▼
66. DIVING GIRL. (Ivory and red
sandalwood. 2 1/4". Signed: Yukoku. B 1326.) A diving girl
(ama) drying herself after a
plunge into the sea. The body is
ivory; the skirt, red sandalwood.

▼
67. SPIDER AND POEMS. (Boar tusk. 4" long. Signed: Iwami Kawaigawa Seiyodo
Gansui. B 384.) A natural boar tusk from which a spider has been carved in high
relief. The microscopic writing consists of representative waka (thirty-one-syllable
poems) by the thirty-six most famous poets of Japan.

82

▼
68. MONKEY DOLL. (Cherry wood. 1 9/16″.
Signed: Miwa. B 710.) A simplified sim-
ian form suggesting a rag doll of the
type that was popularly made in earlier
days by the young girls of certain regions
of Japan and was called saru ningyo or
monkey doll.

▼
69. ELEPHANT. (Ivory inlaid with various materials. 1 5/8″. Signed: Shibayama. B 954.) A typical Shibayama
netsuke inlaid with coral, tortoise shell,
pearl, metal, and other materials.
Although Shibayama is the family
name of the artist who originated or
popularized mosaic inlay, the term
Shibayama is now used generically to
indicate the technique. The signature
appears on an inlaid oblong pearl
plaque.

70. RYUAN. (Ivory. 2 1/4″. Signed: Kaigyokusai Yasunaga. Yasunaga was the artist's adoptive
name, which he rarely used. B 430.) This is probably
▶ a representation of the sennin Ryuan, who com-
pounded the elixir of immortality and, after drink-
ing it, rose into the clouds. His pet rooster pecked
at the dish containing the elixir and also rose to
heaven.

83

71. NIO AND ONI. (Cherry wood. 2 7/8". Signed: Miwa. B 710.) This portrayal of
a Nio and an oni wrestling symbolizes the struggle between good and evil. Although
the oni appears to enjoy the advantage, in the classic sumo position represented—
the kawazu throw—the Nio is about to gain the fall.

▼

72. KABUKI ENTERTAINER. (Wood and ivory. 1 ⁵/₁₆″. Signed: Ho-ichi. B 241.) A man entertains by playing a Kabuki role. His mask, inlaid in ivory, simulates the special Kabuki make-up called kumadori. It is not a character mask, however, since such masks are not used in the Kabuki, except in occasional dramas adapted from the Noh.

▼

73. GO PLAYERS. (Ivory. 1 ¹/₁₆″. Signed: Issai. B 352.) Two tradesmen (chonin) intent on a game of *go*, a complicated Japanese form of checkers.

85

74. MONKEYS. (Ivory. 1 ³/₈″. Signed: Kaigyokusai Masatsugu. B 430.) In Japan, the monkey
(saru) is traditionally believed to have the power
of dispelling evil spirits and of assuring safe and
easy delivery in childbirth. The kami no tsukai
(messenger of the god) at several of Japan's
famous shrines is a monkey. The netsuke pictured here displays the extreme care with which
Kaigyokusai did his carving.

75. GOAT AND YOUNG. (Ivory.
1 ¹/₄″. Signed: Kaigyokusai.
B 430.) This netsuke, like the
one shown in Fig. 74, exhibits
the striking naturalism with
which Kaigyokusai portrayed
his subjects.

76. DARUMA. (Inlaid wood, ivory, and other materials. 1 9/16″. Signed: Tokoku. B 1184.) A yawning Daruma made of inlaid wood, ivory, glass, red lacquer, metal, and other materials. Daruma is often represented yawning, as though in mock sympathy for the nine long years he spent in public meditation in his efforts to gain recognition for the Zen sect. For the same reason Daruma is often represented with atrophied legs; he is the roly-poly of Japan. For other illustrations of Daruma see Fig. 40, 115, and 128.

77. DIVING GIRL. (Ivory, wood, and other materials. 2 9/16″ long. Signed: Gyokuso. B 160.) A diving girl holding an abalone in her arm sleeps on a huge dried salmon. The material is ivory, wood, pearl, tortoise shell, and a type of iridescent pearl shell that imparts a most realistic appearance to the fish eyes.

78. KAPPA. (Staghorn. 1 $^7/_{16}$" long. Signed: Rensai. B 818.) A staghorn netsuke representing a kappa (water imp) caught in the grip of a giant clam—a predicament that must delight every Japanese youngster who has been frightened away from swimming by his mother's warning that a kappa will get him by the leg and drown him.

79. CLUSTERING RATS. (Ivory. 1 $^3/_4$" long. Signed: Tomochika. B 1195.) The subject is a group of seven clustering rats. Counting tails, legs, and heads, there are forty-two appendages that might be subject to breakage and entanglement, yet the design is so cleverly contrived that the result is a smooth, round, "perfect" netsuke. See text, page 159.

80. RONIN. (Whale tooth. 2 $^1/_8$" long. Unsigned, but attributed to Issai Ogasawara. B 352.) The figure probably represents a ronin (masterless samurai), turned robber and disguised as a farmer, lying in ambush with his half-drawn sword concealed beneath him. The netsuke was purchased in Wakayama, the home of Issai Ogasawara, from a family that had owned it for more than three generations.

▼ ▼

81. BLIND MAN. (Wood. 2 ¹/₈″. Signed: Shoko. B 1010.) The blind man stands on a single wooden clog (geta) in order to remove a stone lodged in the other. This is a good example of balance as mentioned in the text on page 108. Note the netsuke, tobacco pouch, and pipe case worn by the blind man as seen in the side view.

82. HANDAKA SONJA. (Ivory. 1 ⁵/₁₆″. Signed: Issai. B 352.) Handaka Sonja, one of the sixteen Rakan (main disciples of Buddha), entices the dragon from his bowl by showing the ◀ sacred jewel. Shaven heads, long drooping eyebrows, and large earlobes are some of the attributes of the Rakan.

83. ONO NO TOFU. (Wood. 2". Unsigned.) A humorous treatment of the story of Ono no Tofu, the celebrated calligraphist, who learned perseverance from a frog which continued jumping until it reached the branch for which it aimed. The figure balances on a single geta. See text, page 108. See Fig. 226 for another illustration of Ono no Tofu.

84. GIGAKU MASK: OTOKO. (Wood treated with red lacquer. 1 11/16". Signed: Choka copied this mask after a mask owned by the Tamukeyama Temple.) A Gigaku mask for the character Otoko, an old man. Gigaku, an ancient form of the dance-drama, is no longer extant in Japan, but a number of its masks have survived.

85. NOH MASK: KAMINARI. (Ivory; eyes inlaid in pearl and black coral. 1 1/2". Signed Kyogyoku.) The netsuke represents a Noh mask for the character Kaminari, who is actually Raijin, the god of thunder, under a stage name.

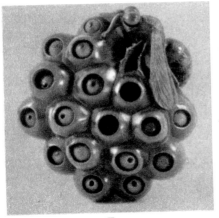

86. WASP AND HIVE. (Wood. 1 ⁷/₁₆″. Signed: Toyomasa. B 1254.) Although the larvae are loose and can be rattled, they do not fall free. See text, page 108.

87. NOH MASK: GEDO. (Wood. 1 ³/₄″. Signed: Masayuki. B 644.) The mask portrayed in this netsuke is probably that of Gedo, a heretic.

88. KYOGEN MASK: HYOTTOKO. (Wood. 1 ⁵/₈″. Signed: Masakazu. Kakihan. B 596.) Kyogen are the comic interludes in a Noh performance. The earthy Kyogen presents a strong contrast to the formal, ethereal Noh. The mask portrayed in this netsuke is also used by the street performers called manzai, a group of whom appear in Fig. 101. The character represented here is Hyottoko, a man with a twisted mouth and a popping eye. See Fig. 5 for another example of a Kyogen mask.

89. GAMA SENNIN. (Porcelain. 2 $^1/_{16}$''.
Unsigned.) The netsuke is made of
Hiradoyaki, a fine porcelain ware of
Korean origin produced on the island
of Hirado near Kyushu. The subject is
a Gama Sennin, a happy "immortal"
associated with the toad (gama). Note
the toad peeping from the sennin's
sleeve. See Fig. 178 for another illustration of Gama Sennin.

90. SENNIN WITH SACRED JEWEL.
(Wood, lacquered and inlaid with
pearl, ivory, shell, and other materials. 4 $^5/_{16}$''. Unsigned.) This netsuke is of the kind that is loosely referred to as the "Shuzan" type. Its
claim to the classification rests only
on size, subject, and the fact that it is
colored. Compare Figs. 143, 144, and
145. The subject is one of the Chinese
"immortals" holding a sacred jewel
(tama) in his hand.

91. OTAFUKU. (Porcelain. 1 ³/₄". Signed: Kenya. B 479. See text, page 76.) The subject is Otafuku, also known as Ofuku, Okame, and Uzume. The name means "big cheeks" and is applied to ugly, ungainly women. For other illustrations of Okame, a favorite subject of the netsuke carver, see Figs. 120, 132, 150, and 196.

92. COCK AND HEN. (Wood. 1 ³/₁₆″. Signed: Masanao. B 613.) This representation of a cock and a hen in a coop is a good example of a trick netsuke that separates into two parts.

93. TSUBA. (Ebony. 2 ¹/₈″. Signed: Yoshu Kotetsu.) A netsuke in the design of a tsuba or sword guard. Note the simulated fish-roe (nanako) ground. The piece is most likely the work of a metal artist. The signature is highly enigmatic and is a good example of some of the problems encountered in reading netsuke signatures. The roots and radicals of the characters are transposed, as in seals. The characters are read "Yoshu Kotetsu," and the meaning seems to be "old (ko) iron (tetsu) from Yoshu (a district of China)."

94

▼
94. HORNED DEMON. (Wood. 1 ¹/₂″. Signed: Ryumin. B 864.) An oni regards himself in a mirror as he struggles to extirpate his horns. This is the identical subject carved by Seizui Hamano, the metal artist, and referred to in the text on pages 113–14.

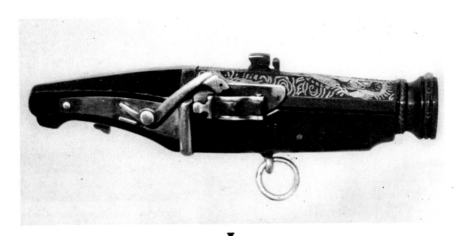

▼
95. PORTUGUESE GUN. (Red sandalwood and metal with damascene inlay. 2 ¹⁵/₁₆″ long. Signed: Murasada.) It was the Portuguese who, around 1542, introduced the Japanese to firearms. This netsuke is a replica of one of the weapons that caused great excitement upon their appearance in Japan.

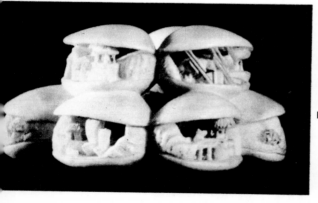

96. OMI HAKKEI. (Ivory. 1 3/8"
long. Signed: Nagamitsu. B
731.) The netsuke represents
the famous Omi Hakkei, the
eight beautiful views around
►Lake Biwa, minutely carved
inside a group of clamshells.
This is an example of anabori
or "cavern carving." Most
anabori netsuke are carved in
a representation of a shell.

97. ROCK BASKET. (Wood. 1 3/8".
Signed: Kyokusai. B 565.) Carved
from a single block, the netsuke
represents a basket of rocks used for
damming rivers. The "rocks" are ◄
loose and move about within the
basket. A good example of superb
mechanical ingenuity in carving.
See text, page 108.

98. LANDSCAPE. (Red sandalwood. 1 11/16". Signed: Goto
Masayoshi.) A landscape design of clouds, mountain, and
village executed in the style of
a Chinese painting. There is
no conclusive evidence that a
►metal artist did the carving except for the signature Goto
Masayoshi, which is a combination of the names of Ishi-
guro Masayoshi and Goto, who
represented two families of
great metal artists.

▼

100. TSURU SENNIN. (Ivory. 1 $^7/_{16}$".
Signed: Mitsuhiro. B 685.) The Tsuru
Sennin (or Teirei) is an "immortal"
usually portrayed riding on or accompanied by a crane (tsuru). In this representation the sennin holds a Buddhist
scepter or nyoi.

▼

99. OISHI KURANOSUKE. (Wood;
sword and crest inlaid in ivory. 2".
Signed: Soko. B 1100.) Oishi Kuranosuke, the leader of the Forty-
seven Rōnin, as a young man. Kuranosuke, called Yuranosuke in the
Kabuki version of the story (Chu-
shingura), is positively identified by
the crest on the back of his kimono.
The characters of the artist's signature, though they read "Soko," are
different from those given for Soko
Toshiyama in Biography 1100. The
artist may have exercised a common
prerogative in changing the characters of his name to suit his whim.

▼

101. MANZAI. (Ivory. 1 $^9/_{16}$". Signed:
Meikeisai. This is an artist name of Hojitsu. B 243.) The netsuke portrays a
group of itinerant entertainers (manzai)
singing, dancing, and playing on the
drum.

97

▼

102. HORSE. (Ivory; eyes inlaid in amber and black coral. 1 $^7/_{16}$" long. Signed: Rantei. B 812.) The horse has long been a highly admired animal in Japan, both as a steed for warriors and as an object of worship. The sacred white horse found at many shrines is a relic of the ancient Shinto ritual of purification and has the role of hearing the confessions of the worshippers. In the netsuke pictured here, the artist has rendered his subject in flowing classic lines.

▼

103. NOH DANCE. (Wood. 1 ⁵/₈″. Signed: Hozan saku. B 290.) The lion-mask dance from the Noh play *Shakkyo*. Note the diapering on the kimono, a carved substitute for the sumptuous woven patterns of the original. Compare the same subject treated in lacquer, Fig. 119.

104. IKKAKU SENNIN. (Ivory. 3 ¹¹/₁₆″. Signed: Rantei. B 812.) The story of Ikkaku (the Single-horned) Sennin relates that he lost his magical powers when ◄ he succumbed to the temptations of a beautiful woman. Note the sennin's horn, which is partially concealed by his head covering.

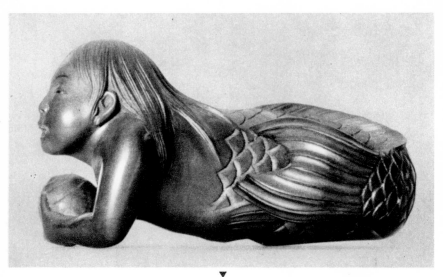

▼

105. MERMAID. (Wood. 2 ¹/₈″ long. Signed: Kokeisai Sansho. Kokeisai is the artist name of Sansho Wada. B 903.) A mermaid holding a sacred jewel. There is a Japanese legend to the effect that one who eats the flesh of a mermaid will enjoy eternal youth.

▼

106. THE MIRACULOUS TEAKETTLE. (Ebony. 1 ¹/₂″ long. Signed: Mitsuhiro. B 685.) The netsuke illustrates the fable of the miraculous teakettle (bumbuku chagama) that turned into a badger when a priest put it on the fire to boil water for tea. The himotoshi is inserted on the inside of the cover of the teakettle. The ebony of which the piece is carved has been cleverly treated to simulate iron. The eyes are inlaid in amber and black coral.

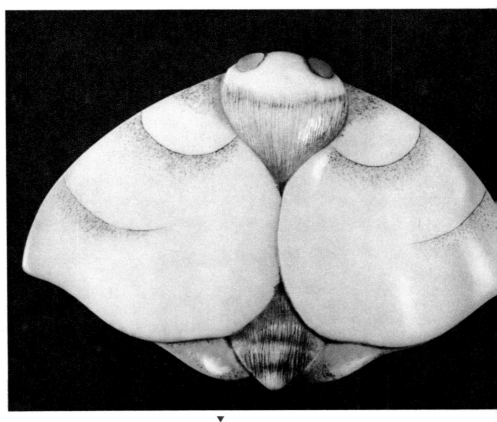

107. Moth. (Ivory; eyes inlaid in pearl. 1 $\frac{3}{4}''$ long. Signed: Dosho. B 89.) A lightweight netsuke suitable for use with an inro. See text, page 64.

108. DRIED SALMON. (Black coral. 2 ½" long. Signed: Tomotada saku. B 1216.) A dried salmon carved from black coral
(umimatsu). The fish scales are realistically carved so that they
are smooth or rough to the touch depending on whether the
finger is moved in the direction of the tail fin or of the head.

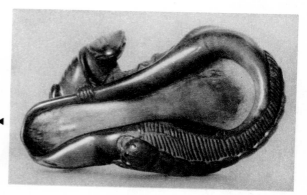

109. LIZARD AND CENTI-
PEDE. (Wood. 2 ³/₁₆"
long. Signed: Yoshinaga.
B 1302.) A lizard and a
centipede on opposite ◄
sides of an elephant-ear
leaf. The stem of the leaf
forms the place of attachment of the cord.

110. SNAKE AND FROG. (Wood.
2 ¹/₁₆" long. Signed: Masanao.
►B 612.) In an episode of primitive savagery, a snake devours
a frog on a straw sandal.

102

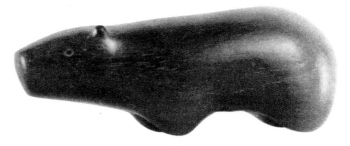

111. BEAR. (Red sandalwood. 1 ⅝″ long. Signed: Ichiraku. B 310.) This stylized representation of a bear effectively illustrates the imaginative design, the balance, and the rounded shape that characterize the best of the netsuke carvers' creations. The design was probably borrowed from the ancient clay burial figures called haniwa. This netsuke carries the artist's signature in a lacquer cartouche.

112. TENNIN. (Ivory. 1 ⅝″ long. Signed: Hojitsu. B 243.) The tennin, who are the angels of the Buddhist paradise, are accomplished musicians and dancers. The one depicted in this netsuke plays a hand drum of the type called tsuzumi. The most famous of Japanese tales about the tennin is the one told in the Noh play *Hagoromo* (The Robe of Feathers).

113. INK-STICK NETSUKE. (Ebony. 1 ¾″ long. Signed: Made by Kyusai, Naniwa, Imperial Japan. Naniwa is the old name for Osaka. B 576). The solid ink called sumi is made from the soot produced by burning pine wood or oil. This is mixed with a glue extracted from fish bones and pressed into sticks which are carved with various designs. Fine old ink sticks are collectors' items in the Orient. Liquid ink is produced by rubbing the stick in a small amount of water. Compare this netsuke with the one shown in Fig. 197.

103

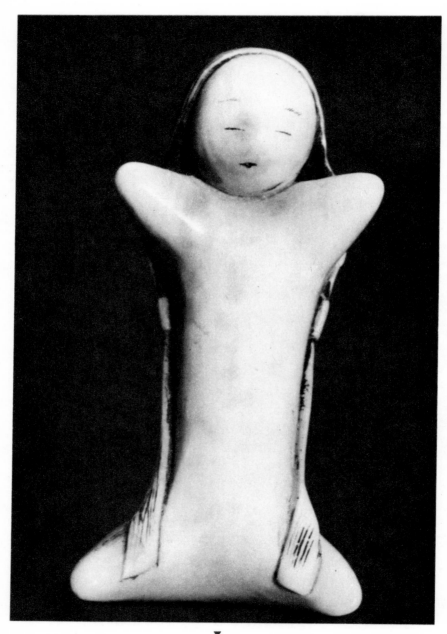

114. AMAGATSU. (Ivory. 2 ¹⁄₄". Signed: Masanao. B 609.) The netsuke illustrated here simulates an amagatsu, a stylized doll which in former times was placed near the head of a newborn child in supplication to the gods to protect him and grant him good health. This childbirth symbol is said to be an ancestor of the dolls that are displayed in the annual Doll Festival on March 3.

115. DARUMA. (Wood. 1 ⁵/₁₆″. Signed: Joso saku. B 400.) Daruma, who should be meditating, is reading an erotic "pillow book" and "biting the laugh." The netsuke provides an example of the jocular freedom with which religious figures may be caricatured and mocked in Japanese art.

116. KIYOHIME AND THE BELL OF DOJO-JI. (Wood. 1 ⁹/₁₆″. Signed: Tadatoshi. B 1146.) The temple called Dojo-ji is the traditional site of the tragic climax of the temptress Kiyohime's love for the chaste priest Anchin. Here, after he had spurned her advances, Anchin took refuge from Kiyohime beneath the temple bell. She, turning herself into a demon serpent, wrapped herself about the bell and melted it in the flames of her fury, while the luckless Anchin burned to death inside. The story forms the plot of a drama famous in both its Noh and its Kabuki versions.

117. ONI AND CLAM. (Coral. 2 5/16″ long. Unsigned.) A coral netsuke of a pale pink hue. A devil (oni) is in distress, his loincloth caught and held by a massive clam. The expression on his face reflects his desperate plight.

118. SHOJO. (Lacquered ivory with coral mask. 1 5/8″. Signed: Koteisai.) The Noh dance of the red-faced, red-haired drunkard called a shojo. See Fig. 162 for another illustration of a shojo.

7: Netsuke Subjects and Designs

THE NETSUKE has no function by itself but is used together with a sagemono or suspended object which it supports between the hip and the sash. Functionally, any object that can support the sagemono serves as a netsuke. But the netsuke developed ornamentally as well as functionally and in this way grew into an art form.

Since inro, pouches, and purses were worn and used in public, preferences grew toward the beautiful and the luxurious. Consequently, carvers expended great effort to create new ideas and designs in netsuke. In the early days most netsuke were made for pleasure and amusement by painters, metalworkers, and other artists. Thus improvements in mechanical techniques were not to be expected. More attention was given to subject and design than to mechanical ingenuity. Subject and design were considered the essence of netsuke. The reason is therefore clear why one sometimes finds netsuke of superb design amounting to great art in miniature.

The design of netsuke, like that of other art forms, falls into three artistic levels: reproduced realities, imaginary or exaggerated extensions of realities, and abstractions and impressions. One finds the designs of most netsuke on the second of these levels. It is quite rare to find designs that reproduce reality photographically, as is often the case in the art of the Occident.

In view of its function, certain restrictions must be observed in designing a netsuke. It must be limited to a particular small size; it must pass easily between the obi and the hip; and the shape must be smooth, rounded, and free of jutting points or sharp edges. (See Figs. 64 and 79). The form of the netsuke must be of a type that will not be damaged by the friction that accompanies its use. Indeed, a small amount of rubbing should impart a refinement to it. Again, the netsuke must be sufficiently sturdy to suspend and support the sagemono by the cord that passes through it. The holes for the cord must not mar or detract from the design, and they must be made on that side of the netsuke that fits snugly against the body. For example, if the netsuke portrays a standing figure, the holes are usually made at the back of the figure so that the face side will be visible when the netsuke is worn. Thus, unlike other art forms that are free from the limitations imposed by use and are only to be looked at, the netsuke must conform to certain restrictions imposed by its function.

Particular designs sometimes impose special limitations. Balance is often carefully considered in producing a netsuke. Examples of proper balance are the figures that stand on one leg (Figs. 81 and 83). There are many designs that have required mechanical triumphs for their accomplishment; for example, figures with loose tongues or movable heads, as well as seeds in lotus pods, bees in hives (Fig. 86), and mushrooms in baskets—all of which, though loose, do not fall free from the netsuke.

It has already been noted that design is the essence of netsuke. Painters and other artists created designs which they carved into netsuke or at least created designs that were suitable for use by the carvers. Very often, once a good design had been created, the netsuke carver repeated it again and again, and even his students and followers copied the identical design.

At the end of the Tokugawa period, reference books containing netsuke designs were published to keep carvers abreast of the work of painters and other artists who created original designs for this purpose. These publications included illustrations for other crafts as well as for that of making netsuke. The *Banshoku Zuko* (Illustrations of Multitudinous Occupations) is based on the original drawings of Hokusai Katsushika published by Gungyokudo Roko in six volumes between 1835 and 1850. At the conclusion of the text appears a clear statement that the volume is intended as a reference for netsuke carvers and other artisans. The two-volume *Bambutsu Zukai Isai Gashiki* (Isai's Designs for Everything) was published for the same purpose in the autumn of 1864. The *Bijutsu Chokoku Gafu* (Art of Sculpture Illustrated) by Takeda Denuemon was published in 1892. In the introduction by Okamoto Kasai it is stated that sculpturing from paintings and drawings is a characteristic of the art of our country which, from sentiment and patriotism, we should seek to develop and improve. All these books contain designs suitable for netsuke and are intended to be used as references by the netsuke carvers.

The subjects of netsuke cover the entire range of shapes and forms, including, as they do, representations of things of the imagination as well as of actuality. Thus netsuke portray deities, *sennin* (wizard hermits), human beings, birds, animals, insects, fish, fruits, mountains, rivers, landscapes, and innumerable other subjects, including even family crests. Among the human figures depicted are Shoki, Daruma, Kanzan and Jittoku, meditating priests, blind masseurs, Ashinaga and Tenaga (Longlegs and Longarms), ratcatchers, Tartars, puppeteers, Ofuku, devils, and endless others. In the non-human class there are badgers, wolves, lions, butterflies, bees, cicadas, turtles, shellfish, frogs, animals of the zodiac, catfish, gulls, sparrows, hawks, and other living things too numerous to name. As for masks, those of Ofuku are the most popular, but there are many others from the Bugaku, the Noh, and the Kyogen, including Hannya, Okina, and the fox (Figs. 85, 87, 88, etc.). The people we call *asobinin* (drifters and gamblers) particularly liked snake and skull netsuke because of a prevailing superstition that they brought luck to gamblers. The animals of the zodiac were also popular, and purchasers ordered netsuke depicting the animals in whose years they were born. Masanao of Ise (B 612) efficiently prepared a catalog of his carvings of animals so that his customers could order from it.

An artist who exercised great influence on the subject and design of netsuke was Shuzan Yoshimura of Osaka. He was primarily a painter, a pupil of Tanyu Kano. He was honored for his painting with the artist rank of *hogan*. Netsuke carving was only his hobby. His designs were chiefly of sennin and other subjects taken from the *Sankaikyo* (a Chinese publication in eighteen volumes containing illustrations of sennin, ghosts, and legendary animals) and other books. The wood he used was cypress, which he tastefully colored with enhancing effect. Shuzan is considered a great master of netsuke carving, and his work is frequently copied. His influence on the netsuke carvers who followed him was great. His netsuke were never signed, and they are now very scarce. It is most difficult to judge the genuineness of netsuke purporting to be Shuzan's (Figs. 143–145). The Imperial Museum in Tokyo has a group of netsuke attributed to him.

In addition to the netsuke mentioned above, rats by Ikkan (B 321), cows by Tomotada (B 1216), monkeys by Kaigyokusai (Figs. 74 and 146), monkeys and turtles by Tomokazu (B 1206), Ofuku by Shugetsu (B 1042), quails by Okatomo (B 784; Fig. 206), animals of the zodiac by Masanao of Ise (Fig. 92), tigers by Kokei (B 524), loquats by Mitsuhiro (B 685), cicadas by Tomiharu (B 1191), Noh dolls by Toen (B 1177; Fig. 29), skulls by Gyokuzan Asahi (B 164), masks by the Deme family (Fig. 41), and *anabori* (interior carvings) by Hoshin (B 275) are particularly famous. It is said that a netsuke carver named Insai (B 345) devoted his entire life to the repeated unsigned carving of a single subject, a monkey trainer, in two designs. I shall speak in more detail about the netsuke carvers in a later chapter.

As examples of innovations based on simple designs, we find a Daruma with revolving eyes or a representation of the priest Anchin and the scorned Kiyohime of the Dojo-ji tragedy in which, through a tiny aperture simulating damage to the bronze bell, one may see the face of Anchin in successive colors of red, white, and blue as the bell hanger is turned. These two novelties are credited to Minko (B 661). Again, there are wicker baskets with loose stones inside that rattle with a lovely sound (Fig. 97) and various other elaborations. The carpenter's inkpot and the Portuguese gun (Fig. 95) are netsuke whose merit is found in the unusual subject matter itself rather than in the carving.

The "combined use" netsuke mentioned in Chapter 4 is deserving of attention in considering design and subject. This type of netsuke has a secondary function in addition to its basic use as a netsuke. Examples are the abacus, the tinderbox, the sundial, and the yatate.

Kagamibuta and manju netsuke were generally made subsequent to the Ansei period (1854–1859). These were usually shaped by lathe before final carving. My impression is that most of the netsuke in Edo were destroyed in the great earthquake of Ansei. The production of these types of netsuke could be rushed, and therefore kagamibuta and manju were produced in large quantities.

The three hundred years of the Tokugawa era constituted a period of tranquillity in which art flourished. With regard to painting, for example, the Kano of Tokyo were protégés of the shogun, the Tosa were sponsored by the Imperial Household in Kyoto, and there were many artists who found patronage among the daimyo. Artists thus sponsored were bound to conform to the artistic style and tradition of their families. The styles of painting were not the natural styles of individual members but were patterns developed by the family. We are therefore seldom able to find anything new or unusual in the paintings of the sponsored artists.

On the contrary, netsuke were popular among the common people, although not with the samurai and royalty. Exclusive employment or sponsorship of the netsuke carver was almost unheard of, despite the fact that the system of exclusive employment was a product of the peaceful life of the Tokugawa era. By exception, Hojitsu (B 243; Figs. 101, 112, and 182) may almost be considered to have been in the employ of the shogun in the later years of the Tokugawa period. His, however, was a most unusual case. Most of the netsuke carvers were free and independent, unfettered by any traditions, and able to choose any subject worth representing and any technique worth applying to a new art form. The netsuke warrants our special interest as an expression of the essential character of the Tokugawa era.

The work of the master carvers is of course the most meritorious. Nevertheless, because of the enormous public demand, netsuke making became a wholesale trade, and as a result many netsuke of inferior quality were carved, and repetitious subjects were mass-produced. Many netsuke makers worked for their daily bread rather than for the spiritual satisfaction of the artist. It is of course understandable that in the days of the peak popularity of the netsuke, wholesalers would deal in inferior pieces to satisfy the great demand.

The large number of erotic netsuke that had "hidden pleasures" for their subject must also be considered. Like the ukiyo-e woodblock prints, the netsuke developed through popular appeal during the Edo period. I have seen an Otafuku (Ofuku) netsuke of this kind on which was inscribed: "Minko made this at the request of a daimyo for his amusement." This is an unusual case, and it is doubtful that Minko was actually the carver. I have also seen a netsuke by Hojitsu in the shape of a papier-mâché dog that opened to reveal a very erotic design. I also once saw an ivory netsuke carved to simulate a menuki in the form of Ofuku with a lewd design on the reverse. It bore the fraudulent signature of Kaigyokusai. I believe that the application of erotic themes to netsuke was discouraged because netsuke were worn publicly and openly before the eyes of women and children. At a later date, when netsuke were exported, erotic subjects were more frequently carved. Even so, the subject was usually concealed within the netsuke, and only rarely was an exposed "hidden pleasure" design of complete figures carved.

8: The Netsuke Artists

To SUMMARIZE, the use of netsuke grew out of practical necessity. At first gourds, shells, and other natural objects were utilized by the simple expedient of attaching a cord. By gradual stages netsuke developed ornamentally as well as functionally. More attention was given to subject and design, and the netsuke grew into an art form. It was first used with the purse, pouch, and other sagemono. Its artistic level improved when it came to be used with the inro.

In the early days the carving of netsuke was for the most part an amusement or hobby of the makers of Buddhist images, painters, and metalworkers. From Genroku through Shotoku netsuke became very popular. As the general taste for artistic netsuke grew, considerations of design and subject became more important, and numerous original and elaborate designs were created. Starting with Horeki, the vogue for tobacco pouches resulted in an enormous demand for netsuke, which brought about the birth of the specialized netsuke carver. Nevertheless, the fine artist who carved netsuke for his own pleasure or as a hobby continued as before, unaffected by the specialists who devoted themselves exclusively to the production of netsuke. This accounts for the great variation in quality among netsuke. It is the variation between art and craft.

We have already discussed Shuzan Yoshimura, who occupies the forefront in the field of netsuke. Hogan (artist title) Shugetsu (Fig. 4) is another artist who carved netsuke as a diversion. Shugetsu first lived in Osaka and then moved to Tokyo. Most of his carvings are masks of Ofuku. His descendants continued carving through four notable generations.

There were quite a few metalworkers who carved netsuke as a hobby. Seizui Hamano (B 938) is an instance. One of his superior creations is an *oni* (demon) regarding himself in a mirror as he tries to extirpate his horns (Fig. 94). The material is the wood of the mountain cherry tree. Another instance is Tou Tsuchiya (B 1244), whose artist name is Yasuchika Tsuchiya. He is known in metal art as one of the "three greats" of Nara. Yasuchika tried his hand at carving netsuke for pleasure, using bamboo and other woods. His creations are of an invariable excellence and are usually signed: "Made by Tou for fun." Mitsuoki Otsuki (B 701) was a noted metalworker of the Kyowa era (1801–1803). He used boxwood to carve a netsuke depicting a frog perched on a skull. The depth of the eye socket of the skull is marked by a barely visible pinhole—a most difficult feat. His technical skill is so remarkable as to be almost unattainable by artists limited in experience to the media of wood and ivory. In addition to netsuke, Mitsuoki made many metal discs for kagamibuta.

Tomotada (B 1217), another metalworker, carved boxwood netsuke and inro in bold designs as a hobby. Many other metalworkers were carvers of netsuke (Figs. 93 and 98). There is a netsuke bearing the signature "Kaneyuki, living at Maruyama, Kofu." (See B 445.) The addition of the word "living" usually denotes the work of a metal artist. Of course, many noted metalworkers executed the metal parts of kagamibuta netsuke in bas-relief, inlay, or etching (Figs. 10–12).

There were numerous mask carvers who also made netsuke. Deme Uman (B 77) is one of the best. He was a Noh-mask carver of Tokyo, and his mask netsuke usually bear the signature "Tenka-ichi Deme Uman" (Deme Uman, best in the world). Deme Joman (B 69; Fig. 41) also made mask netsuke. There were a number of other members of the Deme family who carved netsuke. One frequently finds mask netsuke bearing the signature "Tenka-ichi Deme Saman" (B 75). Although this artist wished to indicate a relationship between himself and Uman, his work is far below the standards of Uman.

There have been quite a few dollmakers who also carved netsuke. One of the earliest was Hinaya Ryuho, whose real name was Nonoguchi Ryuho (B 779). He was nicknamed Hinaya (dollmaker) because his vocation was the creation of fine dolls. Extant examples of his work are very scarce. Ryuho was also proficient at painting and poetry. Chikayuki Fukushima (B 33), who lived at Asakusa in Tokyo, excelled at making Asakusa dolls but was also a carver of netsuke. There were many others among the makers of Nara dolls (Fig. 29) and Uji dolls (Fig. 61) who also carved netsuke.

Among the many ceramists who made netsuke were Ninsei (B 761; Fig. 36), Mokubei (B 712), Hozen (B 293), Dohachi Niami (B 81), Kitei (B 494), Kenya (B 479; Fig. 91), Zoroku (B 1339), and others. However, a good many netsuke bearing the seals of Raku and Kiyomizu earthenware were actually made by other potters. The famous potters usually devoted themselves to making utensils for the tea ceremony, but some of them also made fine netsuke. Among porcelain netsuke, those of Hiradoyaki are the greatest in number (Fig. 89). Hirado netsuke have been produced since the old days, but very few examples bear signatures.

The numerous lacquer artists who created netsuke include Kajikawa (B 432), Haritsu (B 826), Yoyusai (B 1319), Kansai (B 449; Fig. 196), Zeshin (B 1337; Fig. 197), Hashi-ichi (B 197), and Taishin (B 1153). Many lacquer netsuke bear no signature.

Netsuke artists took great pains and expended great energy in originating ideas and creating new subjects. Numerous preliminary sketches were often necessary. An instance of the netsuke carver's painstaking efforts occurred in the life of Tomokazu (Fig. 136), who lived in Gifu and devoted himself almost exclusively to animal subjects. One day Tomokazu left home without a word, as though going to the neighborhood bath. To the consternation of his worried family and friends, he was missing for several days. On his return, he explained that he wanted to carve netsuke in the form of deer and that, for this reason, he had climbed Mt. Kinka in order to observe deer at first hand and to study their behavior in their natural environment. So anxious was Tomokazu to preserve his observations while they were still fresh that he had begun carving on the spot and had neglected eating for several days. His neighbors listened to the story with open-mouthed admiration. Such was the artist spirit: so far beyond the limitations of ordinary people.

A noted actor, the leader of a Kabuki troupe in Osaka, was from childhood much interested in carving. He was acquainted with Soko Toshiyama (B 1100; Fig. 99) and frequently ordered special carvings from him. About the year 1902, this actor asked Soko to carve for him a representation of the legend of the demon of Rashomon. Soko's forte was carving historical subjects, and he investigated exhaustively in the interests of authenticity. He was too fine an artist to repeat some common version of the subject incorporating the demon's severed arm. After deep thought, Soko decided on a design combining a helmet with a *kinsatsu* or prohibitory signboard. He inquired concerning the type of helmet worn by Watanabe no Tsuna, the hero of the legend. Although the helmet worn in the theatrical version of the story is spade-shaped, Soko considered the probability that Watanabe no Tsuna had not worn a spade-shaped helmet, since helmets of this type were reserved exclusively for generals. He questioned scholars and students of historical paintings, but no one was certain about the point. He finally consulted Matsumoto Hoko, a recognized authority on historical painting. Matsumoto was certain that Watanabe no Tsuna's helmet was crescent-shaped, that it was decorated with a silver crest centering around a halberd, and that it had a three-sectioned neck protector. As for the prohibitory signboard, Soko learned that the To-ji in Kyoto owned the precise object, which was revered almost as a national treasure. But it was not on public display. Soko visited the temple and humbly besought permission to view the treasure on the special grounds that he was investigating historical facts essential to his art. The priestly guardian listened sympathetically and finally granted Soko permission. The signboard was crumbling with decay but still sufficed to recall its original aspect. With absolute assurance of authenticity, Soko made a quick copy of it. He was now ready to begin work on his carving, and he discussed with his patron his ideas for creating an accurate netsuke based on his research and study. The actor insisted that the helmet be spade-shaped and that the characters on the signboard be in gold as depicted on the stage—both in disregard of authenticity. Soko absolutely refused to make an unauthentic netsuke. The actor was equally adamant, and they parted in rancor.

There are many instances similar to this. Various carvers expended unstinted, even prodigious, efforts in carving netsuke. On this ground alone, the netsuke merits our tribute. It is a superb example of the arts of Japan in the Tokugawa period. Nevertheless, the study of netsuke has been neglected in our country.

Some netsuke were carved as a pastime; some were signed with false or misleading signatures; some were signed only with a *kakihan* (written seal mark); and some were not signed at all. Thus there are many master carvers whose identity is almost entirely unknown. In the study and appreciation of netsuke, discovering the true identity of these artists is a most difficult task although at the same time a most exciting and rewarding investigation.

Although the netsuke is only a miniature art form, the time required for its creation is a long one in comparison with that of other objects of industrial art. In painting, the subject—whether mountain, river, landscape, flower, or bird—is drawn upon a single surface, but in carving a netsuke there are six surfaces to consider: front, back, sides, top, and bottom. Furthermore, the most complicated and delicate designs are carved with nothing more than a cutting edge and a cleaning brush.

A common method of staining netsuke is to mix gardenias, mangrove bark, and water in an earthenware vessel and to boil the netsuke in the mixture for twenty-four hours. Afterwards, it is dried and polished. Soko Morita (B 1101; Fig. 198) and his school and followers utilize this method.

Usually it takes one or two months to make a single fine netsuke. Greater ability and effort than can be easily imagined is required to express a clear emotion. That the netsuke carver's earnings were very meager deserves sympathy. This was especially true of the more gifted and conscientious carvers whose time-consuming and painstaking work often received no commensurate reward. Consequently, many fine artists led a very poor existence. The public generally ignored the netsuke carver and his wretched condition. After his death, however, it frequently discovered the great merit of his work, and the artist would then receive posthumous plaudits from the very people who had ignored him when he was alive. Such cases were not infrequent.

Let us now consider the subject of signatures. Shuzan Yoshimura never signed his netsuke. Many noted netsuke carvers, in accordance with the prevailing custom, did not sign netsuke which they fashioned at the special order of a daimyo. Nevertheless, when sold, signed netsuke commanded higher prices. For this reason, artists signed those netsuke that were made for sale as distinguished from those made at the order of noble patrons.

When the eldest son of a netsuke artist succeeded his father, he usually continued to use the identical name without distinguishing himself by adding "the Second" or "the Third" to the signature. In such cases, the particular generation can be identified only by style and technique or by calligraphic characteristics shown in carving the signature. Thus it is often most difficult to identify the artist. There were numerous artists who used several names concurrently or who changed names repeatedly at their whim. A majority of the netsuke made at Ujiyamada are signed Masanao.

Honorary titles often used with signature are hogan (法眼), hokyo (法橋), and tenka-ichi (天下一). The titles of both hogan and hokyo were first bestowed upon Jocho, a sculptor of Buddhist images. Later these titles were conferred upon painters. The netsuke carvers who held the title of hokyo were Ryukei (B 853), Sessai (B 955), and Hozan (B 290; Figs. 5 and 103). Those who held the title of hogan were Rantei (B 812; Figs. 102 and 104), Shuzan, Toki (B 1183), and Tadayoshi (B 1149; Fig. 223). Sometimes the artist included his title with his signature.

The title tenka-ichi, dating from the Ashikaga period, was given only to mask and mirror makers of outstanding ability. Tenka-ichi was the highest possible honor for an artist in this field. At first the title was not intended to honor netsuke carvers, but in later periods the excessive bestowal of it culminated in a prohibition against its use. Representatives of the Deme family of mask makers were probably the only carvers in the field of netsuke who properly used this title.

Another source of confusion lies in the identical signatures belonging to quite different artists. Some netsuke bear only a kakihan or written seal. Some include the appellation "old man," which is written okina (翁), so (叟), or rojin (老人). Some include the character saku (作), meaning "made"; to (刀), meaning "knife-cut"; or sha (写), meaning "copied." Some bear the characters 應需 (oju), meaning "at the request of," or 應好 (oko), meaning "to please the taste of." Others include the information 門人 (monjin), meaning "pupil of," or に模す (ni mosu), meaning "imitated," or such other information as the date or place where the netsuke was carved, or the age of the carver. There are numerous other additions that are sometimes made to signatures.

9: The Regional Characteristics of Netsuke

NETSUKE EXHIBIT regional characteristics according to the area where the carver was trained. Within a given region, those produced in cities and local areas tend to exhibit further specialization. A brief discussion by regions follows.

THE KANSAI AREA

This area includes Osaka, Kyoto, Wakayama, Nara, Sakai, Uji, and other cities of west central Honshu.

OSAKA: In the art of netsuke carving, Osaka occupies a predominant position. The city produced a large number of master carvers. An Osaka man, Inaba Tsuryu, published in 1781 the *Soken Kisho,* the only book in our country dealing with the subject of netsuke. In recent times, Kaigyokusai Masatsugu (Figs. 32, 70, 74, 75, and 146), Mitsuhiro Ohara (Figs. 100 and 106), Gyokkin Iida, Ryukei Tanaka Mondo (B 714), Dosho Kagei (B 89; Figs. 107 and 216), Sansho Wada (B 903; Fig. 105), Soko Toshiyama (Fig. 99), Kyusai Hirai (B 576; Figs. 54, 113, and 210), and others were bred in Osaka. Other masters carve there at the present time.

Shuzan Yoshimura studied painting under Mitsuhiro Kano, who was a pupil of Tanyu Kano. As a painter, Shuzan was honored with the title of hogan. He was fond of carving netsuke in his leisure time. Most of his subjects were taken from the *Sankaikyo* and the *Ressendenzu* (Pictures of Numerous Sennin). He modified the designs to suit his taste when he executed them in seasoned cypress, his preferred material. He completed his carvings by the application of unusual colors of striking vividness. As his netsuke aged through use and exposure, the colors mellowed and thus enhanced the pleasing effect. In the *Soken Kisho* are several drawings of Shuzan netsuke made by his son, Hogan Shukei. Shuzan discontinued netsuke carving in his middle years. He died in 1776.

As Shuzan's fame as the greatest of the netsuke carvers solidified, many imitators adopted his style. His design and colors proved to be good models, just as cypress proved to be good material for the aspiring netsuke carver. In short, Shuzan's netsuke were used as models for the study of the various techniques of carving. Of course, much of the copying was not for practice but for purposes of deception. Since Shuzan did not sign his work, neither did his students and imitators. The copiers may not originally have intended to deceive, but those who appraised the netsuke as genuine pieces by Shuzan deceived themselves and others—errors for which the copiers bear no responsibility. Ever since the middle of the Meiji period and up to the present time, a certain exporter has engaged an Osaka netsuke carver to live at his home and to devote himself in secret to the manufacture of Shuzan-style netsuke. This exporter has sold the netsuke as the genuine work of Shuzan, earning unwarranted profits. I learned these facts directly from one of the persons engaged in the fraud.

In summary, Shuzan, whose work has been copied and imitated by many, initiated the basic patterns of netsuke carving in the Kansai area and greatly influenced the entire art form.

Next we consider Kaigyokusai Masatsugu, who is pre-eminent among netsuke artists. He was born in Osaka in 1813. He did not follow the usual pattern of learning the art as an apprentice but was entirely self-taught. He sketched and carved prolifically. His work is pure and polished beyond description. Kaigyokusai had many pupils, but a large number of them deserted and went to Tokyo about 1887. As did Okyo Maruyama in painting, Kaigyokusai developed a highly personalized style. The power and influence of his beautiful carving carried as far as Tokyo, and many carvers imitated his technique in Tokyo as well as in Osaka. Some observations on Kaigyokusai's work follow.

He selected his material very carefully, avoiding types that tended to break, decay, or become worm-eaten; for example, water-buffalo horn. When he carved boxwood or ivory, he cut away soft, spongy, or uncertain parts. He frequently selected for use only a small piece from a great mass of material, since only choice material satisfied him.

Each of his ivory netsuke is made of the best tokata despite the scarcity and the exorbitant cost of this material.

Kaigyokusai made numerous preliminary sketches of the object to be carved, including the back and the underneath parts. He spared neither time nor effort. In making rats, rabbits, and other animals, he carved the whiskers realistically in raised lines instead of merely indicating the hairs by etching, as less gifted carvers commonly did.

Kaigyokusai generally utilized the natural configuration of the subject in arranging for attachment of the cord, thereby avoiding the inartistic disfigurement caused by the *himotoshi* (holes through which the cord passes). Examples of this are found in his carving of various quadrupeds in which the natural postural separation of the leg from the balance of the body is used for passing the cord. There is no known instance of Kaigyokusai's using a separate material for lining the cord holes.

Kaigyokusai used hoten for inlaying the eyes of rabbits, rats, and other animals whose eyes are red. For the black pupils of animal eyes, he used umimatsu in preference to horn, which is susceptible to damage by worms. For the eyes of birds and frogs, he used a special yellow pearl (kigai), with umimatsu for the pupils. In carving such subjects as snails, butterflies, and cicadas, he occasionally inlaid various materials or attached wings of contrasting material. However, he avoided the type of mosaic known as Shibayama.

He did not color his wood or ivory. Since he used only the finest materials, the warm, beautiful luster of the ivory or the lovely grain of the wood was artistically sufficient. He colored only when color was essential to his purpose; for example, in order to give boxwood the appearance of smoked bamboo.

Since his animal carvings were thoroughly sketched and prepared in advance and then carefully executed, his representations of animals are natural in posture, anatomic structure, and weight distribution. They are never slanted or otherwise distorted. Lines for the representation of hair, whether straight or curved, are clean and even in spacing and in depth. A sensitive, deft, and powerful hand is clearly indicated.

All of Kaigyokusai's work is beautifully finished and polished. The work of knife and brush is scrupulously completed. His signature is strong and accurate. In etching his seal, he made the border lines square, straight, and firm. He occasionally used ink to emphasize the characters of the signature Masatsugu, but not of the signature Kaigyoku or Kaigyokusai. The characters for these last two are completed just as etched in the ivory.

These are general observations and therefore not without exceptions. Nevertheless, his netsuke are masterpieces and are always true netsuke. I have heard that Kaigyokusai was a most dutiful son. On studying his netsuke, I am sure that this must be true.

Mitsuhiro Ohara, who also lived in Osaka, did some exquisite and beautiful work, often in a realistic style. He has left some remarkable pieces. In his declining years he returned to his birthplace, Onomichi, where he died.

Gyokkin Iida came from Omi. He devoted himself to making tea utensils in the Chinese style, which were popular at that time, but he also made netsuke. His preferred material was bamboo. Many of Gyokkin's pupils also made tea utensils.

Dosho Kagei (Figs. 107 and 216) came to Osaka from Izumo. He usually carved in ivory. He studied Shibayama mosaics and may be considered the peerless artist in Osaka in inlaying ivory in the Shibayama style. Sansho Wada studied under Dosho.

Soko Toshiyama came to Osaka from Kanazawa to study the art of carving. His forte was the carving of historical subjects. He mastered both simple carving (subori) and painted carving (saishoku) and made good use of the burin in his work. He also excelled in painting and calligraphy.

Kyusai Hirai carved in wood, bamboo, and tusk. He was skillful in carving small objects such as tea-ceremony utensils, okimono, netsuke, and obidome (obi clasps). He was greatly influenced by the styles of Kaigyokusai and Gyokkin and taught many pupils.

SAKAI: Kyubei Tobutsu (Fig. 21), after long study, perfected a bronze alloy similar in quality to that of Chinese Ming bronzes. Using this material, he made numerous metal netsuke cast from a wax mold. Among the shapes he designed were helmets, pots, dishes, drums, shells, and gourds. The helmets and pots doubled as ash trays. He decorated many netsuke with chains of circles, arabesques, and rain dragons. These designs were executed in openwork in order to lighten the weight of the netsuke and were made by the lost-wax process. Therefore no two are identical. His netsuke were cast as completed designs and were never assembled from partial castings. Kyubei did not sign his netsuke.

Ichiraku created netsuke from rattan *(to)* and wisteria vines *(fuji-zuru)*. Rattan work grew in popularity and was later used in producing pipe cases *(tsutsu)* and other such articles (Figs. 27 and 28).

WAKAYAMA: Issai Ogasawara was skilled in carving netsuke from elephant and other tusk, but netsuke bearing his signature are rarely found (Figs. 73, 80, and 82). Matauemon Kishu (B 650) was also a skillful netsuke carver.

NARA: The style of carving known as the *Nara ningyo* (Nara doll) was carried on by the Okano family (B 993–1005) for thirteen generations. The material used was invariably cypress, which was shaped with a single instrument—a knife—and was finished by painting.

Hohaku Shoju (B 1001), representing the ninth generation of the Okano family, improved the conventional Nara ningyo. He also carved Noh and Kyogen actors. Hokyu Shoju (B 1002), of the tenth generation, is reputedly the finest of the line. Toen Morikawa (Figs. 29 and 40) diligently studied the carvings of Hohaku and Tsunenori (B 1003), who was of the eleventh Okano generation. Toen mastered their methods and evolved a new style of his own. He devoted himself to Nara ningyo and to copying ancient carvings. People say that his work could not be distinguished from the original ancient models. Toen may aptly be called the foremost of the Nara ningyo makers. He was also a professional Kyogen actor and was once honored by being called to perform in the imperial presence. His other talents included painting, writing poetry, and playing the *sumakoto* (single-stringed harp), the samisen, and the *tsuzumi* (hand drum). He was also proficient in flower arrangement and calligraphy.

KYOTO: Master carvers in Kyoto prior to Temmei (1781–1788) were Tomotada (B 1216; Fig. 108), Okatomo (Fig. 206), Yoshinaga (B 1302; Figs. 109 and 224), Masanao (B 609; Fig. 114), and others. Later came Rantei and Hakuryu (B 181). Kyoto also produced such noted ceramists as Hozen, Ryonyu, Kitei, Zoroku, and others, all of whom made many artistic netsuke in porcelain.

UJI: Gyuka (B 167), a tea-ceremony master at Uji who was adopted by the Kamibayashi family, made a doll out of seasoned tea wood in the form of a tea picker, as a souvenir of Uji. He painted it and presented it to the shogun in 1842. The shogun was lavish in his praise, and as a result Gyuka received many orders from daimyo and other officials. His work was quite artistic and later earned the appellation of *Uji ningyo* or Uji dolls. Such dolls are made in great numbers even today. The quality of the later work, however, is quite inferior to that of Gyuka's (Fig. 61).

TAMBA: During Temmei and Kansei (1781–1800), Toyomasa (B 1254; Fig. 86), who lived in Shinoyama, made a variety of wooden netsuke of excellent quality. Toyokazu (B 1253), his pupil, followed Toyomasa's style.

THE EDO AREA

Edo was the city to which many people migrated from local districts all over Japan in order to engage in business. The new settlers augmented the demand for inro and tobacco pouches, and this mounting demand resulted in the production of netsuke by wholesale methods. Netsuke carvers sprang up, their talents varying from those of master craftsmen to those of inferior artisans.

The commercial netsuke maker lived solely by producing netsuke, making as many of them as possible in order to increase his earnings. He used molds to cast them more speedily and bought waste ivory from the manufacturers of samisen. This waste ivory was usually in pieces of triangular shape—a fact that accounts for the huge output of triangular-shaped designs. Such commercialism rarely resulted in good netsuke. On the other hand, exquisite pieces were made by master carvers as an avocation. These fine netsuke were acquired by daimyo, wealthy tradesmen *(chonin),* and dandies who squandered their means on tobacco pouches.

A great many Edo netsuke were destroyed in the huge fires that followed the great earthquake of Ansei in 1854, and a sudden shortage resulted. In order to meet the sharp demand, dealers were forced to use natural materials such as ivory and horn cut in round sections about three-eighths of an inch thick and having a simple hole or metal fitting for the cord. From the end of the Tokugawa period through the Meiji period, netsuke became an export item, and many carvers earned their livelihood by making netsuke for the export trade.

Prior to Temmei, the master netsuke carvers of Edo were Miwa and Uman. Later came Tomochika I (B 1195; Figs. 79 and 137), Jugyoku (B 408; Figs. 155 and 164), Ryukei (B 852), Tokoku (B 1184; Figs. 50 and 76), Joso (B 400; Fig. 115), Kokusai (B 527; Figs. 20 and 26), Ryo (B 830; Fig. 192), Koun (B 555), Kyuichi (B 575), Mitsuaki (B 350; Fig. 167), and Gyokuzan (B 164; Fig. 19). Even now we have so fine an artist as Soko Morita (B 1101; Fig. 198).

Miwa made netsuke as a hobby. His work is superb, and he is considered the originator of the Edo-style netsuke. His subject matter is quite different from Shuzan's. Shuzan took his subjects from Chinese legend and history; Miwa, from the daily Japanese scene. Prior to Miwa the chief material for netsuke was cypress, but because it proved fragile and subject to erosion by rubbing, he decided to use cherry wood or occasionally boxwood, Chinese woods, and others. Another of his innovations was the use of dyed ivory or horn inserted as a lining for the himotoshi which served as a strong channel for the smooth passage of the cord without erosion. Miwa kept his method for lining cord holes a secret.

Uman was an apprentice in a family of mask carvers. He made netsuke in the form of masks as an amusement. His work has an unassuming charm.

Hojitsu was a subject of a small fief directly under the control of the shogun. Using ivory and boxwood with equal facility, he made netsuke that were realistic but refined. He was patronized by the shogun and may even have been in his employ. He also enjoyed the patronage of Marquis Tsugaru. Hojitsu had a considerable number of pupils, and some fine carvers emerged from his studio.

The first Tomochika was born in Edo in 1800 and became a netsuke specialist. He carved principally in ivory and selected subjects from Hokusai's *Manga*. His style emphasizes the large outline rather than the small detail. His output was large. Both the second and the third Tomochika also became netsuke specialists and trained many apprentices (Figs. 79, 137, and 220).

Kokusai specialized in the carving of horn. His characteristic style became extremely popular and gave rise to the term *Kokusai-bori,* or

Kokusai carving. Joso excelled at carving small objects, particularly netsuke and ojime.

Koun, the most renowned sculptor in wood during Meiji and Taisho, was an honorary professor at the Tokyo Art Academy and an artist for the Imperial Household. He trained many young students and made other important contributions to the art of sculpture. Koun carved a number of netsuke, particularly in his younger days.

Gyokuzan had no teacher but developed his skill by studying drawing. He is particularly famous for his many skull netsuke and for his fine sculpture in ivory during Meiji and Taisho. A prize was bestowed upon him by Prince Yoshihisa in the presence of the Emperor Meiji for his small okimono of a skull displayed at the Second Domestic Industrial Exhibit. He headed the Tokyo Carvers' Association and was one of the first professors at the Tokyo Art Academy. Gyokuzan moved to Kyoto in his later years, studied mosaics from examples at the Shosoin (at Nara), and became quite expert at inlay techniques.

Kyuichi was also one of the first professors of the Tokyo Art Academy. He was a faithful follower of the Nichiren sect of Buddhism, and the bronze statues of Nichiren at Hakata and Ushijima are his work. He began his career as a netsuke carver and devoted himself diligently to the study of netsuke throughout his life. He deserves recognition as one of the foremost netsuke students of our country.

Although Soko occasionally carved in ivory, most of his work is in wood. He sometimes colored his netsuke with excellent effect. His choice of subjects was from nature, which his style closely imitated. He studied under Joso but was also influenced by Hojitsu and Kaigyokusai. He carved with great delicacy, and each single stroke of his knife was executed with the utmost care. The Kannon of Eleven Faces that he made some years ago is only one inch in height. It is said that the eleven faces on the Kannon's head cannot be seen by the naked eye. Soko is generally conceded to be the supreme netsuke artist of the present day.

THE CHUKYO AREA

The Chukyo area includes Nagoya at its center, Ise, Mino, Hida, and other localities. Most of the netsuke produced in this area are made of boxwood. The boxwood grown at Mt. Asakuma, near Ise, is reputedly the finest in our country. In Hida, however, yew is also used for netsuke carving, although in the Chukyo area other woods and ivory are seldom used. Netsuke produced in the area are generally based on sketches of living subjects, particularly animals. The carvings are carefully finished on all six sides, and many days are spent in faithfully reproducing each subject. The results are vivid representations that include many masterpieces. I think that it was difficult for the Chukyo artists to obtain such reference books as Hokusai's *Manga* and others from Tokyo. They therefore made netsuke from drawings of the living subject. Once a good design was created, it was repeated many times.

NAGOYA: In old Nagoya, Tametaka (B 1159; Fig. 142) was the most famous carver. Later there appeared many master hands like Hogan Tadayoshi, Tadatoshi (B 1146; Figs. 116, 121, and 130), Ikkan, Bokuzan (B 19), Tomotada (B 1217), Masatoshi (B 630), and Masakazu (B 596; Figs. 88 and 120), each of whom left wonderful netsuke. The Nagoya artists often employed a secret technique by which they cleverly carved their signatures in raised characters.

Tametaka must be regarded as the pioneer among the Nagoya netsuke artists. He employed an embossing technique to produce arabesque kimono designs that brought him fame. He also made okimono. He was an eccentric whose constant companion was the sakè bottle. His method of signing by means of raised characters, as he did in his later years, is regarded as his characteristic device.

Tadatoshi's work is based on careful observations and drawings from nature. His carving is strong and true. Ikkan also relied on drawing from nature, and most of his netsuke are quite realistic. In his younger days, his favorite subject was the sleeping *shojo* (a mythical creature renowned for its fondness for sakè) and in his later years, the rat. Tomotada was a metal artist, but he made netsuke and inro as a pastime. His carvings in boxwood are finely detailed.

Masatoshi and Masakazu were brothers. Masatoshi visited China and made musical instruments for the performance of Ming and Ch'ing compositions. Masakazu carved in both wood and ivory. He made many netsuke for export, particularly using the rat as a subject and repeating it numerous times because it was so well liked by foreigners.

ISE: At Ise, in the old days, the Minko school was the more famous, but in recent times it is the Masanao school. Almost all of the netsuke carvers of Ise were attached directly or indirectly to one or the other of these two schools. They produced many fine netsuke.

Minko (Figs. 124 and 138) began his career with the carving of Buddhist altars. His work made a favorable impression upon Marquis Todo, the feudal lord of the Tsu clan, and it appears that Minko moved to Tsu to take employment with this clan. He made netsuke, *tonkotsu* (tobacco cases), scabbards, and decorative wooden swords. He created various designs in boxwood and red sandalwood and also inlaid foreign woods, tusk, horn, and other materials in articles of paulownia wood. His netsuke were not based upon sketches from nature but upon designs and neat effects.

Masanao (Fig. 110) lived in Yamada and carved netsuke of popular appeal during his lifetime. His favorite subjects were the animals of the zodiac, and his carving is crisp and skillful. The second, third, and succeeding generations were also known as Masanao and continued the production of netsuke (Fig. 92).

Kokei (Figs. 122 and 123) considered Minko as his ideal. He followed his lead but placed some reliance on sketching from nature. He carefully finished his netsuke on all six sides. Kokei lived in Kuwana.

MINO: Most of the netsuke carvers of Mino painstakingly prepared for carving by making preliminary sketches from real life. To this extent, they were largely self-taught, and it is very difficult to determine the existence of teacher-student relationships. For example, Tomokazu (Fig. 136), Bazan (B 10; Fig. 125), and Tessai (B 1173) appear suddenly on the scene as mature artists.

Tomokazu was born in Gifu. His carving, based on sketches from real life, included many animal netsuke, particularly turtles and monkeys. His work is quite clever. Boxwood was his favorite material.

Bazan was born in the Motosu district and later lived at Ogaki. His work was also based on nature drawings, and many of his netsuke are finely detailed.

Ittan (B 377) was a Toba clansman. He came to Nagoya and later moved to Gifu. Most of his subjects were figures and animals skillfully executed in wood. His favorite subject was the sleeping shojo. The first Masanao of Ise learned carving from Ittan.

HIDA: Sukenaga (B 1124; Figs. 126, 127, and 219), lived at Taka-yama and studied carving with Suketomo (B 1128). He regretted the loss of power and effectiveness in the Nara ningyo caused by the ad-dition of colors. After diligent experiment, he developed the so-called Hida ittobori (single-knife carving), using yew wood from Hida. He cleverly used the reddish and whitish tints of this wood, thus preserv-ing the full power of the carving. Later, ittobori carvings became one of the most noted products of Takayama, and quite a few carvers of the district devoted themselves to this technique.

OTHER DISTRICTS

A considerable number of netsuke were produced in districts other than those mentioned above, and there are many master carvers whose biographies are not well known. Some of these are noted below, although the information about them is very scant.

IWAMI DISTRICT: Tomiharu (B 1191) first became a priest, but since he loved carving, he went to Edo and studied the technique of woodworking. Later he returned to his home district and took up residence in the Naga area. He resigned the priesthood and reverted to the status of layman, devoting himself exclusively to netsuke carv-ing. Basing his work on sketches from nature, he carved in ebony, black persimmon, and boar tusk. His favorite subjects were frogs and cicadas (Fig. 139). His daughter Bunshojo (B 28; Fig. 135) learned his techniques and did excellent work. Kamman (B 440) was a student of Tomiharu and was greatly influenced by his master's style.

SANUKI DISTRICT: Zokoku (B 1338) was a lacquer dealer who excelled at carving. He made various articles in tsuishu (red lacquer) and tsuikoku (black lacquer), as well as many detailed and delicate carvings by special order for the daimyo of the Takamatsu clan. He was raised to the status of a samurai and was admired by the people of his district as a great lacquer artist and sculptor.

ECHIZEN AND ECHIGO DISTRICTS: Sessai (B 955) served Marquis Echizen and was granted the title of hokyo. He excelled at carving and was famous for his depiction of snakes. His son Sekka

(B 949) was first a carpenter and later became a carver. His output, though scant, was excellent in quality. Masayoshi's (B 638) favorite subject was the shishi with a loose ball under his paw. This loose or free ball was carved by perforating a fixed outer ball. Masayoshi's carvings were quite intricate. Masamitsu (B 604) was at one time Masayoshi's adopted son but later returned to his natural family. He made other carvings as well as netsuke.

OTHERS: Besides those carvers mentioned above, there were Otoman (B 788; Figs. 190 and 218) at Hakata, Beisai (B 11) at Itsukushima, Sekiran (B 945) at Mito, Totenko (B 1243) at Kazusa, Hidari Issan (B 203; Fig. 128) at Aizu, and Toun (B 1247) and his pupil Hokufu (B 250) at Oshu. Each of these left fine netsuke.

Subjects of local interest are usually the messengers of the deities of the shrine of a particular district. Examples are the netsuke representing the deer that is the holy messenger of the Kasuga Shrine at Nara and the frog that fulfills a similar role at the Okitama Shrine of Ise Futami. The Uji doll previously mentioned is also a good example of a netsuke of local interest. The wood of the tea bushes of Uji—famous for its green tea—is used for the carving of netsuke in the design of women tea pickers (Fig. 61). Similarly, carvings in the yew wood of Hida exemplify netsuke of local interest, since this wood is a famous product of the district.

119. Lion Dancer. (Gold lacquer. 1 ¹/₂″. Signed: Koma Bunsai. B 27.) A masked
Noh actor performs the lion dance in the play *Shakkyo*. Compare Fig. 103.

120. OKAME. (Wood. 2 3/8″. Signed: Masakazu. B 596.) According to Japanese legend, the sun goddess once hid herself in a cave in a fit of anger at the unruly behavior of her brother. In the ensuing darkness that covered the world, the gods tried in vain to lure her out. Finally the goddess Okame performed a licentious dance that provoked the uproarious laughter of the assembled deities. This in turn aroused the curiosity of the sun goddess and enticed her to peek from the cave, whereupon one of the gods seized her by the hand and dragged her forth. Thus light was restored to the world, and Okame came to be a symbol of mirth and good humor. For other names and illustrations of Okame, see Figs. 91, 132, 150, and 196.

121. SNAIL. (Wood. 1 11/16″ long. Signed: Tadatoshi. B 1146.) A realistic snail, the parts cleverly treated to give the impression of hard shell and soft body. The artist's signature appears in raised characters.

122. GOAT. (Wood. 1 $^{13}/_{16}$″ long. Signed: Kokei. B 524.) In this representation of a reclining goat, the natural point of division of the leg from the body forms the place for the attachment of the cord. See text, page 108.

123. DIVING GIRL. (Wood. 1 $^{11}/_{16}$″ long. Signed: Kokei. B 524.) A diving girl holding an abalone while she struggles against the embrace of a salacious octopus.

124. Ox. (Ebony; eyes inlaid in gold and black coral. 1 ⅝″ long.
Signed: Minko. Kakihan. B 661.) The ox or cow (one word—
ushi—does for both in Japanese) figures prominently in Japanese
legendry. It was one of the twelve animals that hastened to be present at Buddha's side when word went out that he was dying, and
it thus assumed a place of honor in the Oriental zodiac. In the
recumbent position in which it is shown here, it is associated with
the statesman Sugawara Michizane, who rode on an ox when he
was driven into exile. It is also an emblem of the Zen sect.

125. Snail and Pear. (Wood. 1 ½″ long. Signed:
Bazan, in raised characters. B 10.) A snail on a rotted
pear. The speckled skin of the pear is realistically
represented by raised spots.

134

126. BADGER PRIEST. (Wood. 1 ³/₄″. Signed: Sukenaga. B 1124.) A badger disguised as a priest has difficulty in con-
▶ cealing his tail. The netsuke is an example of modified ittobori carving. For more typical examples of this style of carving, see Figs. 29 and 40.

▼
127. FROGS. (Wood; eyes inlaid in shell and black coral. 1 ⁹/₁₆″ long. Signed: Sukenaga Matsuda. B 1124.) A group of three frogs. In what might be construed as an example of mother love, the large frog endures without complaint the small one on her back, which holds a foot against her eye.

135

128. DARUMA. (Wood. 1 5/8".
Signed: Hidari Issan. B 203.)
A roly-poly Daruma. For other
illustrations and comment on
Daruma, see Figs. 40, 76, and
115.

129. CROSSING THE RIVER SANZU. (Ivory. 1 5/8" long. Signed: Toun.
B 1248.) A group of oni carry a wealthy tradesman in grand style
across the bridge over Sanzu no Kawa (the Japanese River Styx),
which separates this life from the hereafter. The proverb illustrated
is "Jigoku no sata mo kane shidai," which can be translated as
"Even the judgments of hell are influenced by money."

130. THE DANCE OF RANRYO. (Wood. 2 $\frac{1}{4}$". Signed: Tadatoshi. B 1146.) Ranryo, a character in the ancient court and temple dances called Bugaku (and still performed today), was a legendary Chinese prince whose victory in battle was always assured by his wearing a mask like the one shown here. His dance in the Bugaku is called Ranryo no mai. Note the diapering on the dancer's costume.

137

131. Fox Priest. (Wood. 3 7/8″. Signed: Komin. B 530.) The fox, traditionally believed capable of assuming a startling number of disguises, is shown here in the ◄ garb of a priest. The figure and the staff are carved from a single block of wood. See text, page 161.

▼

132. Doctor's Model. (Wood. 3 1/2″ long. Unsigned.) Okame poses as a Chinese doctor's model. In former days, the modest Chinese lady patient used such a model to indicate the seat of her pain. The netsuke has a secondary use as a fudekake or rest for a writing brush.

138

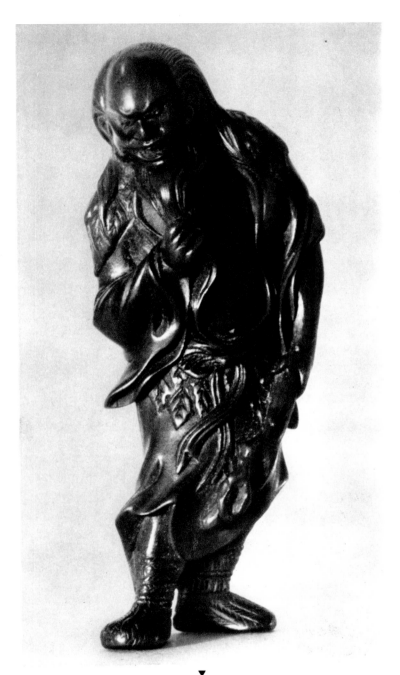

133. Bearded Sennin. (Wood. 2 7/8″. Signed: Genryo *to*. This is an artist name of Minkoku. B 667.) A bearded sennin wearing a coat of leaves and carrying a branch in his hand.

134. DIVING GIRL AND OCTOPUS.
(Ivory; barnacles and himotoshi
inlaid in shell. 2". Signed: Choku- ◄
sai. B 55.) An erotic design of a
diving girl and a grasping octopus.

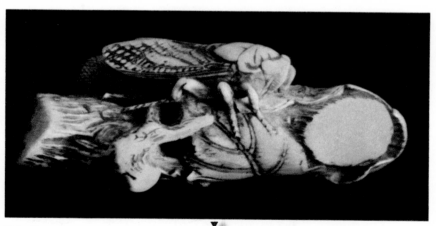

135. CICADA AND PINE. (Ivory. 2 1/8" long. Signed: Seiyodo Bunshojo. B 28.)
Cicada on pine branch with leaves and cones. The artist was one of the few women
carvers of netsuke.

136. BLIND MAN AND BAKEMONO. (Wood. 1 $^{15}/_{16}$″. Signed: Tomokazu. B 1206.)
The fiend has an extensible neck. The blind man is unaware of his danger. The
netsuke illustrates the Japanese proverb, "Mekura hebi ni ojizu," or "A blind man
does not fear a snake," which can be taken as the equivalent of "Ignorance is
bliss." The bakemono represented is probably Rokuro Kubi or Whirling Neck.
For comments on bakemono and on the Japanese attitude toward the blind as
represented in netsuke, see the captions to Figs. 46 and 225 respectively.

137. A BASKET OF MONSTERS. (Ivory. 1 1/4". Signed: Tomochika. B 1195.) The netsuke illustrates an episode from the famous Japanese folk tale about the tongue-cut sparrow, "Shitakiri Suzume." The assemblage of monsters are those who fell upon the wicked and greedy old woman as punishment for her having mutilated the sparrow.

138. BOY IN DRAGON'S COILS. (Wood. 1 9/16" long. Signed Minko. B 661.) A young boy saves himself from the coils of a dragon by reciting the magical phrase, "Namu Amida Butsu" (Save me, O merciful Buddha).

139. BASKING FROG. (Ebony. 2 9/16" long. Signed: Sekiyo Kawaigawa Seiyodo Tomiharu chokoku. B 1191.) The frog figures in a number of Japanese sayings and stories and perhaps most notably in Basho's famous haiku poem about the frog jumping into the old pond. The proverb, "Ido no kawazu taikai o shirazu" (A frog in a well knows not the great sea), is often used to describe a man of limited experience and narrow views.

142

140. SNEEZING MAN. (Wood. 1 $\frac{11}{16}$". Signed: Gyokkei. B 130.) A good example of Japanese humor. A man holds a ▶ slender ivory stick with which he tickles his nostrils to make himself sneeze. The artist's signature appears on an inlaid ivory plaque.

141. SCULPTOR. (Wood. 1 $\frac{1}{8}$". Signed: Gyokusai. B 155.) A wood sculptor appraises the head of a huge Nio (Deva King) that he has carved.

142. RYUJIN. (Wood. 1 $\frac{7}{8}$". Signed: Tametaka. B 1159.) A representation of Ryujin, the Dragon King of the Sea. The dragon headdress worn by Ryujin is only partially visible in the illustration. In his hand he holds the "tide-ruling jewel." See text, page 161.

143

143–145. THREE NETSUKE ATTRIBUTED TO SHUZAN YOSHIMURA. (Fig. 143 boxwood; Figs. 144–145: cypress. 3½–4″. Unsigned.) The netsuke shown in Figs. 143, 144, and 145 may be attributed to Shuzan Yoshimura (B 1092). Since Shuzan never signed his netsuke, only attribution is possible, and most attributions are at least disputable. In the case of the netsuke in Fig. 143, which portrays Shoki the Demon Queller preparing to bottle an oni, the attribution may be questioned because the material is not cypress, which Shuzan customarily used, but boxwood. The human-headed kirin (a fabulous animal) pictured in Fig. 144 is of cypress, but the carving lacks power and seems to have a refinement associated with a later period than that of Shuzan. For this reason, attribution to Shuzan is disputable. With regard to the human-headed kirin shown in Fig. 145, attribution to Shuzan may be questioned on the ground that, although the netsuke is of cypress, it does not stand by itself and thus fails to pass one of the tests of a good netsuke. This failing, however, may be due to wear. One of the best tests to determine the genuineness of a Shuzan netsuke is based on the age and authenticity of the paints and colors applied to it.

146. MONKEY. (Amber. 1 $^1/_2$". Signed: Kaigyokusai Masatsugu. B 430.) The virtues of seeing, hearing, and speaking no evil combined in a single monkey. The fine amber material is of an unusually uniform color and quality. See text, page 77.

147. KARAKO ON A DRUM. (Ivory. 1 ¹/₁₆″. Signed: Gyokuyosai. B 163.) The mirthful face of this karako (Chinese ▶ boy) unmistakably registers the happiness that he symbolizes. Karako are still among the most popular toys for young children and are often used as okimono.

148. GENROKU SAMURAI. (Wood. 2 ³/₁₆″. Signed: Gyokuso. B 160.) A young samurai dandy, probably of the Genroku period. Genroku was the brief (1688–1703) but exciting era that saw the ◀ evolution of the typical ukiyo-e style, the flourishing of the fabulous gay quarters of the Yoshiwara, and the development of the Kabuki theater to a paramount position in Japanese cultural life.

146

149. HAWK AND DOG. (Ivory. 1 9/16″. Signed: Hidechika. B 206.) A powerful hawk has ▶ seized a young mountain dog in its fierce talons. Note the care with which the textures of feathers, talons. and hair are suggested.

150. SETSUBUN. (Ivory. 2 1/4″. Signed: Hidemasa. B 212.) Setsubun is the bean-throwing festival that marks the beginning of spring according to the lunar calendar. The scattering of the beans is designed to drive away evil spirits and ◀ invite good fortune into the household. It is accompanied by shouts of "Fuku wa uchi, oni wa soto," meaning "Happiness in, evil out." Here an exuberant Okame hurls beans at an oni who tries to take refuge under her kimono.

151. JUROJIN, GOD OF LONGEVITY. (Wood. 1 9/16″. Signed: Homin. B 263.) Jurojin is one of the Seven Gods of Fortune. The two views show the cleverness of the design in this netsuke. On the one side is carved the shape of a turtle, one of the attributes of Jurojin and a symbol of longevity; on the reverse, Jurojin with his elongated beard. The artist's signature appears on an inlaid ivory plaque.

152. OGURI HANGAN AND THE STALLION. (Ivory. 1 3/4″. Signed: Isshu. The signature stands for Isshusai. B 372.) This striking netsuke portrays the celebrated exploit of the hero Oguri Hangan, who tamed a vicious stallion so thoroughly that he could bring the animal to stand on a board used for the game of *go*.

153. Butterfly Dance. (Wood. 1 15/16″. Signed: Gyokuso. B 160.) This netsuke portrays the ancient kocho no mai (butterfly dance), in which the dancers wear wings and flutter like butterflies.

154. SENKYO. (Wood. 1 $1/2$".
Signed: Joryu. B 395.) Two
coolies carry a "passenger" between them by means of a pole
stuck through a hole in his
chest. This is an example of the
psychological function of the
inro netsuke as good "medi-◄
cine." The user is amused at
the netsuke, and his sense of
well-being improved. The people portrayed are Senkyo, a
legendary race of foreigners
who, according to Chinese
fable, had large holes in the
middle of their chests.

▼
155. ARIOMARU AND THE OCTOPUS. (Wood; octopus eyes inlaid in ivory and black coral. 1 $9/16$" long. Signed: Jugyoku. B
408.) Ariomaru, the servant of the exiled priest Shunkan,
overcomes and kills the octopus that has seized his master's
leg. The story of the exile of Shunkan is the subject of a well-
known Noh play.

156. FALCON. (Wood; eyes inlaid in black coral. 2 1/4". Signed: Harumitsu. B 194.) A member of the hawk family, probably a ◄ falcon. The surface of the netsuke is scarred and stained to simulate natural markings.

157. BUDDHIST GONG. (Bamboo. 2 1/8" long. Unsigned.) This gong (mokugyo), in the shape of a monster's head, has ► been carefully hollowed out so that it gives off an authentic sound. See text, page 162. For other types of gongs, see Figs. 24, 48, and 210.

151

158. KIDOMARU. (Ivory. 1 $^5/_8$". Signed: Chiku-unsai. B 42.) Kidomaru, charmed by the beautiful music of his brother's flute, is diverted from his attempt at fratricide. This legendary bandit was ultimately killed by Watanabe no Tsuna. See text, page 116, and Fig. 54.

159. NICHIREN. (Ivory. 1 $^5/_{16}$". Signed: Chomin.) Nichiren was the celebrated priest who founded the sect of Buddhism that bears his name. He is represented here sailing into exile in the midst of a violent storm which he quelled by prayer.

▼   ▼

160. ANIMALS OF THE ZODIAC. (Ivory. 2 $^1/_8$". Signed: Kagetoshi. B 421.) The twelve animals of the Japanese zodiac are the rat, the ox, the tiger, the rabbit, the dragon, the snake, the horse, the sheep, the monkey, the fowl, the dog, and the wild boar. All of them appear (and the monkey twice) in this netsuke, of which two views are shown.

161. ONI. (Ivory. 1 $^9/_{16}$". Unsigned.) This netsuke features a clever design for attachment of the cord, ◄ which the oni holds in his powerful grip. For other illustrations of oni, see Figs. 117, 163, and 172.

162. SHOJO. (Wood. 1 1/8″. Signed: Kazutomo.) A flowing waterfall of sakè which opens ▶ to reveal an inebriated shojo with an overturned sakè cup on his head. For an illustration of the shojo dance as performed in the Noh, see Fig. 118.

163. ONI AT SETSUBUN. (Ivory. 1 3/8″. Signed: Kohosai. B 516.) An oni cowers in great distress as he is pelted with beans at the ◀ Setsubun festival on the eve of the lunar spring. See Fig. 150 for another illustration and comment on the Setsubun festival.

164. BLIND MEN GROOMING AN ELEPHANT. (Wood. 1 5/8″. long. Signed: Jugyoku. Kakihan. B 408.) In this amusing variation on the ▶ famous old story, the blind men, instead of forming mistaken impressions about the elephant's appearance, are grooming it as if in preparation for a festival.

165. TADAMORI AND THE OIL THIEF. (Ivory. 1 $^{11}/_{16}$". Signed: Hidemasa. Kaki-han. B 212.) Taira no Tadamori, undaunted by the reports of a fire-breathing monster lurking in the vicinity of the Gion Temple, bravely attacks the creature, which turns out to be a common temple servant in the act of stealing oil.

155

166. CAMELLIA. (Ivory. 1 ⁵/₈″ long. Signed: Kyokusai. B 565.) Camellias, though admittedly very beautiful, did not grace the samurai garden. At full bloom the blossoms break off at the stem, falling suddenly like the flash of a sword. The abrupt demise of the flower at the peak of its bloom reminded the samurai family of the fate of decapitation that might befall their warriors at the height of their youth and vigor.

167. MONKEY. (Ivory. 1 ⁵/₁₆″. Signed: Komei. The signature may also be read as Mitsuaki. B 350.) This beautifully carved monkey has neither been smoothed nor polished, so that the original knife cuts remain visible.

168. BAT. (Wood; eyes inlaid in black coral. 1 $7/16$″ long. Signed: Horaku. B 268.)
A bat resting with one wing partially extended. The bat in various designs is a favorite subject of Horaku.

169. TOY DOG. (Lacquer. 1 1/4″ long. Unsigned.) A red-lacquer (tsuishu) netsuke representing a ▶papier-mâché toy dog. This toy should not be confused with the inu-hariko, which is a dog-doll box having childbirth and erotic associations.

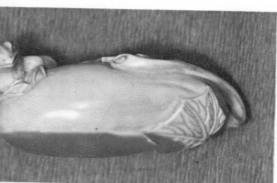

170. FROG AND SQUASH. (Hornbill casque. 2 1/2″. Unsigned.) A netsuke carved from the casque of the hornbill (hōten). The bright orange-red and yellow are ▶characteristic. Usually honen is found in ojime, as shown in Fig. 31, since it is infrequently of sufficient bulk for netsuke. In some fine animal netsuke the red part of this material is used to inlay the eyes. See text, page 78.

171. MANJU. (Lacquer inlaid with shell. Diameter: 1 5/8″. Unsigned.) A lacquer manju decorated in Somada inlay,. which is named after Somada◀ Hisamitsu, who developed and gave his name to the technique of inlaying netsuke and inro with intricate designs in tiny cut pieces of iridescent shell.

10: The Appreciation of Netsuke

THE NETSUKE has no proper function except as a unit in an ensemble. It is not a free art form. In this respect it differs fundamentally from the okimono. The purpose of the okimono is only to give pleasure as a decorative "placed object." Regarded as a cube, the netsuke is carved and finished on all six sides. Unlike the okimono, it is usually examined on all of its surfaces. Because of its specific use, it must conform to rigid limitations. For these reasons the netsuke merits special appreciation as a miniature art form.

Since the netsuke is made to be carried at the hip, it is essential that the shape be rounded, smooth, and free of sharp points, edges, and appendages which might be broken off or which might catch or tear kimono sleeves. As an object of wear, the netsuke must not be brittle or fragile, but must be strong and sturdy. For example, the carver who creates a netsuke in the form of a rat must design the tail so that it curls in some manner about the body. If the tail protrudes, it may catch on the wearer's kimono, or it may be broken (Fig. 79). A carving that is fragile or brittle fails in an essential requirement of a good netsuke. Such a carving is more truly described as a simple ornament or okimono. All the great netsuke artists were careful to make sturdy, smooth carvings free of protuberances and rough edges.

Moreover, netsuke intended for use with delicate lacquer inro are required to be light in weight and smooth in outline. Metals, ceramics, and other hard materials are unsuitable for use as inro netsuke. Ivory netsuke for use with inro are usually free of rough edges, relatively small in size, and deeply carved in order to minimize weight.

Perhaps the single most important point to bear in mind in the appreciation of netsuke is to consider the problems confronting the artist, who must create an interesting design yet observe many fixed limitations. The netsuke must be small, smooth, sturdy, light, rounded, and free of points, edges, or protuberances. It must not be fragile or brittle. How much more difficult the task of the artist who creates an attractive design within the confines of these various limitations!

Another limitation on the netsuke artist's freedom is the need for carving two holes or some other place of attachment for the cord by which the sagemono is suspended. The okimono needs no place of attachment, since it rests on the flat surface upon which it is placed. By contrast, the netsuke is attached to the sagemono by means of a cord which passes through it. The matter of carving the holes in the netsuke for passage of the cord is most important. In some cases special holes for the cord are not cut, but in lieu of these some natural conformation of the netsuke is utilized for attachment of the cord (Figs. 43 and 161). For example, the natural posture of an animal depicted in a netsuke may provide a space between limb and body for attachment of the cord. In many cases the two holes are about the same size. In other cases one hole is larger than the other in order to accommodate the knot by which the cord is tied. Occasionally the holes of a wooden netsuke are decorated or strengthened by the addition of ivory sleeves. In forming the cord holes it is essential that the cord pass easily and smoothly, that the bridge between the cord holes be of sufficient strength and durability to bear the weight of the sagemono, that the holes do not mar the beauty of the design, and finally that the holes be placed in such a way that the best portion or "face" of the netsuke is exposed to view as it is worn.

It is obvious that daily wear and exposure will cause some appreciable change in netsuke through handling and rubbing. It is noteworthy that the master carvers considered the effect of constant use and fashioned the netsuke in such a way that daily wear served to smooth and refine it as it aged. How perfect was the understanding of the master carvers of the essential nature of the netsuke!

A netsuke must be shaped so that it is not awkward or bothersome when worn. A ball shape is unsatisfactory because its constant rolling is an annoyance (Fig. 217). The manju shape, a modification of the ball shape, proved very stable and comfortable. For reasons of comfort, metal netsuke were cast in openwork to eliminate the heaviness of solid metal.

The artisans who collected the ivory waste from the samisen factories used the ivory most grudgingly, wasting nothing. Since the raw ivory waste was triangular in shape, so too were the finished netsuke. Curiously enough, the custom of carving triangular-shaped ivory netsuke influenced work in wood as well, so that even this inexpensive material was frequently carved in a triangular shape (Fig. 142).

To appreciate netsuke, we must consider the status of the netsuke carver, which differed substantially from the status of the painter, the lacquerer, and other artists. For example, the painter was often granted a land tenure by the shogun or daimyo who employed him, or he held office in the Imperial Household Art Section. No such fine opportunities were available to the netsuke artist. While he was thus confined to relative poverty, he was, on the other hand, free of the restraints imposed by traditions of style, by the demands and instructions of superiors and sponsors, by fear of ostracism from the school of art to which he belonged, or by fear of the loss of his royal patronage. This freedom from social and financial restraints accounts for the interesting and endless variety of netsuke—certainly a point of appreciation.

Many mechanical and technical secrets are sometimes incorporated in the design of a netsuke. An example is the beehive netsuke. The numerous little larvae are loose, so that the netsuke sounds like a rattle when shaken, yet they are not removable from the hive (Fig. 86). Another example is the lotus-pod netsuke, in which the loose seeds rattle but do not fall free. The mechanics of such carvings were jealously guarded and executed in secrecy. The same secretiveness applied to the techniques for staining ivory, for carving ivory sleeves and lining the cord holes, for inlaying contrasting materials, for imitating and simulating various materials (Figs. 58 and 106), for embossing signatures, and for carving many other "trick" netsuke (Figs. 97, 136, and 210).

Netsuke are required to be sturdy. They are usually carved from a single block of material, and inlay and mosaic are generally avoided. Lovers of netsuke do not ordinarily approve of netsuke composed of separate parts joined together. In carving a *tekkai sennin* (a hermit who leans on an iron staff) it is relatively easy to carve the staff separately and to attach it to the figure in a simple operation. However, the staff may then be easily broken. The netsuke artist therefore carves both staff and figure out of a solid block of wood or ivory, although his labor is thereby doubled (Fig. 131). It is a different matter, however, if the effectiveness of the design is enhanced by the inlay, or if the artist purposely works out an elaborate design in order to demonstrate his artistry with inlay or mosaic.

In carving netsuke in the shape of Buddhist gongs *(mokugyo)* the inside is hollowed out with as much care as the exterior is designed, so that when the gong is struck, the sound is authentic (Fig. 157). This is an example of the conscientious attention to detail that is so characteristic of the art of the netsuke carver.

So neglected has been the study of netsuke in Japan that numerous fine netsuke are unknown to the public. They are dispersed here and there, unseen, undescribed, and unpublicized.

Signatures and seals on paintings and tea-ceremony articles, or on the original boxes containing these, are considered of prime importance. Netsuke, on the other hand, do not suffer from the absence of a seal or signature. An exception exists in the case of those netsuke carved by artists known to have customarily inscribed their signature or seal. Since netsuke were made for daily wear, it was rare for them to be provided with boxes. Still, boxes were sometimes supplied for netsuke to be used by tea-ceremony masters and devotees.

Many remarkable netsuke are not signed. For this reason, forged signatures on netsuke prior to Meiji are rare—unlike the situation prevailing in the case of paintings, calligraphy, and tea-ceremony articles. Nevertheless, many forgeries of the names of the famous old netsuke carvers are found, especially of those listed in the *Soken Kisho* and of those who, like the Deme family, are widely known to the general public. Despite these exceptions, forged signatures occur much less frequently than in the case of paintings, calligraphy, and tea utensils.

Following the Meiji period it became common practice for the carver to furnish a signed box with his netsuke, just as in the case of paintings, and the value of a netsuke was lessened by the absence of the original box. The development of an export trade in netsuke led to the widespread forging of famous signatures, and great quantities of netsuke bearing spurious signatures were shipped abroad.

In determining the age of an art object, the various indications of use and wear are considered important guides. It is quite difficult, however, to determine the age of a netsuke by signs of use and wear alone. Often fine netsuke were not used at all, although made long ago and although made to be worn. Many an old netsuke has never been worn. On the other hand, many a comparatively recent netsuke has been given such hard use that the guides of use and wear lead to completely contrary conclusions. It is therefore quite difficult to judge the true age of an unsigned netsuke. This also is an important point to keep in mind when appraising netsuke.

11: The Decline of the Netsuke

THE NETSUKE reached the zenith of its popularity during Bunka and Bunsei, the periods which spanned the years from 1804 to 1829. At the end of the Tokugawa period in 1867, this popularity began to decline. I believe that the main reasons for the decline may be outlined as follows.

In the past, identical leather or brocade was used to make both the tobacco pouch and the pipe case, and they were suspended together at the hip by means of the netsuke. Later the style changed, and the pipe case came to be made of wood, horn, ivory, or other tough material, and it was attached to the tobacco pouch in place of the netsuke. Beautiful pipe cases of ivory, horn, bamboo, wood, rattan, and twisted paper (Nagato cases) were carved or lacquered and tended to supplant the netsuke. As the use of fine decorated pipe cases increased, the need for netsuke decreased.

The "black ships" of a foreign country (Commodore Perry and his men-of-war), coming to our land in 1853, had an unsettling effect. Our people became uncertain and troubled over the restoration of imperial rule. Luxuries lost their popular appeal, and netsuke, being a kind of luxury, gradually disappeared from the social scene. The former appreciation of art objects gave way to a concern with articles of commerce and financial gain. Art appreciation sank so low that fine lacquer scrolls and other art objects were mutilated, if not ruined, in order to strip from them their precious metal decorations. This disastrous trend was precipitated in 1876 by an edict abolishing the wearing of swords, the very lifeblood of the samurai tradition. Art objects lost their appeal. Furthermore, the number of people who could afford costly tobacco pouches diminished. The use of netsuke almost came to an end during the last days of the Tokugawa government and the early days of the Meiji Restoration.

Prior to the Meiji era, the inro was invariably worn with ceremonial dress *(kamishimo)* at all formal ceremonies and important occasions. After the Meiji Restoration in 1868, either Western-style clothes or coat *(haori)* and pleated skirt *(hakama)* replaced the kamishimo. The inro was out of place without the kamishimo and thus fell into disuse. Naturally the inro's inseparable companion, the netsuke, also fell into disuse.

With the Meiji Restoration and the beginning of trade relations and commerce with foreign countries, the smoking of cigarettes instead of pipes found favor. As a consequence the tobacco pouch was discarded. The new practice adversely affected the popularity of netsuke. When Western-style clothing was adopted by the middle and upper classes, more people who had formerly purchased fine tobacco pouches and netsuke began to smoke cigarettes. The decrease in the use of tobacco pouches was marked by a parallel decline in netsuke.

As previously mentioned, the use of netsuke is steadily declining. Formerly an article of utility, netsuke are now treasured only by collectors and connoisseurs. They are greatly appreciated by foreigners, who are completely removed from any connection with their practical use.

12: The Export of Netsuke

IN 1853, WHEN Commodore Perry of the United States led his black ships to Uraga, Mikawaya Kozaburo was the head porter of the shogunate government. He provided for the needs of the foreigners in various small matters. At that time even persons such as carpenters, plasterers, and porters were caught up in the craze for tobacco pouches. Mikawaya Kozaburo was no exception. He wore a costly tobacco pouch to which he attached a fine mask-group netsuke. One of the Americans accompanying Commodore Perry was fascinated by Kozaburo's mask-group netsuke and earnestly beseeched Kozaburo to give it to him. At that time the Japanese, never having seen foreigners before, were afraid of them. Kozaburo mistook the American's pleading for a roaring rage. He feared that the American might kill him if he refused. He reluctantly handed over his treasured netsuke to the American.

The American was elated and in return gave Kozaburo many presents of unusual things from the United States. Kozaburo related the incident to his fellow workers, and the story came to the notice of some officials of the shogunate government, who were incensed. They charged that Kozaburo had flouted the shogunate government by trading with a foreigner without permission. The government was negotiating with Perry for the opening of ports and the commencement of trade, but a formal agreement had not yet been signed. Having incurred the displeasure of the authorities, Kozaburo was thrown into prison. The authorities rejected his explanation that he had been coerced into the exchange, that he had not meant to trade with the American, and that he had not intended any offense to the shogun. The American was sorry for Kozaburo's plight. He explained the situation to the officials and finally secured Kozaburo's release. Later Kanagawa was designated as a foreign trade port.

One day Kozaburo happened to meet the American. He thanked his friend for securing his release from prison and invited him to his home. The American remarked that all his shipmates found the netsuke unusually interesting. He asked if it were possible to accumulate a large number of netsuke. Kozaburo answered that he could do so, provided he had sufficient funds at his disposal. This conversation was the birth of the trade in netsuke. Kozaburo purchased netsuke at various localities with funds furnished by his American associate. He packed them in an orange crate and sent them to Kanagawa. In this way the first netsuke were exported to foreign countries.

Kozaburo later established a trading company named Sanko Shokai at Kanda, Tokyo, specializing in overseas shipments of various art objects including netsuke. After some hardships he also opened an art shop at Yushima specializing in pouches of all kinds.

Kozaburo was very small of stature, and he stuttered. At first sight he appeared to be a rustic, but he always wore his hair in a large topknot in true samurai style and, like a samurai, fought against injustice, always endeavoring to rectify wrongdoing and dishonesty. He possessed the fine character of a samurai and gentleman and was an accomplished swordsman. At the time of the upheaval that led to the Meiji Restoration, he sided with the shogunate. While engaged in trade he found deep pleasure in providing the objects desired by others. He died in 1889 at the age of sixty-seven. I understand that Koun Takamura, the great wood sculptor, carved a large number of okimono for export at the request of Kozaburo.

Netsuke were among the first articles to be exported, and they continued to be the subject of commercial transactions in increasing quantities. Their value at that time was greatly depressed. At the time of the Meiji Restoration the whole nation seethed in a turmoil of uncertainty over the restoration of imperial rule, the abolition of clans, the establishment of prefectures, and the inception of foreign trade. People were not in the mood for art and showed little interest in art objects. Even swords, formerly considered the purest of art objects and the very soul of the samurai, were ignored. Artists fell upon wretched days, eking out a bare existence. However, since large numbers of netsuke were required for the overseas trade, wood carvers and metalworkers fared better than other artisans, and numerous netsuke, particularly in ivory, were made for export to foreign lands.

Export netsuke were made for the most part in the large cities such as Tokyo and Osaka. Chuichi (B 62), a resident of Osaka, was proficient in making turtle netsuke and produced them for the export trade. Masatoshi of Nagoya and his pupil Seikei (B 915) specialized in the subject of the ratcatcher for export. In Osaka some fairly prominent carvers turned out netsuke in the style of Shuzan Yoshimura which were sold as genuine by dealers to foreigners at exorbitant profits. I learned these facts from a couple of the participants in the fraud.

Most of the netsuke made from the end of the shogunate (1867) through the first half of Meiji were exported to foreign countries, very few being retained for domestic use. It is a strange phenomenon that our netsuke carvers at that time were better known abroad than in Japan. Even in recent days one occasionally hears of a foreign tourist purchasing five hundred or a thousand netsuke to take back to his home country. Many such netsuke are coarsely carved for the foreign buyer.

Nevertheless, netsuke exported in quantity to foreign countries included both good and bad examples. There are a considerable number of collections of netsuke on display in foreign museums. Good books on the subject of netsuke are published abroad, and articles on netsuke with many illustrations are carried in foreign magazines. In our country, on the other hand, there is no comprehensive publication on netsuke, and I regret very much to say that the collection of netsuke at the Imperial Household Museum is quite poor.

13: Observations on Netsuke by Periods

FOR THE PURPOSES of discussion, it is convenient to divide the history of netsuke into three periods: early, middle, and late.

EARLY PERIOD

This division covers the period from the birth of the netsuke through the Kansei era, which ended in 1800. Early in the Tokugawa period, many Chinese priests visited Japan and taught the Chinese classics. Chinese literature and history became widely known. The dissemination of books containing numerous illustrations with explanations in simple language stimulated interest. Among such books were the *Sankaikyo*, the *Ressendenzu*, and the *Doshaku* (Drawings of Saints of Buddhism and Taoism). A great variety of Chinese legends and historical episodes were ultimately Japanized to become part of our own heritage. The absorption of Chinese literature and legend greatly influenced the development of netsuke. Shuzan Yoshimura, for example, carved netsuke using sennin and other Chinese figures from the *Sankaikyo* as models. Shuzan was awarded the title of hogan for his painting, but he was also renowned as a netsuke carver. Influenced by Shuzan's great reputation, many other netsuke carvers copied his style and his practice of portraying Chinese legend and fantasy.

Our people admired not only the Chinese classics but also Chinese *objets d'art*. Netsuke designs were greatly influenced by art objects imported from China. Seals, sword handles, cane heads, formal dress ornaments, pendants, and similar articles of Chinese origin were used in their original condition as netsuke by the simple addition of cord holes. The influence of Chinese art objects explains the widespread adoption of the shishi design in ordinary netsuke and in seal netsuke (Fig. 51).

Basho, the great *haiku* (seventeen-syllable verse form) poet of the Tokugawa period, had many pupils who went on walking tours through the countryside, spreading the charm of the haiku verse form. Strangely enough, Basho's poetry had a marked influence on the design of netsuke. The haiku's subtlety, harmony, and concern with the seasons permeated all art forms, including netsuke. The fine netsuke carvers followed the trend by creating designs of subtlety, seasonableness, delicacy, and charm.

The carving of Buddhist images and of architectural decorations was at that time in a state of decline. On the other hand, the carving of netsuke was progressing. The sculptors of Buddhist images and of architectural decorations found leisure to carve netsuke as an avocation or amusement. They were concerned with the design of netsuke rather than with techniques and mechanics of carving. The early users of netsuke also appreciated design above all, and they frequently thought out interesting ideas which they requested their favorite artists to interpret in netsuke. In this period, design was paramount.

Minko of Ise concentrated all his creative forces on designs for netsuke. He despised realistic sketching as a dissipation of creative energy. It is said that he expelled any of his pupils who dared to carve a realistic design. The Daruma with revolving eyes is one of the designs created by Minko.

To summarize, in the early period many artists carved netsuke as a hobby. The subject matter was taken mainly from Chinese legend and history and from haiku and *waka* (verse form of thirty-one syllables). Besides, imported Chinese art objects were often either adapted as netsuke, or their designs were modified for carving as netsuke. The early period may be characterized as the period of design in contrast to technique. We may describe it as a preparatory period for the golden age to follow: the middle period.

MIDDLE PERIOD

The middle period represents a span of sixty-eight years from Kyowa through Bunka and Bunsei until the Meiji Restoration. Netsuke carving as an amusement and an avocation increased during this period. Many of the artists who enjoyed the patronage of the shogunate carved netsuke as a pastime. For such artists, the main concern was the design, and they created many fine netsuke of superb quality. Many artists whose entire productivity was confined to netsuke made their appearance at this time. They were the netsuke artists, and the golden age of netsuke had arrived.

In the field of painting, Okyo Maruyama of Kyoto (1733–1795) had established the sketching school: the pictorial school of art. He had many followers who spread the tenets of the pictorial school throughout Kyoto, Osaka, Nagoya, and Tokyo. Both Matsumura Gekkei and his brother Keibun devoted themselves to real-life sketching and taught many pupils. Such noted painters as Chikuden Tanomura and Kaioku Nukina espoused the ideas of the sketching school, and it appeared certain that pictorial art must overwhelm all other approaches to painting. Naturally the pictorial school of painting exerted a strong effect upon the creation of netsuke, which came to be fashioned more and more after real-life models and sketches.

The influence of the ukiyo-e, which was then at its zenith, also profoundly affected the carving of netsuke. The *Manga* and other illustrated books of Hokusai Katsushika were used as source books and models for netsuke designs. The waka and the comic poems of Moto-ori Norinaga and Shokusanjin also furnished ideas from their enormous range of subject matter, covering everything from daily activities to imaginary beings—all of which were carved into netsuke.

Chikamasa Shominsai (B 30) of Tokyo made his appearance in this period. He taught his brother Tomochika Yamaguchi his technique, and ultimately Tomochika concentrated solely on the production of netsuke. Ryukei of Tokyo also specialized in netsuke, and both Tomochika and Ryukei trained a large number of pupils.

In addition to netsuke of the type described above, Nara dolls were made from the beginning of Bunka (1804), and Uji tea-picker dolls were designed by Gyuka Kamibayashi. In Hida, at Takayama, single-knife carvings were produced, and at Otokoyama small pigeon netsuke were made.

Most of the netsuke of Edo were destroyed by fire at the time of the great earthquake of Ansei in 1854. It was virtually impossible to meet all at once the sudden and enormous requirement for netsuke that followed the destruction by the earthquake. As a makeshift, ivory, narwhal, and horn were cut into simple round slices into which holes were drilled to form impromptu netsuke. Manju and kagamibuta netsuke became popular because these types could be manufactured quickly, especially by the use of lathes. Only a token amount of decoration or carving was done on these netsuke—a quite pardonable practice under the circumstances.

To summarize, netsuke carved in the middle period grew into an original art form that compared favorably with sword furnishings and other art forms. The materials and designs of netsuke were tremendously varied, and great numbers were produced. The number of artists who fashioned netsuke as an avocation or amusement increased, and there arose a class of artists who devoted themselves exclusively to the art of netsuke: the true netsuke artists. In Tokyo, Osaka, and Kyoto there were prominent dealers who specialized in netsuke. Certainly this was the golden age of the art.

LATE PERIOD

This period covers the time from the Meiji Restoration to the present. As previously mentioned, the early years of Meiji witnessed a decline in art, and the netsuke lost its importance. Moreover, the vogue of carrying the netsuke and tobacco pouch declined when cigarettes replaced pipes. Ultimately the tobacco pouch and the netsuke fell into almost complete disuse.

Under these circumstances, the metal and the netsuke artists gradually lost their patronage and were reduced to a harsh struggle for their daily food. At this point, fortunately, foreigners visited our country, and their interests fastened on Japanese art objects, which they bought up in large quantities. Numerous art objects were carried to foreign shores in the space of only a few years. The netsuke, as a characteristic art form of Japan, found immediate favor in the eyes of foreigners. It thrived so well on the new export boom that not only netsuke artists but also metal and other artists turned to the fashioning of netsuke as a means of livelihood.

Since ivory was the preferred material for carving netsuke for export, there was a consequent development of skill in the handling of this material. Ivory carving, which had in the past been limited to netsuke, was now expanded to include okimono, and a new epoch in the history of Japanese sculptural art began. At an art exposition held in 1877, only one ivory carving was on display. In 1881, just four years later, half the items displayed at an art exposition were ivory okimono. Foreign orders for okimono were usually filled by the simple device of copying netsuke in a large size and omitting the cord holes. Thus netsuke served as the models and standards for later ivory carvings.

Our artistic world was at this time frozen and lifeless. Through the efforts of Ernest F. Fenollosa—an American employed by the Ministry of Education—Okakura Kakuzo, and others, an art school was established at Kobu University in 1876. In 1887, legislation establishing the Tokyo Art Academy was enacted, and classes were begun the following year. The traditional method of training artists through a master and apprentice relationship was discarded. Instead, the cultivation of artists and sculptors by means of modern educational methods was instituted. Students studied drawing, Western sculpture, ancient Nara carving, and other subjects. Stylized Buddhist sculpture and traditional architectural ornamentation were replaced by an individual and independent approach.

Kyuichi Takeuchi, the first professor of the sculpture department of the Tokyo Art Academy, was originally a netsuke carver, and other faculty members like Gyokuzan Asahi, Tessai Kano, and Mitsuaki Ishikawa had devoted themselves to this art. In 1890, the system of the court artist was instituted, and in 1907, an art committee was established as a section of the Ministry of Education. A little later, regular art exhibitions were sponsored by the Ministry of Education.

The Tokyo Carvers' Association was organized in 1877 with Kaneda Kanejiro, Mitsuaki Ishikawa, Gyokuzan Asahi, and other carvers as charter members and with the support of about twenty dealers in ivory carvings. The members met on the 20th of each month at Kaneda's home. Each brought his latest work, which was passed around for study and criticism. The membership grew, and the meeting place was changed in 1879 to Shinobazu-no-Ike at Ueno in Tokyo. The name of the association was changed to "Club for the Encouragement of Art" and later to "Carving Contest Meeting Association." Sometimes connoisseurs like Fenollosa were asked to lecture. A general meeting was held annually at which each artist displayed his best work, and a prize was awarded to the winning artist.

In February 1887, the governing regulations were revised, and the name reverted to "Tokyo Carvers' Association." A contest in carving was held every year, and there were also monthly meetings for study and lectures. The association sponsored foreign exhibitions of the carvings of its members and thereby greatly stimulated this art form. It also held study meetings at the Seibikan, a showroom where the work of the members was on constant display. It received encouragement from the Imperial Household, which favored it with occasional orders.

In 1923, the Seibikan was destroyed in the Great Earthquake. The following year, the association was merged with the Japan Art Association, and thus ended the glorious Tokyo Carvers' Association. Needless to say, the encouragement that it gave to the art of the carver in Japan was inestimable.

To summarize, in the later period the netsuke lost its practical *raison d'être* and became a collector's item. It was collected by both Japanese and foreigners. The netsuke artists of this period may be divided into two groups, the first being those who studied and developed in the traditional apprentice system; the second, those aspiring artists who received regular instruction in the new art schools. Both groups carved netsuke as a hobby or avocation. Since the netsuke was no longer bound by the strict limitations imposed by use, the artists created more elaborate designs. Complicated and unusual ones were devised, and many old designs were simply copied with a greater wealth of detail. Moreover, netsuke for export were made in large numbers and sold to foreign tourists. Export netsuke were usually made of ivory and carved with a view towards saving as much time and labor as possible, the main consideration being the financial return. In this period the majority of netsuke were made for foreigners. Nevertheless, the master carvers continued carving for pleasure or as an avocation.

172. ONI WITH A CLUB. (Negoro lacquer. 3 $\frac{3}{16}$". Unsigned. See B 758.) This netsuke, which portrays a powerful demon armed with a club, illustrates the Japanese saying, "Oni ni kanabo" (literally, "a demon with an iron rod") or "the strong made stronger." The expression is analogous to "gilding the lily." The negoro lacquer of which the netsuke is made is named after the priests of Negoro in old Kii Province (now Wakayama Prefecture), who developed the process of polishing red lacquer on a black base to attain a pleasing blotched effect.

173. Sотова Komachi. (Wood. 1 3/16". Signed: Masahiro, in embossed characters. B 590.) The famed poet and beauty, Ono no Komachi, as an ugly old woman. She is represented here as ▶ Sotoba Komachi (Grave-Post Komachi). Having rejected her numerous suitors at the height of her fame and beauty, she now faces death loveless and forlorn. See Fig. 174 for another episode in the life of Komachi.

174. Book-washing Komachi. (Wood. 1 13/16". Signed: Masatami. B 623.) Ono no Komachi, a celebrated poet of the 9th century, was the only woman included among the Rokkasen or Six Great Poets of ancient Japan. Represented here is Soshi-arai Komachi or the Book-washing Komachi, so named for an episode in which a rival poet accused ◀ her of plagiarism. Having heard her recite one of her poems, he copied it into an 8th-century book and presented this as evidence to support his charge. Komachi asked that water be brought, and with it she washed away the fresh ink, thus vindicating herself completely. For other representations of Komachi, see Figs. 173 and 199.

175. Octopus. (Wood; eyes inlaid with horn. 2 9/16″. Signed: Ikkyu. B 343.) An octopus that stands upright on its sucker-bearing arms.

176. WILD BOAR. (Wood; tusks inlaid in ivory. 1 $^{15}/_{16}$" long. Signed: Masakiyo B 598.) The wild boar, which occupies the last position among the twelve animals of the Japanese zodiac, is noted for rushing headlong to the attack, looking neither to right nor left. For this reason, it is regarded as a symbol of rash but courageous action, and persons born in the Year of the Wild Boar are traditionally believed to have a brave but reckless character.

▶177. SANSUKUMI. (Frog and snake: wood; snail: ivory. 1 $^1/_2$". Signed Chokusai. B 55.) The combination of snail, snake, and frog, known in Japanese as sansukumi, symbolizes an endless system of check and countercheck. The snake can eat the frog, and the frog can eat the snail, but the snail is poisonous to the snake. Therefore, in combination, the three are mutually deterrent. The group is also a reference to the story of Jiraiya. The artist's signature appears on an inlaid ivory plaque.

178. GAMA SENNIN. (Ivory. 1 $^3/_8$". Signed: Gyokumin. B 148.) Gama Sennin, the ▶ "immortal" hermit whose attribute is the toad. For another illustration of Gama Sennin see Fig. 89.

179. BADGER AND DRUM. (Wood. 1 ⅝″. Signed: Masakatsu. B 594.) A badger holds a Japanese hand drum (tsuzumi). The allusion is to the ◄ popular legend that the badger is able to inflate his belly and beat it like a drum in the night.

180. COILED DRAGON. (Wood. 1 ⅝″ long. Signed: Gechu, in embossed ► characters. B 113.) The animal is represented coiled for use as a netsuke.

181. KINTARO AND THE CARP. (Ivory. 1 ⅜″. Signed: Doraku. Kakihan. B 85.) Kintaro (Golden Boy) was a legendary child of prodigious strength who was nurtured by a mountain ► witch (yama uba). He grew up as a playmate of the wild animals of the forest. Kintaro is also known as Kintoki. Legend has it that other Japanese heroes such as Benkei and Yoshitsune also subdued huge carp while still children.

182. HOTEI, GOD OF HAPPINESS.
(Ivory, wood, and semiprecious
stones. 1 1/2". Signed: Meikei.
This is an art name of Hojitsu. B
243.) The household god of happi-
▶ ness, Hotei, is one of the Seven
Gods of Fortune. The rosary he
wears in this netsuke is made of
semiprecious stones. For another
illustration of Hotei, see Fig. 36.
The artist's signature appears on
an inlaid ivory plaque.

183. ROKKASEN. (Wood. 1 5/16". Signed: Masayuki. B
645.) The Six Famous Poets of 9th-century Japan are
known collectively as the Rokkasen. Here they are fanciful-
ly represented in a free-for-all, as if struggling for poetic
supremacy. A pun on their title, which can also mean
"six battles," is suggested. The artist's signature appears
on an inlaid ivory plaque.

184. SEA HORSE. (Wood. 3 ³/₈″. Signed: Isshin. B 361.) The
design of the sea horse is stylized for function as a netsuke.

185. Bon Odori. (Ivory. 1 3/4". Signed: Minkoku. B 667.) A man and a woman celebrate the festival of O-bon ▶ with the folk dance called bon odori. For an illustration of a more religious phase of the O-bon celebration, see Fig. 198.

186. Woman Traveler. (Ivory. 2 3/8". Signed: Minkoku. B 667.) A well-to-do woman of the Tokugawa period dressed for travel. She carries her lacquered ◀ traveling hat and a bamboo walking stick and wears a scarf to protect her head from dust and sun.

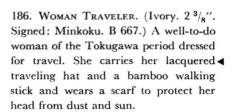

187. Cow. (Ivory. 1 $7/_8''$ long. Signed: Mitsusada *in*. B 702.) A stylized cow simulating the clay toys sold as souvenirs at the Fushimi Shrine near Kyoto.

188. BASKET OF FISH. (Ivory; eyes inlaid in black coral. 2″ long. Signed: Mitsutoshi. B 707.) Carp and catfish in a wicker basket, possibly for presentation as a congratulatory gift.

189. LION DANCE. (Ivory. 2″. Signed: Nobumasa. B 771.) The shishimai (lion dance) is often performed by itinerant entertainers. The dancer wears a lion-head mask and shakes a sacred Buddhist rattle to enhance the effect. The rattle indicates the probable religious origin of the dance. It is said that the lion dancers drink vinegar to keep their bones soft and supple for the dance. See Figs. 103, 118, 119, 130, 153, and 212 for depictions of other dances.

190. ASAHINA SABURO. (Ivory. 2 1/8″ long. Signed: Otoman Matsushita. B 788.) The legendary figure of Asahina Saburo is a kind of Japanese Gulliver and Hercules combined. He appears in both the Kyogen (comic interludes) of the Noh theater and the famous collection of tales called the *Azuma Kagami*. Here he is shown enjoying a tug-of-war with a demon—probably one of the assistants of Emma-o, the King of Hades.

184

191. CARP. (Ebony. 3 ¹/₄″ long. Signed: Kiyoshi *in.*) The carp, because of its ability to fight its way up swift streams, is a symbol of courage and virility and is thus a fitting emblem for the Boys' Day festival.

192. WOMAN BLACKENING TEETH. (Ivory. 1 $3/4$". Signed: Ryo. B 830.) An old woman blackening her teeth as she looks into a bronze mirror. Married ▸ women formerly blackened their teeth and shaved their eyebrows as indications of fidelity to their husbands. These strange customs have not been practiced since the end of the Meiji period.

193. FOREIGN BARBARIAN. (Wood; eyes and buttons inlaid in horn and ivory. 4 $5/8$". Signed: Ryusai.) Namban (southern barbarian) was a term usually applied by the Japanese to the indigenes of the South ◂ Sea Islands but, by extension, was also used for the Portuguese and the Dutch when they first visited Japan. The "barbarian" here carries a monkey and a quiver filled with arrows.

186

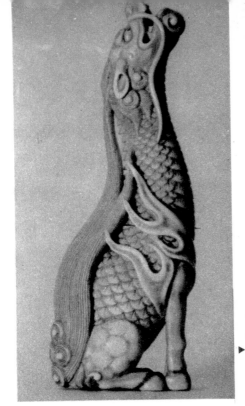

194. KIRIN. (Ivory. 4 1/8". Signed: Yoshimasa. B 1300.) The kirin is one of the four auspicious animals of ▶Chinese origin which include the turtle, the crane, and the phoenix. It bears vague similarities to the unicorn and the giraffe.

▼

195. CICADA ON TILE. (Ivory. 1 9/16" long. Signed: Shigemasa. B 968.) Roof tiles in Japan are often thrown to the ground by wind, rain, or earthquake. This may account for the frequency with which they are represented in netsuke as perches for cocks, bats, cicadas, etc.

187

196. OKAME. (Gold lacquer. 2 9/16″. Signed: Kansai saku. ▶B 449.) Okame half conceals her face behind a sleeve in mock modesty. Compare Figs. 91, 120, 132, and 150.

▼

197. INK STICK. (Black lacquer. 1 13/16″. Signed: Zeshin. B 1337.) A fine black-lacquer (tsuikoku) netsuke simulating an ink stick. The ink stick is rubbed in a small amount of water to produce a black ink. The signature of the carver is in his distinctive sharply incised characters.

▼

198. Nio and Oni at the O-bon Festival. (Boxwood. 1 $^{15}/_{16}$″. Signed: Soko saku. Morita, the carver's surname, appears in a gold seal. B1101.) A Nio (Deva King) and an oni, the representatives of good and evil, embrace fondly as they prepare to pour water and place flowers at the graves of the departed—one of the principal ceremonies of the O-bon festival in remembrance of the dead. The netsuke illustrates the Shinto belief that the dead are beyond good and evil and are worthy of reverence from both friends and enemies. To the passive Roman maxim, "About the dead, say nothing but good," the Japanese add active ancestor worship.

189

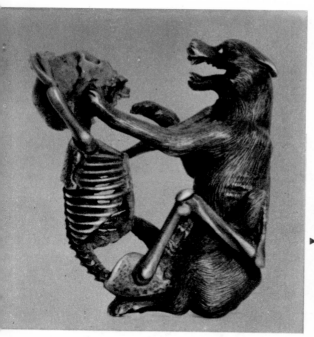

199. Skeleton and Wolf. (Wood. 1 15/16″. Signed: Shoko. B 1010.) Most probably an allusion to Komachi and Fukakasa Shosho. Fukakasa was a tempestuous general who lost his life in a vain effort to prove ▶his love for Komachi, while she survived into a loveless old age. To the Japanese the tempestuousness of Fukakasa, symbolized by the wolf, and the pride of Komachi, symbolized by the skeleton, allegorize the vanity of life.

200. Enshi. (Wood. 1 15/16″. Signed: Ryukosai. B 860.) Enshi is one of the Twenty-four Paragons of Filial Piety. To secure the deer's milk which was the sole remedy for ◀ his mother's eye disease, Enshi disguised himself in a stag skin and mingled with the herd. For other examples of netsuke portraying filial piety, see Figs. 11 and 53.

190

201. KAN-U MOUNTED. (Wood. 2 7/8″. Unsigned.) Kan-u, the famous Chinese military strategist of the Han period, mounted on his horse and stroking his long black beard. See Fig. 9 for an illustration of Kan-u as a standing figure.

202. HANDAKA SONJA. (Wood inlaid with ivory, pearl, yellow shell, and black coral. 1 3/8″. Signed: Soshin.) A representation of Handaka Sonja, one of the Rakan. He is seated in a teppatsu, a Buddhist begging bowl, through the cracks of which a dragon may be seen. For another illustration of Handaka Sonja, see Fig. 82.

203. POLISHING A BELL. (Ivory. 1 1/16″. Signed: ▶Shuosai. B 1073.) A temple servant with a grotesque face polishes a massive bell.

192

204. RAIJIN, GOD OF THUN-
DER. (Wood. 1 3/8″ long.
Signed: Rakumin. Kakihan.
B 794.) Raijin, the god of
thunder (also called Kaminari), peers through the
clouds for a good place to
hurl his thunderbolts. See
Fig. 85 for a mask of Raijin
as used in the Noh drama.

205. LION DANCER. (Ivory. 1 1/2″ long. Signed: Shuosai. B
1073.) A Japanese version of Pygmalion's sculpture of Gala-
tea. The lion dancer is so wondrously painted that he
springs to life out of the kakemono. He holds a branch of
peonies, the flower associated with the lion or shishi. The
association stems from the concept that, just as the lion is
king among beasts, the peony is king among flowers. The
lion dance is the high point of the Noh play *Shakkyo* (The
Stone Bridge). Note the "lion-hair" design on the actor's
kimono.

193

206. QUAILS. (Ivory. 1 ⁵/₈″ long. Signed: Okatomo. B 784.) A ◄ pair of quails standing on a head of millet.

207. KAPPA AND FROG. (Wood. 1 ¹/₂″ long. Signed: Tamekazu. A kappa and a frog are shown ► hand-wrestling on a lotus leaf. See Fig. 78 for another illustration of the kappa and for comment about him.

208. CHOKARO SENNIN. (Ivory. 1 ⁵/₈″. Signed: Ryomin. B 838.) The netsuke illustrates the story of Chokaro, one of the Taoist "immortals" (sennin), and his magic horse, which carried him ► thousands of miles yet could be tucked into a gourd. A popular Japanese saying based on Chokaro's horse emerging from the gourd—"Hyotan kara koma"— means an unexpected occurrence.

209. SOUTH SEA PRIMITIVE. (Ebony inlaid with coral and ivory. 1 $^{11}/_{16}$" Signed Unkoku.) A South Sea Islander (namban or more particularly kurombo, the term applied ◄ to natives of the South Pacific Islands.) holding a branch of coral. For other comment on namban, see Fig. 193.

▼

210. BUDDHIST GONG. (Wood. 1 $^{7}/_{16}$". Signed: Kyusai. B 576.) One of the many types of Buddhist gongs known as mokugyo. A side panel opens on a hinge to reveal a string of 108 tiny mokugyo. The number 108 has a magical significance in some sects of Buddhism. For other representations of Buddhist gongs, see Figs. 24, 48, and 157.

211. FUGEN BOSATSU. (Ivory. 1 $^{3}/_{8}$". Signed: Gyokuso. B 160.) A travesty on Fugen Bosatsu, a sacred Bodhisattva rep- ◄ resented seated on an elephant. Here the figure is a courtesan reading not a sutra but a love letter.

195

212. Noh Dancer. (Ivory. 1 $^{13}/_{16}$″. Signed: Shizumori.) A Noh dancer wearing the mask of Okina, the happy old man. See Fig. 4 for another illustra-◄ tion of the Okina mask. For other representations of dances, see Figs. 103, 118, 119, 130, 153, and 189.

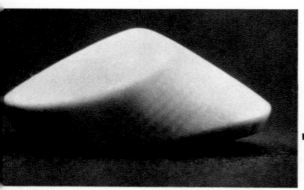

213. Abstract Chestnut. (Ivory. 1 $^{1}/_{8}$″ long. Signed: Ryomin. Kakihan. B 837.) A chestnut in an ▶ interesting abstract form. A popular confection made of sweetened chestnut and similarly shaped is sold in Japan.

214. Sleeping Deer. (Ivory. 1 $^{3}/_{8}$″ long. Signed: Heita.) The deer is the kami no tsukai (god's messenger) ▶ of the Kasuga Shrine at Nara, where it is regarded as a sacred animal and wanders freely about in herds, unmolested and quite tame.

215. Boy and Bird Cage. (Ivory. 1 $^5/_{16}$″. Signed: Kojitsu. B 520.) A young Japanese boy◄ holding a bird cage. His kimono is decorated with auspicious symbols.

216. Puppy. (Ivory. 1 $^1/_2$″ long. Signed: Dosho. B 89.) Since ancient times in Japan, the dog has been the symbol of good health, and robust children are commonly described as being◄ healthy as puppies. For this reason, it has long been the custom to present newborn babies with toy dogs as a charm to insure their healthy growth.

217. Ryusa Netsuke. (Ivory. Diameter: 1 $^1/_4$″. Signed: Nao-tsugu.) A ball-shaped ryusa netsuke in an allover chrysanthe-►mum flower and leaf design. A poor shape for a netsuke, however, since its constant rolling about would cause annoyance. See text, page 160.

197

218. TIGER. (Ivory; eyes inlaid in amber and horn. Signed: Otoman. B 788.) The tiger, not native to Japan but well known from early days through reports from China, is naturally the symbol of fierceness and strength. In Japanese art, the tiger is conventionally portrayed in association with the bamboo. One interpretation of this association is that the tiger beneath the bamboo symbolizes the power of faith.

219. FROG ON A MUSHROOM. (Wood; eyes inlaid in shell and black coral. 1 $\frac{3}{4}$" long. Signed: Sukenaga Hida. B 1124.) The frog portrayed here is sometimes called a rain frog because its singing is believed to presage rain.

220. SLEEPING STUDENT. (Ivory. 1 $\frac{1}{4}$". Signed: Tomochika. B 1197.) A first-year student has fallen fast asleep over his "alphabet" after having written the first four characters: i, ro, ha, ni. The Japanese alphabet is actually a syllabary composed of forty-seven signs, of which i, ro, ha, and ni are the first four. The writing is carved in reverse since the wet black ink shows through the thin sheet of exercise paper.

▼
221. KAIBUTSU. (Wood. 2 1/2″. Unsigned.) Fantastic animals are known in Japan as kaibutsu. Most kaibutsu represented in netsuke are modeled after old Chinese drawings. The one illustrated here is found in the *Soken Kisho*, from which it may have been copied, if not from an earlier Chinese book.

▼
222. NOH MASK: Jo. (Ivory. 1 5/8″. Signed: Mitsuyuki.) Jo, the husband, and Uba, the wife, are the happy old couple in the Noh play *Takasago*, which is often performed at New Year celebrations because of its auspicious character. In the drama, Jo is revealed to be the god of Sumiyoshi and his wife the goddess of Takasago. The netsuke has a metal pin and a ring inserted on the reverse side for attachment of the inro cord.

223. CLAMS. (Lacquered wood. 1 1/4″ long. Signed: Tadayoshi. B 1149.) The realistic effect of this netsuke in lacquered wood attests to Tadayoshi's skill in carving
▶ shells. His signature appears on the netsuke in raised characters and includes the name of his birthplace, which is partially indecipherable.

199

224. SHOKI THE DEMON QUELLER. (Ivory. 1 ³/₈″. Signed: Yoshinaga. B 1302.) Shoki, a legendary Chinese figure dating from the days of the T'ang dynasty, reputedly has the ▸ power of overcoming and expelling devils. During the Boys' Day festival his image is placed in a position of honor in the household in order that the sons of the family may be protected from evil and grow up to be strong enough to fight demons, as Shoki himself does. See Figs. 62 and 143.

225. BLIND MAN AND DOG. (Bamboo. 2″. Signed: Yurin.) A blind man frightened by a dog. The Occidental tends to be appalled at the mockery of the plight of blind men as represented in netsuke. It must be remembered, however, that the ◂ role of moneylender was monopolized by the blind through Tokugawa edict. Moneylenders are never popular. Massage was another profession once restricted to the blind.

226. ONO NO TOFU. (Ivory. 1 ³/₄″. Unsigned.) A variant of the story of Ono no Tofu, the famous calligraphist ▸ who learned perseverance by watching a tree frog finally reach a high branch after many successive failures. Here the frog is attempting to jump on Tofu. For another illustration of Ono no Tofu, see Fig. 83.

14: Literature on Netsuke and Netsuke Collectors

AN AUTHOR FROM the West writes that although Japan is the home of netsuke, the Japanese neither study nor collect them. Many of the art critics of our country disparage or ignore netsuke, regarding them as an inferior form of art. It cannot be denied, however, that netsuke attained their growth and popularity during the Tokugawa period, an era of peace during which our culture, detached and isolated, matured free from all foreign artistic influences. For these reasons, the netsuke is the art form that is most purely Japanese and most representative of our basic artistic characteristics.

Until recently the *Soken Kisho* was the only book on the subject of netsuke written in our country. It was published by Inaba Tsuryu in 1781 and consists of seven volumes. The first five of these deal with swords and sword furnishings, the sixth with leather pouches and inro, and the seventh with netsuke and ojime. The author writes as follows: "Inro, purses, and hanging things are suspended by objects called netsuke. In the *Meibutsu Rokujo*, however, the term *kensui* (suspending) is used. There are many artisans who carve netsuke and who have become popular. Now I shall give the names of some of these craftsmen and illustrate some of their carvings for your appreciation, without regard to the quality of their workmanship."

The author of the *Soken Kisho* lists the names of fifty-three netsuke carvers, giving a brief history of each and illustrations of his work. In addition, he writes about sundial netsuke and Chinese-style *(tobori)* netsuke, furnishing various illustrations. The *Soken Kisho* contains prefaces by the famous Confucianist Ryukobi and others, as well as postscripts written by Inaba's brothers, Tsuho and Rinzo. According to these postscripts, Inaba Tsuryu lived at Nishi Shinsai-bashi, Shiomachi, Osaka. His popular name *(tsusho)* was Shinzaemon, and his pen name *(go)* was Shisuikan Shujin.

Inaba engaged in the business of assembling and decorating swords, having inherited his master's trade as well as his fine character. He was ever at pains to improve his judgment and did not concern himself with selling an article until he had investigated in detail the quality and authenticity of the smallest item. He deplored the fact that those who had developed knowledge and judgment kept their criteria and information secret, imparting nothing to others. In protest, Inaba reduced his various studies to writing and devoted himself to the compilation and editing of information. The *Soken Kisho* has been quoted in many Japanese and Occidental books about netsuke. Its publication benefited principally the making of sword furnishings but also the making of netsuke. In May, 1934, its author was posthumously honored by the Osaka Arts and Crafts Association for his distinguished service in the encouragement of arts and crafts.

Inaba Tsuryu also wrote *Samekawa Seigi* (Commentary on Sharkskin) and *Sarasafu* (Album of Calico). He died on February 22 in 1786 at the age of fifty-one. He was buried at the Hongaku-ji in Osaka and was given the posthumous Buddhist name of Tsushinin Kenryu Hiki.

During 1852 an old man named Kogetsu wrote *Sakasuikoshu* (Brief Biographies of Old Tea Masters). It consisted of five volumes to which he added a supplement in 1882. The fourth volume is illustrated with some pictures of netsuke, but the names of the carvers and most of the illustrations are merely reprinted from the *Soken Kisho*. Kogetsu's new material on netsuke comprised only brief biographies of two or three carvers.

The late Kyuichi Takeuchi, a former professor of the Tokyo Art Academy, made an exhaustive study of netsuke. He lectured occasionally on the subject and contributed articles on netsuke to the magazines. His exposition of netsuke appears in one of the encyclopedias. I understand that the collection of netsuke maintained by the Tokyo Imperial Household Museum was assembled by Takeuchi's assistants.

In April, 1934, I wrote *Shumi no Netsuke* (Netsuke as a Hobby), and in January, 1936, Sasaki Chujiro, Professor Emeritus of Tokyo Imperial University, brought out his *Netsuke of Japan*. The latter should be regarded as a catalog rather than a study. The explanatory material is extremely simple. Since Sasaki is a long-time scholar of natural history, he was able to make drawings of netsuke from his collection in lieu of photographs. His book is a good guide for netsuke designs.

There are no books on netsuke other than these. However, many books were published in early Meiji to supply models and sources of netsuke designs. For this purpose, Hokusai's *Manga* was in demand. Other reference books included the *Banshoku Zuko* (Illustrations of Multitudinous Occupations), the *Bambutsu Zukai Isai Gashiki* (Isai's Designs for Everything), and the *Bijutsu Chokoku Gafu* (Art of Sculpture Illustrated). These books were used principally by the netsuke carvers of Tokyo and not by those of Kansai and Chukyo. Nevertheless, I have seen a mushroom netsuke made by the first Masanao which has exactly the same design as a mushroom illustrated in the *Bambutsu Zukai Isai Gashiki*.

The minute, delicate, patient art of netsuke carving, lovingly carried out by skilled Japanese hands, is not an art duplicated by foreigners. Nevertheless, netsuke appeal to the fancy of the West and have been exported since the late Tokugawa period. Connoisseurs in Europe and America began the collection and study of netsuke. In 1905, a German, Albert Brockhaus, brought out a huge volume entitled *Netsuke* that comprises 500 pages and 272 illustrations, of which 53 are in color. In his preface, Brockhaus states that the netsuke as an art form existed at only one time and in only one place: Tokugawa Japan. The depth of his study is revealed in many portions of his book, and its publication was a great service to netsuke. Moreover, Brockhaus is himself a great collector, and his fine collection is a glory to his country.

In 1924, another book entitled *Netsuke* was published in English. The author was F. M. Jonas, an Englishman who lived in Kobe for a long time and devoted himself to the study and collecting of netsuke. Another edition of the Jonas book was published in 1928. I met Jonas on two or three occasions and learned a great deal about the subject from him.

Besides these, the Frenchman Louis Gonse gives a comprehensive description of netsuke in his book, *L'Art Japonais,* which was published in 1886, and the Englishman Edward Dillon does the same in his *Arts of Japan.* The Japan Society in London published a special issue on netsuke and inro as Volume III (Fourth Session, 1894–1895) of its *Transactions and Proceedings.* Unfortunately, the pieces illustrated in the *Transactions* are not masterpieces. Even my limited acquaintanceship indicates that excellent studies of netsuke like those mentioned above have been published in the Occident.

In our country it must be conceded that the best netsuke collection is the one maintained at the Tokyo Imperial Household Museum. The total number is quite small, and the majority of these originated in the Tokyo area. In my view, the number of carvers represented in the collection is much too small, and the quality of the pieces is much too poor for the Imperial Household Museum. Other museums have no netsuke collections whatsoever. I understand that Baron Go has a private collection of about three thousand netsuke, but I have not seen them. Mr. Jonas collected about a thousand, but I do not know whether he still retains them. A few years ago, I examined the collection of Sasaki Chujiro, which numbers about fifteen hundred items. Most of them are badly defaced by wear. Sasaki also collected sashi netsuke, and his present aim is to collect ancient wooden ones.

Fujii Zensuke of Kyoto owns about two hundred netsuke, most of which are very old pieces. Some of them are superb. Tanigawa Kiroku of Nara has collected numerous carvings by Toen Morikawa, the famous Nara artist, of which some fifty to sixty are netsuke. In addition to the work of Toen, Tanigawa owns works by many other carvers. Yamaguchi Kichirobei of Ashiya, Hyogo, has one hundred netsuke, including many in porcelain by well-known ceramists. He also has examples of netsuke by Kaigyokusai and Mitsuhiro. Yasuda Tasaburo of Osaka has about two hundred metal netsuke made by Kyubei, an artist about whom he is making a special study. In addition to the collectors mentioned above, I have met about fifty or sixty others, each of whom owns about a hundred items. Ejima Shojiro of Osaka is limiting his collection to netsuke made by Kaigyokusai.

In the West, I am informed, the museums of Germany, England, and the United States have excellent netsuke collections. Ivan Le-Page of Brussels has on several occasions written to me, enclosing photographs of more than a hundred netsuke in color and asking my opinion. I have a high regard for his intense interest. I understand that Mr. LePage makes a specialty of collecting netsuke made from water-buffalo horn.

Some of the literature to which I have referred in the text is listed in the bibliography on pages 313–314.

15: Reminiscences of Netsuke Carvers

A VISIT TO KOUN TAKAMURA

DURING THE MONTH of January, 1933, I called at the residence of Koun Takamura in Hayashi-cho, Komagome, Tokyo. Traces of snow remained among an interesting placement of stepping-stones and garden trees. After passing the trees, I came to the entrance, where a servant greeted me. I said that I should like to see the *sensei,* since I wanted to learn about netsuke, and that I had some specific questions in mind—and that this was my only excuse for asking to meet him despite my not knowing him or even carrying an introductory letter. I was promptly conducted into the drawing room, and soon afterwards the master entered. I saw his serene face for the first time.

This kindly, virtuous face, with generously puffed cheeks, flowing beard, and gentle smile, affected me like a refreshing breeze. My thoughts turned to my late father, who resembled the sensei, and I felt that I was seeing him again. As if to further the impression, Takamura treated me like a son. He encouraged me to ask questions freely, just as I should have done if he had been my real father.

The sensei answered my questions courteously and brought to my notice interesting points that had escaped me. Being insufficiently informed on the subject of netsuke, I was embarrassed to mention that I should like to write something on the subject. Takamura suggested that it would be most difficult to produce the ultimate book on netsuke at our present stage of limited research but that, even so, it would be a worthwhile effort to publish what was known. For example, he pointed out, a carver justly famous in one district might be completely unknown outside that district. In such cases, proper investigation could be undertaken only in the artist's neighborhood. Takamura urged me to write my book, and simultaneously I took the project to my heart. I asked the sensei to write the epigraph. He declined on the grounds of his lack of proficiency in writing, but I urged him to disregard the niceties of calligraphy and to write as the greatest authority on sculpture in our country. I asked for his epigraph to be of a size suitable for mounting as a kakemono, since I should like to preserve it for my descendants. He seemed a little disturbed, and he said: "Then it becomes more difficult." Within a few days, he sent me two epigraphs written on half-size kakemono. On one he had written: "Art is endless," and on the other: "Art equals spirit."

At the time I am writing about, Takamura was eighty-one years old. Although it was a bitterly cold day, the sensei made a list of names and addresses of people among his friends who might help me in my work. He showed me a netsuke representing a group of walnuts made by Soko Morita. He prized this netsuke as one of his finest possessions, and he promised to introduce me to Soko. Takamura talked to me about netsuke for fully half a day.

While working on my book, I learned that the sensei was ill. Thinking of his advanced years, I rushed the publication of my book in order that he might see it, and in April, 1934, I completed and published *Netsuke as a Hobby*. It was far from perfect, but I was happy that I could present a copy to Takamura. Perhaps it helped to divert his thoughts from his illness. I am filled with gratitude when I recall that I, unknown and uninvited, called on the most renowned sculptor, a member of the Arts and Crafts Committee of the Imperial Household and a man of venerable age, and had him give to me unstintingly of his sage advice and counsel. His nobility of character was on a level with his greatness as a sculptor.

After my visit I occasionally received letters about netsuke from Takamura written in his own hand, and my regard for him deepened. I neglected to mention above that I asked the sensei whether he had ever carved a netsuke. He said that he had and that he had consigned some to a pouch shop named Maruka and others to Otaki Tokusaburo. I inquired at Maruka's and was disappointed to learn that most of Takamura's netsuke had been lost in the Great Earthquake.

BESTOWAL OF POSTHUMOUS HONORS
by the Osaka Arts and Crafts Association

To commemorate the tenth anniversary of the founding of the Osaka Arts and Crafts Association, the society held a ceremony on May 9,

1934, to confer posthumous honors upon deceased artists and craftsmen who had rendered distinguished service in the promotion of artcrafts. The city of Osaka contributed to the event by permitting a display in the main hall of Osaka Castle of the works of those posthumously honored. Among those honored, the following were noted as netsuke carvers or persons who had in some way promoted the appreciation of netsuke: Shuzan Yoshimura, Shugetsu Higuchi, Mitsuhiro Ohara, Gyokkin Iida, Kaigyokusai Yasunaga Masatsugu, Sekka Shima, Toen Morikawa, Doraku Anrakusai, Dosho Kagei, Masakazu Sawaki, Masatoshi Sawaki, Ryukei Tanaka Mondo, Kyubei Tobutsu, and, for his promotion of artcrafts, Inaba Tsuryu.

The bereaved families or their descendants were invited to attend the ceremony and were presented with certificates of posthumous honors. Unfortunately the families of Tsuryu, Shuzan, Shugetsu, and Mitsuhiro could not be found. At a later date, however, the families of Tsuryu and Mitsuhiro were located.

INABA TSURYU: Through the assistance of the Local History Society of Osaka, the gravestone of Tsuryu was located at the Hongaku-ji in Osaka. With the gravestone as a starting point, investigation was begun, and it was determined that Tsuryu was born in Osaka in 1736, the first son of Inaba Tsushu; that his childhood name was Ichitaro; that he took the name of Shinuemon upon reaching his majority; that his nickname was Kyuho but was later changed to Shunkin; and that his *nom d'artiste* was Shizui. Although the family trade was the practice of medicine, which Tsuryu would normally have been expected to follow, he deserted the path of his doctoruncle Hayashi Tansui and interested himself in the business of swords, sword furnishings, and related articles. Later in life, Tsuryu delegated the management of the business to his younger brother, Tsuho Rinzo, and spent his time in writing. He wrote *Samekawa Seigi* and *Sarasafu* (also entitled *Shinto Sarasa Hinagata*) in addition to the *Soken Kisho*. He died in 1788 in his fifty-first year and was given the posthumous Buddhist name of Tsushinin Kenryunikki.

Tsuryu's wife Ren, whose posthumous Buddhist name was Tsuzein Myokinichiyu, bore him two children. The first of these died in infancy, while the second called himself Nidai Shinuemon and operated a shop dealing in swords. Nidai's descendants continued until Meiji, when the family line was extinguished in the fifth generation, since there was no successor to Godaime Kichisaburo. However, the descendants of Tsuryu's younger brother thrived, and the present head of the family, Inaba Inosuke, lives at Sumiyoshi in Osaka. On November 9, 1941, the family held a memorial service for Inaba Tsuryu at the Hongaku-ji along with an exhibit of his writings.

SHUZAN YOSHIMURA: The *Gravestone Annals of Famous Families of Naniwa* (Osaka), compiled by Miyatake Gaikotsu and published in March, 1911, relates that the gravestone of Shuzan Yoshimura is located at the Komyo-ji, Osaka. The *Character Sketches of Osaka Citizens,* compiled by Ishida Seisai, and the *Historical Relics and Monuments of Osaka* give the same information, but the *Brief Account of Visits to Osaka Gravestones* and the *Complete History of Osaka* do not confirm this point. In January, 1942, I visited the Komyo-ji and scraped away the dirt from each of the gravestones but failed to find Shuzan's. The temple officials could not help me. It is doubtless true that Shuzan's gravestone was located at the temple prior to 1911, but thereafter it was probably dismantled as an abandoned stone.

MITSUHIRO OHARA: Since it is known that Mitsuhiro in his later years returned to his birthplace, Onomichi, and died there, I made inquiries there and learned from Hino Gettei, a local priest, that Mitsuhiro's gravestone could be found at the Tennen-ji. Officials of the temple put me in contact with Mitsuhiro's family and advised me of the location of some of his surviving works. I wrote to the family and on November 27, 1941, had the pleasure of a visit from Ohara Shuzu, one of Mitsuhiro's surviving relatives, to whom I handed the Certificate of Posthumous Honor awarded by the Osaka Arts and Crafts Association. Thus there was a delay of seven years between the announcement of the award and the actual delivery to the family. The four sides of Mitsuhiro's gravestone read as follows:

Front: Sessado Mitsuhiro Shinji (posthumous name).
Back: August 2, Meiji 8 (1875). Grave of Mitsuhiro Ohara.
Right: Erected by Ohara Tosuke.
Left: A strange wind blows across my body. Today is the day that
    I depart for the cool world.

KAIGYOKUSAI YASUNAGA MASATSUGU: I heard that the gravestone of Masatsugu could be found at the Hoju-in in Osaka. I could not find it in the section of the cemetery to which I had been directed. I then checked each gravestone until I found it. The faces of his stone read as follows:

Front: Tokuo Kaigyokuzen Jomon (Kaigyokusai's first posthumous name). Tokuju Kakureizen Joni (wife's first posthumous name).
Back: Erected October 8, Meiji 15 (1882).
Right: Takuzen Hokaku Shinshi (Kaigyokusai's second posthumous name). Tongaku Myojo Shinshi (wife's second posthumous name).

HOJITSU YAMADA: On September 10, 1942, Soko Morita and I visited the grave of Hojitsu at the Renkyu-ji of the Nichiren sect in Osaka. The stone is made of natural marine rock and must have been erected by his students and relatives in 1894. Portions of the stone are chipped, and some of the characters have become undecipherable.

Part Two: AN INDEX OF NETSUKE CARVERS

An Index
of Netsuke Carvers

EXPLANATORY NOTES

NAMES: The artist in Japan may be known by various names during his lifetime, and this can be a cause of much confusion to the student of netsuke. The following list of terms used in the biographies given here should be an aid to the understanding of the names and signatures of many of the netsuke carvers. Other terms will be found in the index.

Azana: Nickname.

Chomei: Carved signature. The name, including inscription, that the sculptor or carver engraves or embosses on his work.

Go: Art name or pseudonym. The artist may use and discard several *go* during his lifetime.

Hanko: See *in.*

In or *hanko:* Seal. An engraved seal cut into some hard material such as wood, ivory, stone, or metal. The *in* is covered with a pastelike red ink and stamped on the document or object to be identified. As sometimes used in the biographies, *in* means a signature carved on the netsuke in the style of an impressed seal—in other words, carved in *tensho* (seal character) script.

Inkoku: Seal-like characters carved on the *objet d'art* itself to simulate an impressed seal.

Kaimyo: Posthumous name. A name conferred in a Buddhist ceremony after death.

Kaisho: Printed or square style of writing characters.

Kakihan or *kao:* A written or carved seal as distinguished from an *in* or impressed seal. *Kakihan* are often added to the artist's signature and in this case cause no problem of identification. *Kakihan* standing alone and unaccompanied by signatures, however, are almost impossible to identify unless the artist's *kakihan* is widely known or unless it is composed of parts of, or elaborations of, the characters forming the artist's *chomei,* in which cases the application of much puzzle-solving cleverness and much calligraphic astuteness may lead to an uncertain identification.

Kanji: Chinese characters used in the written Japanese language.

Kao: See *kakihan.*

Kundoku: Native Japanese readings of Chinese characters used in the Japanese language.

Mei: The name, including inscription, with which the artist signs his work. The term *mei* is applied to artists in general, including painters and writers as well as sculptors, while the term *chomei* is limited to sculptors and carvers.

Mosha: Facsimile signature. An exact copy of the *chomei* or the *mei.*

Na: Given name.

Ondoku: Chinese readings, in Japanized pronunciation, of *kanji* used in the Japanese language.

Raku-in: Similar to a *yaki-in.* The seal, engraved in copper, is heated and burned into the object as a brand.

Sosho: "Running hand" or cursive style of writing characters.

Tensho: Style of writing used for impressed seal characters.

Tsusho: Popular name or "calling" name.

Uji: Family name or surname.

Yago: Shop name. The name by which many shopkeepers were known, particularly among the tradesmen *(chonin)* of pre-Meiji days, who were not permitted to use *uji* or family names. The custom persists even today. Such names always end in the suffix *ya.*

Yaki-in: Brand or heated seal. Usually found on porcelain or pottery netsuke.

Yomyo: Infant or childhood name.

DATES: Specific dates are given whenever they are known. In other cases the artist may be dated by the period or era with which he is most associated and for which corresponding Western dates are inserted in parentheses. In those cases where it is impossible to give either specific dates or eras, the artist is classified as early, middle, or late. As stated in Chapter 13, the early period covers the years from the birth of the netsuke through Kansei (1800); the middle period, the sixty-eight years from Kyowa (1801) until the beginning of Meiji (1868); and the late period, those from the beginning of Meiji to the present. Thus the dating "early middle" means the early part of the middle period—that is, roughly the first half of the period between 1801 and 1868.

The following list of Japanese eras with corresponding Western dates, should prove useful as a handy reference; other eras and periods are noted in the index.

Genroku	1688–1703	Bunka	1804–1817
Hoei	1704–1710	Bunsei	1818–1829
Shotoku	1711–1715	Tempo	1830–1843
Kyoho	1716–1735	Koka	1844–1847
Gembun	1736–1740	Kaei	1848–1853
Kampo	1741–1743	Ansei	1854–1859
Enkyo	1744–1747	Manen	1860
Kanen	1748–1750	Bunkyu	1861–1863
Horeki	1751–1763	Genji	1864
Meiwa	1764–1771	Keio	1865–1867
Anei	1772–1780	Meiji	1868–1911
Temmei	1781–1788	Taisho	1912–1925
Kansei	1789–1800	Showa	1926–present
Kyowa	1801–1803		

MISCELLANEOUS: Roman numerals following a name indicate the line of succession to that particular name. The succession is not necessarily by generation, nor is it necessarily lineal. A nephew, brother, grandson, or other relative who shows an aptitude for carving may succeed to the use of the founder's name, or a promising apprentice may be adopted or simply honored with the bestowal of the name.

References to biographies are indicated by a capital B followed by the number.

Many of the biographies are quite elliptical—for example, "Baigyoku 梅玉. Late. Ivory. Masks." More fully stated, this would be: "Baigyoku was a carver associated with the late period who worked principally in ivory and is known mainly as a carver of mask netsuke."

The most frequent additions to signatures are listed below. Other inscriptions are translated in full in the individual biographies.

Chokoku: Sculptured or carved.
Gisaku: A copy.
Koku: Carved.
Makie: Gold lacquerer.
Monjin: Pupil of.
Ni mosu: Imitated (from).
Oju: By request (of).
Okina: Old man.
Oko: To please the taste of.

Rojin: Old man.
Saku: Made.
Seisaku: Produced.
Sha: Copied.
So : Old man.
Tenka-ichi: Best in the world (literally "first under heaven").
To : Knife-cut or cut with a knife.
Tsukuru: Made.

梅源　　　　　　　元山

–A–

1. Adachi Tomoshichi安達友七.
Go: Masanobu 正信. See Masanobu (B 616).

2. Anraku 安樂. Middle. Ivory.
Human figures and animals. See
Fig. 55. See mosha (No. 1).

3. Anrakusai 安樂齋. *Chomei:* Kogyoku 光玉. *Go:* Anrakusai 安樂齋.
See Kogyoku (B 511).

–B–

4. Baigen 梅源. Late. Nara dolls.
See mosha (No. 2).

5. Baigyoku 梅玉. Late. Ivory.
Masks.

6. Baihosai 貝寶齋. Early. Wood.

7. Banryusai 盤龍齋. Early.
Ivory.

8. Basui 馬水. Late. Wood.

9. Batoraku 馬頭樂. Middle.

10. Bazan 馬山. *Chomei:* Bazan
馬山, usually in embossed characters. Born in Tempo (1830–1843)
in the district of Motosu, Gifu.
Carved realistic netsuke of excellent
quality in wood. Went to Tokyo in
his middle years but returned to
Gifu disillusioned with the haste
and cheapness of netsuke carving
in Tokyo. Continued carving netsu-

ke despite his struggles with financial difficulties. Never made two
netsuke of the same design. Created
several original mask designs for
ceramist Sekisen Shimizu (B 947).
Died about 1897 at the age of 64.
See Fig. 125. See mosha (No. 3).

11. Beisai米齋. *Uji:* Ogawa 小川.
Na: Ryobei 良平. Late. Horn.
Lived on Itsuku Island. A netsuke
of his is signed as follows: "On Itsuku Island I trapped a deer and cut
off its horns. Beisai, 65 years old,
carved. 以嚴島纝落角削之六十五
叟米齋刀."

12. Bisho 美笑. *Chomei:* Bisho 美笑.
Early middle. Wood.

13. Bokugyoku 卜玉. Middle.
Chestnut wood (kurinoki).

14. Bokugyuken 牧牛軒. *Chomei:*
Toshiharu 利治. See Toshiharu (B
1233).

15. Bokuji 卜二. Some netsuke are
found that bear his signature.

16. Bokuko 墨湖. *Uji:* Ando 安藤.
Born in Gifu. His father was associated with Tessai Kano (B 1173).
Bokuko lived with Kano in Tokyo
and studied his methods. Was a
proficient carver and developed a
fresh and original style. Created a
technique similar to tsuishu carvings. Was also an expert appraiser
of art objects.

17. Bokusai 穆齋. Early middle. Wood. Human figures and sennin. Lived in both Kyoto and Tokyo. His work was fine and sensitive.

18. Bokusai 僕哉. Middle. Mostly wood.

19. Bokuzan 卜山. *Chomei:* Bokuzan 卜山, in raised characters. Middle. Wood. Shells and animals. Lived in Nagoya. See mosha (No. 4).

20. Bokuzan 朴山. Middle. Wood. Carved in the style of Hokusai drawings.

21. Bumpo 文寶. Tempo. Mainly wood.

22. Bumpo 文峰. Late. Ivory.

23. Bun 文. Early.

24. Bunga 文雅. Middle.

25. Bungyo 文魚. Middle. Lived in Tokyo.

26. Bunryusai 文柳齋. Late. Ivory.

27. Bunsai 文齋. Called himself Tani (谷). See Fig. 119.

28. Bunshojo 文章女. *Uji:* Shimizu 清水. *Na:* Onoe 尾の江. *Go:* Bunshojo 文章女 or Iwao Seiyodo 巖青陽堂. *Chomei:* Seiyodo Bunshojo chokoku 青陽堂文章女彫刻. Born in 1764 when her father was 32

years old. Was the eldest daughter of Tomiharu (B 1191), the first Iwao Seiyodo, whom she succeeded as Iwao II. Bunshojo equaled her father as a netsuke artist. Was also an accomplished haiku poet. Drank a great deal of sakè and remained single all her life. Taught carving to Shikazo, the son of her younger sister Yachiyo. Died in 1838 at the age of 75. She left beautiful boar-tusk netsuke carved with spiders. See Fig. 135. See mosha (No. 5).

29. Bunsui 文水. *Uji:* Takahashi 高橋. *Na:* Kichinosuke 吉之助 Born in 1819. Cabinetmaker and wood carver. Lived in Kyoto and later in Tokyo.

–C–

30. Chikamasa 親正. *Go:* Shominsai 松民齋. Bunsei (1818–1829). Son of a juggler. Entered the school of Hiraga Gennai 平賀源内, where he studied carving under the strict discipline imposed by his master. Later carved netsuke exclusively. Enjoyed a reputation as a fine ivory carver.

31. Chikanobu 親信. Middle. Wood.

32. Chikashige 親重. See Ryuho (B 779).

竹
壽

𥴩

7. CHIKUSAI

33. Chikayuki 親之. *Uji:* Fuku-shima 福島. *Tsusho:* Yasusaburo 安三郎. *Go:* Suginoya 杉之舎. Meiji (1868–1911). Was the third son of Rinshun Hanadokoro. Lived in Asakusa, Tokyo. Carved Noh dolls which he called Asakusa dolls. His work is excellent but rarely found. It is said that he made an incense box (kogo) in the shape of a crane, on the outer box of which he wrote: "Chikayuki, maker of Asakusa dolls あさ草人形親之造." On the kogo itself he affixed his seal, which reads: Asakusa. Died on July 9, 1883, at the age of 46.

34. Chikko 竹光. Late. Wood. Masks and other subjects.

35. Chikko 竹江. *Uji:* Takehara 竹原. Lives in Higashi-ku, Osaka. During his youth studied as a pupil of Kaigyokusai (B 430). Later worked independently. Proficient in wood carving. Is alive today and carves tirelessly.

36. Chikko 竹香. *Uji:* Kusakawa 草川. *Na:* Seishichi 清七. *Chomei:* Chikko 竹香. Early Meiji (1868–1911). Resided in Tsu. Was the star pupil of Chikusen Imanaka (B 41). Carved decorations on various types of receptacles. His work had a special refinement and won him wide acclaim. Very few carvers today can emulate the quality of his work.

Only seldom did he make netsuke.

37. Chikuju 竹壽. Late. Nara dolls. See mosha (No. 6).

38. Chikusai 竹齋. See Kiyu (B 498).

39. Chikusai 竹齋. Early. Wood. Human beings and animals. See mosha (No. 7).

40. Chikusai 竹齋. Meiji-Taisho (1868–1925). Resided at Hama-dera. Good at carving beauties. Died in early Taisho (1912–1925).

41. Chikusen 竹仙. Early Meiji (1868–1911). Lived in Tsu. Good at drawing and poetry. Excelled at carving landscapes and floral dec-orations of superior quality on writing brushes, yatate, poetry cards, and other things. Was com-missioned by the Tsu clan to do this type of work. His netsuke are rarely found but are usually carved from bamboo roots and nuts and repre-sent landscapes and the "four gentlemen" (shikunshi)—that is, the orchid, the chrysanthemum, the plum, and the bamboo.

42. Chiku-unsai 竹雲齋. Early middle. Ivory. Human figures. See Fig. 158.

43. Chiku-unsai 竹雲齋. *Uji:* Tanabe 田邊. *Na:* Tsuneo 常雄. Late. Lived in Sakai. Carved

218 · INDEX OF NETSUKE CARVERS

mainly bamboo fittings and vases for flower arrangements. Also made netsuke.

44. Chikuyosai 竹陽齋. *Chomei:* Tomochika 友親. See Tomochika (B 1195).

45. Chikuyuken 竹友軒. See Shunsai (B 1070).

46. Chingendo 珍元堂. *Chomei:* Hidemasa 秀正. See Hidemasa (B 212).

47. Chinkin 椿近. Middle. Ivory.

48. Chisoku 知足. Some netsuke bearing his signature are found.

49. Cho 調. Early. Wood. Masks. Usually identified himself with a kakihan.

50. Chodo 昶堂. Early. Wood. Masks. Signed with a kakihan.

51. Chogetsu 潮月. *Uji:* Yamada 山田. *Na:* Shosetsu 正接. *Go:* Shunkosai 春江齋. Born in 1826; died in 1892.

52. Chohei 猪平. Early. Wood.

53. Chokichi 長吉. *Uji:* Miyashiro 宮代. Middle to late. The fifth generation Chokichi lived in Kanda, Tokyo.

54. Chokosai 長光齋. Early. Wood. Human figures and horses.

55. Chokusai 直齋. *Uji:* Miyagi 宮城. *Na:* Masanosuke 政之助. Born in Osaka in 1877. Because of Chokusai's poor health as a child, his father decided that he should not succeed to his construction business but arranged for him to study carving as a pupil of Isseisai Naomitsu (B 751). Chokusai was sixteen when he became a pupil of Naomitsu and studied with him for four years. Carved in both wood and ivory, which he never colored. Devoted himself almost exclusively to netsuke carving. Kosen Nishimoto (B 545) of Osaka and Okada Naoaki 岡田直明 were both pupils of Chokusai. See Figs. 134 and 177. See mosha (No. 8).

56. Chosen 晁川. Early. Wood. Animals.

57. Chounsai 長雲齋. See Gyokumin (B 150).

58. Chounsai 長雲齋. See Hidechika (B 206).

59. Chounsai 長雲齋. *Chomei:* Jugyoku 壽玉. See Jugyoku (B 407).

60. Chounsai 長雲齋. See Seimin (B 925).

61. Choyo 猪葉. Ivory. Fish and turtles.

62. Chuichi 忠一. Taisho (1912–1925). Born in Osaka. Excelled at carving turtles in wood. Made netsuke for export. Died in Manchuria in the latter part of Taisho. See mosha (No. 9).

63. Chuzan 忠山. Late. Ivory.

– D –

64. Daisen 大泉. Made cast-metal netsuke. See Fig. 23.

65. Dembei 傳兵衛. *Yago:* Taharaya 田原屋. Prior to Temmei (1781–1788). Lived in Osaka. Was a pupil of Kanjuro (B 447). Carved in wood and ivory.

66. Deme Dohaku 出目洞白. Born in Tokyo. Carved mask netsuke.

67. Deme Eiman 出目榮滿. Died in 1705. Although a mere pupil of Deme Mitsunaga 出目光長 he was nevertheless the originator of the mask netsuke.

68. Deme Jokyu 出目上久. Early. Some netsuke bearing his signature are found.

69. Deme Joman 出目上滿. Was a younger brother of Deme Juman (B 71). Carved mask netsuke. There is some opinion that he was the son of Deme Uman (B 77). See Fig. 41.

70. Deme Josei 出目上清. Was a pupil of Deme Uman (B 77). Carved only mask netsuke.

71. Deme Juman 出目壽滿. Early. Mask netsuke. Son of Eiman (B 67).

72. Deme Kunimitsu 出目國滿. Some mask netsuke bear his signature.

73. Deme Mitsuhide 出目滿英. *Uji:* Fujiwara 藤原. Early. Mask netsuke.

74. Deme Mitsuhisa 出目滿久. Early. Mask netsuke.

75. Deme Saman 出目左滿. Carved mask netsuke. Called himself Saman in contrast with Uman *(sa:* left; *u:* right; *man:* 10,000 or completeness). Sometimes carved "tenka-ichi" 天下一 with his signature. However, his work is quite inferior to that of Uman (B 77). See mosha (No. 10).

76. Deme Taiman 出目泰滿. Early. There are wood masks representing Okina that bear his signature.

77. Deme Uman 出目右滿. *Na:* Jirodayu 二郎大夫. Anei (1772–1780). Lived in Tokyo. Was a family pupil of the Deme mask carvers. Was the son of Juman (B 71) and the grandson of Eiman (B

11. DEME UMAN   12. DEME YOSHINARI   13. DOSEN   14. DOSHO

67) of the main family. Carved netsuke as a hobby and made elegant mask netsuke. Often carved his signature followed by "tenka-ichi." See mosha (No. 11).

78. Deme Yoshinari 出目吉成. *Chomei:* Deme Yoshinari saku 出目 吉成作. Most probably late. Carved mask netsuke. See mosha (No. 12).

79. Deme Zekan 出目是觀. Early. Carved masks and mask netsuke.

80. Denko 田耕. Tempo (1830–1843). Mostly wood.

81. Dohachi 道八. A famous ceramist of Kyoto who also made porcelain netsuke.

82. Donraku 鈍樂. Early. Wood. Animals and masks.

83. Donrin 曇林. Temmei (1781–1788). Wood. Human figures. Work is sensitive and refined.

84. Donshu 呑舟. Early. Carved mask netsuke in both rough and delicate techniques.

85. Doraku 道樂. Middle. Excelled in ivory carving. Born in Ono-michi but lived in Osaka. See Figs. 53 and 181.

86. Dorakusai 道樂齋. See Doraku (B 85).

87. Dosei 道成. Some netsuke bearing his signature are in existence.

88. Dosen 道仙. Probably early late. Made delicate carvings of butterflies in inlaid wood. Signed by cutting his signature on an ivory plaque which he inlaid in the carving. See mosha (No. 13).

89. Dosho 道笑. *Uji:* Kagei 景井. *Na:* Juzaemon 壽左衛門. *Go:* Kokusai 古苦齋. *Chomei:* Dosho 道笑 or Dosho *in* 道笑印. Born in 1828 in Izumo but moved to Osaka. Died in 1884. Was taught ivory carving by Anrakusai Doraku (B 85). Also carved in wood, bamboo, turtle shell, horn, and precious stone. Sometimes carved his mei on an inlaid plaque. See Figs. 107 and 216. See mosha (No. 14).

90. Doshosai 道笑齋. Tempo through Keio (1830–1867). Worked in ivory and in Shibayama style inlay. May be the same individual as Dosho (B 89).

91. Dotei 道亭. Middle. Wood.

92. Dozan 道山. *Chomei:* Dozan 道山. Tempo (1830–1843). Wood.

—E—

93. Eigyoku 永玉. Middle. Wood. Proficient at carving netsuke.

a   b

15. EIRAKU

16. FUSHO

94. Ei-ichi 惠一. Late.

95. Eijuken 永壽軒. Early middle. Wood. Carved many masks.

96. Eijun 永惇. *Uji:* Nozawa 野澤. Did inlay work.

97. Einen 英年. Middle. Wood.

98. Eiraku 永樂. *Chomei:* Rakkan Eiraku *in* 落款永樂印 or Kahin-shiryu *in* 河濱支流印. Was a famous ceramist of Kyoto, with a reputation maintained through several generations of his family. See mosha (No. 15).

99. Eirakusai 永樂齋. *Chomei:* Tomotada 友忠. See Tomotada (B 1216).

100. Eisai 永齋. *Uji:* Teramoto 寺本. *Na:* Motojiro 元治郎. Late.

101. Eisai 英齋. *Uji:* Matsushima 松島. *Na:* Masashichi 政七. Middle.

102. Ekisei 易政. *Na:* Senzo 仙藏. *Go:* Kiryosai 貴凌齋. Early middle. Followed the technique of his grandfather, Senzo Shibayama (B 954).

103. Ekishin 易信. Some netsuke bearing his signature are found.

– F –

104. Fuboku 浮木. Early. Wood and ivory. Human figures and animals.

105. Fukai 不皆. Early. Worked in ivory and metal.

106. Fusayuki 房之. Late.

107. Fusho 風昇. *Chomei:* Fusho 風昇. Tempo through Keio (1830–1867). Mostly wood. Good at carving dragons. There is one of his netsuke signed: "Fusho, 71 years old 風昇七十一歲." See mosha (No. 16).

– G –

108. Gado 雅堂. *Uji:* Naniwa 難波. *Na:* Shikazo 鹿三. *Chomei:* Gado 雅堂 or sometimes Furueda *in* 古枝印. Born in Takamatsu in 1888. Graduated from the Kanagawa Prefectural Arts and Crafts School established in Takamatsu. Employed by the Yamaha Musical Instrument Manufacturing Company. Removed to Osaka in 1913. Carved in wood and in bamboo, which he sometimes colored. Made many tea-ceremony articles and occasionally netsuke.

109. Gambun 眼文. Middle. Lived in Kyoto and also Tokyo. Did excellent work in metal as well as in wood and ivory.

110. Garaku 雅樂. Middle. Wood.

111. Garaku 我樂. *Azana:* Risuke 利助. *Chomei:* Garaku 我樂. Anei

我
笑

17. GASHO

(1772–1780). Lived in Osaka. Was a pupil of Taharaya Dembei (B 65). Carved deer, turtles, and other animals in ivory.

112. Gasho 我笑. *Uji:* Taguchi 田口. *Chomei:* Gasho 我笑. Late. Ivory. Probably a pupil of Dosho (B 89). See mosha (No. 17).

113. Gechu 牙虫. Prior to Temmei (1781–1788). Some netsuke bearing his signature are found. See Fig. 180.

114. Gekko 月耕. Early to middle. Wood. Animals.

115. Gemmin 玄民. Middle. Ivory and bone.

116. Gengensai 元々齋. Middle. Wood. Animals of the zodiac.

117. Gen-ichi 元一. *Chomei:* Gen-ichi 元一. Bunsei (1818–1829). Wood.

118. Genko 玄光. Middle. Ivory. Many owl netsuke.

119. Genkosai 玄黄齋. *Uji:* Morino 森野. Late. Wood.

120. Genryosai 元良齋. Middle.

121. Genryosai 玄了齋. See Minkoku (B 667).

122. Gensai 元齋. *Chomei:* Gensai 元齋. Middle. Carved netsuke representing vegetables in ivory,

coral, or metal, and in combinations of these materials.

123. Gessen 月洗. Tempo (1830–1843). Wood. Figures.

124. Getchu 月虫. Early. Wood.

125. Godo 悟道. Early. Ivory and freestones.

126. Goryu 五龍. Early. Ivory. Human figures.

127. Goto Seijiro 後藤清次郎. Middle. Metal artist of the Goto school.

128. Goto Yataro 後藤彌太郎. *Go:* Yoshiaki 義明. Meiji (1868–1911). Traveled extensively, returning to Tokyo in early Meiji, when he devoted himself to carving.

129. Gunsai 葷齋. There are a few netsuke signed with his name.

130. Gyokkei 玉珪. Temmei and Kansei (1781–1800). Wood. Carved human figures, animals, and insects. See Fig. 140.

131. Gyokkei 玉桂. *Chomei:* Gyokkei 玉桂. Temmei and Kansei (1781–1800). Wood. Noh masks.

132. Gyokken 玉ケン. Late.

133. Gyokkin 玉琴. *Go:* Chikurin 竹林 and Gyokkin 玉琴. *Na:* Seijiro 政治郎. *Chomei:* Gyokkin 玉琴.

18. GYOKKIN   19. GYOKKO   20. GYOKKOSAI   21. GYOKUHOSAI

Worked in the kitchen of the Iida family. Went to Kyoto and Nara, where he associated with priest Hakuho and Toen Morikawa (B 1177). Removed to Osaka, where he became acquainted with Umemoto Kotetsu 梅本古鐵 and Zuisho Hotta (B 1342), finally understanding the techniques of carving. Made elegant bamboo carvings and tea-ceremony articles. Always drank sakè to excess and was full of eccentricities. Was openhearted and unaffected by wealth and honors. Managed his personal finances very badly, causing many difficulties, to which he was indifferent. Enjoyed sitting in bamboo groves and playing the gekkin (moon guitar). Spent his declining years in the same carefree manner. Died at the foot of Senririkyo Bridge in Osaka in 1880 at the age of 64. Cremated at the Hofuku-ji. His son Kotaro 康太郎 used the go Kinden 琴田 or Dorin 桐林 and attempted to assume his father's mantle but lacked the necessary ability. See mosha (No. 18).

134. Gyokko 玉光. *Go:* Gyokkosai 玉光齋. *Chomei:* Gyokko 玉光. Tempo through Keio (1830–1867). Ivory and wood. Was extremely proficient at carving netsuke representing human beings, animals, and masks. See mosha (No. 19).

135. Gyokko 玉固. Early. Wood.

136. Gyokkosai 玉光齋. See Gyokko (B 134). See mosha (No. 20).

137. Gyokubun 玉文. Late. Ivory. Specialized in carving Hotei.

138. Gyokuchin 玉珍. Early. Wood. Mostly human figures.

139. Gyokugasai 玉賀齋. See Ryusa (B 871).

140. Gyokugyokusai 玉々齋. Late. Carved in horn.

141. Gyokuho 玉抱. Middle. Ivory and horn.

142. Gyokuho 玉寶. *Uji:* Yamada 山田. *Chomei:* Gyokuho 玉寶. Carved during the first half of Meiji. Studied under Ryuchin (B 843).

143. Gyokuhosai 玉寶齋. This artist is almost certainly the same individual as Gyokuho (B 142).

144. Gyokuhosai 玉寶齋. See Ryuchin (B 843). See mosha (No. 21).

145. Gyokuji 玉治. Prior to Temmei (1781–1788). Lived in Kyoto.

146. Gyokujitsu 玉實. Late. Ivory.

147. Gyokuju 玉壽. Late. Wood.

玉玉
斗斗
a   b

玉藻

玉雲

22. GYOKURINTEI   23. GYOKUSAI   24. GYOKUSO   25. GYOKU-UN

148. Gyokumin 玉民. Middle. It is not certain whether this carver is the same man as Gyokumin (B 149). See Fig. 178.

149. Gyokumin 玉珉. May be the same artist as Gyokumin (B 148).

150. Gyokumin 玉眠. *Go:* Chounsai 長雲齋. Born 1859, the eldest son of Masamitsu Kikugawa (B 484).

151. Gyokurintei 玉林亭 or Gyokurin 玉林. Carved animals and masks in wood. See mosha (No. 22).

152. Gyokuryu 玉龍. Middle.

153. Gyokuryusai 玉龍齋. See Gyokuryu (B 152).

154. Gyokusai 玉齋. *Chomei:* Gyokusai 玉齋. Middle. Wood and ivory. Mainly human figures. Carved many balancing figures that stand on one foot. Quite famous. See mosha (No. 23).

155. Gyokusai 玉哉. Early middle. Wood. Human figures and animals. See Fig. 141.

156. Gyokusen 玉川. Middle. Wood and ivory.

157. Gyokusen 玉泉 or Gyokusensai 玉泉齋. Early. Wood.

158. Gyokushi 玉之. Middle. Ivory. Dragons and oni.

159. Gyokushinsai 玉眞齋. Middle. Horn.

160. Gyokuso 玉藻. *Uji:* Ouchi 大内. *Na:* Jiemon 治右衞門. *Chomei:* Gyokuso 玉藻. Born in 1879, the same year as Soko (B 1101). Studied under Joso (B 400) for about 18 months before carving independently. Later studied netsuke in daily meetings with Soko from 1920 to 1934. His work was exhibited at the Japan Art Association, the Tokyo Arts and Crafts Exhibition, and the Association for the Propagation of Ivory Carving. He received prizes on numerous occasions. He exhibited only netsuke. Gyokuso presently lives in Nerima-ku, Tokyo. See Figs. 77, 148, 153, and 211. See mosha (No. 24).

161. Gyokutei 玉亭. Middle. Wood. Sennin and other figures.

162. Gyoku-un 玉雲 or Gyokuunsai 玉雲齋. Early. Wood and ivory. See mosha (No. 25).

163. Gyokuyosai Mitsuhina 玉陽齋光雛. *Chomei:* Gyokuyosai 玉陽齋. Lived from Temmei until Meiji (1781–1868). Carved netsuke of figures, dragons, and other subjects. Lived in Asakusa, Tokyo.

多尔 (mosha characters)

26. GYOKUZAN

玉山 (mosha characters)

27. GYOKUZAN

Was the teacher of Kokusai Ozaki (B 527). See Fig. 147.

164. Gyokuzan 玉山. *Uji:* Asahi 旭. *Na:* Tomimaru 富丸, but later changed to Tomisaburo 富三郎. *Chomei:* Gyokuzan 玉山, Kyusho 旭生, or Kyugyokuzan saku 旭玉山作. Born in Asakusa, Tokyo in 1843. Ordained a priest but, liking the carver's art, devoted himself exclusively to ivory carving from the age of 24. Carved frogs, snakes, crabs, monkeys, and other animals but was especially proficient at carving skull netsuke. Considered an expert on the subject of ivory carving during Meiji. Was an influential member of the Association of Tokyo Sculptors. Was a professor at the Tokyo Art School. Refused to accept an inferior position offered him on the Imperial Art Committee. His style was quite realistic. The excellence of his work was a source of wonder both to our own people and to foreigners. He won many prizes and awards, including the first prize for a carving of a skull exhibited in 1881. One of Gyokuzan's prizes was awarded to him by His Imperial Highness Prince Norihisa in the presence of Emperor Meiji. Later moved to Kyoto and studied the collections of the Shoso-in and other ancient art, becoming an expert in inlay techniques. Acted as a member of the examining committee for the fourth and fifth exhibitions (1895 and 1903) respectively. Died on August 10, 1923, at the age of 79. See Fig. 19.

165. Gyokuzan 玉山. *Go:* Isshinsai 一心齋. *Chomei:* Isshinsai Gyokuzan 一心齋玉山. Late. Ivory. Daruma was his favorite subject. See mosha (No. 26).

166. Gyokuzan 玉山. Wood. Carved human figures, animals, fish, and masks. See mosha (No. 27).

167. Gyuka 牛加. *Uji:* Kamibayashi 上林. *Na:* Keimei 景命. *Go:* Rakushiken 樂只軒. *Chomei:* kakihan or yaki-in. Born in December 1801 near Iwamura Castle, Mino. Entered the monastery of Mitsu-ji and became a priest. In 1819, he served the family of one of the imperial princes as a priest. Later resigned from the priesthood in order to study the paintings of the Maruyama school. Did well as a painter. Adopted the *go* of Seisen 清泉 and the pseudonym of Shiho 子奉. In 1827 adopted by Kamibayashi of Uji, a famous tea master, since his family had no heir. The shogun approved his succession to the household of the tea master, and he thereupon changed his

a   b

28. GYUKA   29. HACHIGYOKU   30. HAKO

name to Gyuka. In 1843, Tsumura, the Lord of Ise and magistrate of Kyoto, requested Gyuka to carve a souvenir of Uji for presentation to the shogun. Gyuka carved from seasoned tea wood a doll netsuke representing a woman tea picker and presented it to the shogun. Several daimyo found the carving appealing and requested Gyuka to reproduce the same subject for them. The second-generation Gyuka carved many of these dolls, and gradually they became known as Uji dolls. In 1859, Gyuka relinquished the carving of Uji dolls to his successor and removed to Uji, where he died in 1870 at the age of 70. His son succeeded him as the second generation and was called Kyusen Rakushiken (B 578). Gyuka signed with a kakihan or a brand. Since Gyuka was the seventh or eighth generation of Kanamori Sowa 金森宗和 and since Sowa had already originated the Uji doll, it is more accurate to say that Gyuka revived this netsuke form. However, Gyuka's work is much superior to Sowa's by the addition of a pictorial quality.

Gyuka was an enthusiastic adherent of the emperor system and exerted his influence to restrict the use of the tea grown in the Uji district to the Imperial Household instead of the Tokugawa shogunate. See Fig. 61. See mosha (No. 28).

– H –

168. Hachichiku 八竹. *Chomei:* Hachichiku 八竹. Late. Wood. Carved some fine netsuke of wolves.

169. Hachigaku 八岳. Bunka (1804–1817). Wood and ivory. Excelled at carving figures.

170. Hachigyoku 八玉. *Chomei:* Hachigyoku 八玉. Early. Born in Tokyo. Was a mask carver. Made netsuke as a hobby. See mosha (No. 29).

171. Hako 波江. *Na:* Tomiharu 富春. Hako is a *go* accepted in his youth by Shunyodo Tomiharu (B 1191). There is a cicada netsuke carved from black persimmon wood and signed: "Carved by Sekiyo Hako Seiyodo 石陽波江青陽堂彫." He probably made this netsuke while residing in Hane-etsu. See mosha (No. 30).

172. Hakudo 白道. Middle. Wood. Mask netsuke.

173. Hakudosai 白道才. Wood. Mask netsuke. Most probably the same artist as Hakudo (B 172).

174. Hakuei 白英 or **Hakueisai** 白英齋. Middle. Ivory. Mostly figures.

175. Hakugyoku 白玉. Middle. Wood.

176. Hakuko 白紅. Middle. Wood.

177. Hakumin 伯珉. *Go:* Isshosai 一照齋. *Uji:* Sekine 關根. *Na:* Shimbei 新兵衛. Middle. Lived in Tokyo. Was a pupil of Isshinsai Yoshiyuki (B 1318).

178. Hakumo 伯茂. *Chomei:* Hakumo 伯茂. Late. Ivory and seeds. See mosha (No. 31*).*

179. Hakuo 白翁. Tempo (1830–1843). Excelled at carving manju netsuke.

180. Hakuosai 白翁齋. Same carver as Hakuo (B 179).

181. Hakuryu 白龍. *Uji:* Miyasaka 宮坂. *Go:* Shoundo 松雲堂. *Chomei:* Hakuryu 白龍. Ansei (1854–1859). Lived in the Gion section of Kyoto. Best known for his ivory netsuke. Usually carved animals. His work was as highly regarded as the figure netsuke of Rantei (B 812).

182. Hakuryu 白龍. *Chomei:* Hakuryu saku 白龍作. A pair of colored wood netsuke representing the happy old couple of Takasago are in existence. These legendary figures may have been carved for amusement by Hakuryu Miya-

saka (B 181). See mosha (No. 32).

183. Hakusai 白齋. Middle. Wood.

184. Hakusen 白仙. Late. Wood.

185. Hakushin 伯信. Middle. Ivory.

186. Haku-un 白雲. *Chomei:* Haku-un 白雲. Middle. Ivory. Fine carver.

187. Haku-unsai 白雲齋. *Chomei:* Haku-unsai 白雲齋. Worked between Tempo and Meiji (1843–1868). Lived in Kanda, Tokyo. Named Ichijo 一條. Was a skillful carver. His son Kitaro 喜太郎 succeeded him.

188. Haku-unsha 白雲社. Same carver as Haku-unsai (B 187).

189. Hakuzan 白山. Late. Excellent carver. Often carved frogs on lotus leaves in horn. Usually cut his signature on an ivory-inlaid plaque. See mosha (No. 33).

190. Hanryu 畔柳. Middle. Wood.

191. Haritsu 破笠. See Ritsuo (B 826).

192. Haruchika 春周. Lived before Temmei (1781–1788).

193. Harukazu 春一. *Chomei:* Harukazu 春一. Tempo (1830–1843). Mostly ivory.

左
山
一
萬
秀
乃
秀

35. HASHI-ICHI   36. HIDARI-ISSAN   37. HIDE   38. HIDE

194. Harumitsu 春光. *Chomei:* Harumitsu 春光. Early late. Wood. Good at carving the animals of the zodiac and others. Lived at Yamada, Ise. Learned carving from Masanao II (B 613). See Fig. 156. See mosha (No. 34).

195. Haruoki 春興. Early middle. Wood.

196. Harushige 春重. *Uji:* Hisamatsu 久松. *Na:* Heijiro 平次郎. Late. Resided in Tokyo. Was a pupil of Shungetsu (B 1066).

197. Hashi-ichi 橋市. *Uji:* Hashimoto 橋本. *Na:* Ichizo 市藏. *Chomei:* Hashi-ichi 橋市. Born in 1817. Was a son of Matajiro Hashimoto, a lacquerer of scabbards at Shiba, Tokyo. Was an expert lacquerer. A strange man of unusual character. Made lacquer netsuke as a hobby. In his old age he called himself Hashi-ichi II. Died in 1882. His gravestone is found at the Chosenji, Asakusa, Tokyo. See mosha (No. 35).

198. Hassho 八升. Early. Wood. Hermits.

199. Hattori Nobukazu 服部信壽. *Uji:* Hattori 服部. Early middle. Was a samurai in the service of the shogun but also carved netsuke.

200. Heihi 幣非. Early. Wood.

201. Heishiro 平四郎. Lived in Osaka before Temmei (1781–1788). Was a carver of friezes. Excelled at carving flowers and leaves, which accounts for his family name, Kusabana *(kusa:* grasses; *hana:* flowers). Also carved netsuke.

202. Hidari 左. See Masamine (B 603).

203. Hidari Issan 左一山. *Chomei:* Hidari Issan 左一山. Lived during Temmei and Kansei (1781–1800). Came from Aizu. Called himself Tokumitsu 篤光. Carved netsuke and inro in wood, frequently using a turtle design. Also good at carving snails. His work is pictorial and strong. Often used an elaborated form of toku 篤 from Tokumitsu as his kakihan. See Fig. 128. See mosha (No. 36).

204. Hide 秀. *Chomei:* Hide 秀. Middle. Wood. Carved in good taste. See mosha (No. 37).

205. Hide 秀. *Chomei:* Hide 秀. Late. Ivory. Realistic netsuke. His chomei is an abbreviation. See mosha (No. 38).

206. Hidechika 秀親. *Go:* Chounsai 長雲齋. Early. Ivory. A famous carver. See Fig. 149.

207. Hideharu 秀晴. Late. Wood.

208. Hidehiro 秀弘. Late. Wood.

秀
正

209. Hidekazu 秀一. Early. Wood.

210. Hidekiyo 秀清. Early. Wood.

211. Hidekuni 秀國. Middle. Wood.

212. Hidemasa 秀正. *Go:* Chingendo 珍元堂. *Chomei:* Hidemasa 秀正. Early middle. Wood and ivory. Lived in both Kyoto and Tokyo. An excellent carver. See Figs. 150 and 165. See mosha (No. 39).

213. Hidemasa 英正. Middle. Carved nuts.

214. Hidemitsu 秀滿. Middle. Wood.

215. Hidemitsu 秀光. Late.

216. Hidenobu 秀珍. Late. Ivory.

217. Hideo 秀雄. Late.

218. Hidetomo 秀友. Middle. Ivory.

219. Hidetsugu 英次. Early. Ivory.

220. Hideyoshi 英吉. Early. Wood.

221. Higo 肥後. *Uji:* Kameya 龜谷. *Na:* Heisuke 平助. Lived in Osaka prior to Temmei (1781–1788). Was a machinist and dentist. Carved netsuke as an avocation.

222. Hikaku 飛鶴. Early. Ivory. Figures.

223. Hiroaki 廣明. Early. Wood.

224. Hirochika 廣親. Middle. Carved masks from nuts.

225. Hiro-ichi 弘一. Middle. Wood.

226. Hironobu 弘倍. Early. Wood.

227. Hirosada 廣貞. *Chomei:* Hirosada 廣貞. Early. Wood. Mainly masks.

228. Hirotada 廣忠. *Chomei:* Hirotada 廣忠. Middle. Ivory. Excellent carver.

229. Hirotoshi 弘壽. Late. Ivory.

230. Hiroyuki 廣之. Early middle. Ivory.

231. Hiseki 匪石. *Uji:* Sawagishi 澤岸. Kyowa (1801–1803). From Kaga. Sometimes carved in wood inlaid with ivory or tortoise shell.

232. Hoan 法安. Late. Ivory.

233. Hoei 法英. Late. Figure netsuke of this carver are found.

234. Hoen 法延. *Chomei:* Hoen 法延. Temmei and Kansei (1781–1800). Wood. Chinese figures.

235. Hoen 寶園. Middle. Ivory.

法
寶
〵

236. Hogen 法元. Early. Wood and ivory.

237. Hogetsu 法月. Middle. Wood and ivory.

238. Hogyoku 法玉. *Go:* Ikkeisai 一鶏齋. Early middle. Wood, ivory, and metal.

239. Hogyoku 寶玉. Excellent carver in both wood and ivory.

240. Hohaku 保伯. See Shoju IX (B 1001).

241. Ho-ichi 法一. *Chomei:* Ho-ichi 法一. *Uji:* Sakurai 櫻井. *Na:* Shimbei 新兵衛. Lived in Kyoto and also in Tokyo. Was a pupil of Hojitsu (B 243). Excelled in carving both wood and ivory. Made mask and figure netsuke. Died in 1879 at the age of 51. Buried at the Myoyo-ji in Chitosemura, a suburb of Tokyo. See Fig. 72.

242. Ho-in 豐尹. *Chomei:* Ho-in 豐尹. Keio (1865–1867). Mainly wood.

243. Hojitsu 法實. *Uji:* Yamada 山田. *Na:* Izaemon 伊左衛門, but some say Iuemon 伊右衛門. *Go:* Meikeisai 明鶏齋. *Kaimyo:* Zekoin Myotatsu 是光院妙達. *Chomei:* Hojitsu 法實 or a kakihan based on Hojitsu. As Hojitsu was a vassal of the shogun, he may have enjoyed his lord's sponsorship as a netsuke artist. His family crest consisted of a Chinese bellflower in a circle. Also patronized by the Daimyo of Tsugaru. Subjects mostly figures. Influenced by the paintings of Hanabusa Icho. His carving is realistic, refined, graceful, painstaking, and elegant. Considered the best carver of Tokyo, where he resided. Used the *go* Meikeisai, which was adopted from the characters indicating Keiseigakubo, the section of Tokyo where he lived. Died in 1872. Buried at the Renkyu-ji of the Nichiren sect in Tokyo. See Figs. 101, 112, and 182. See mosha (No. 40).

244. Hoju 法壽. Middle. Wood and ivory.

245. Hokei 法珪. Early middle. Teacher of Ryukei (B 852).

246. Hokei 寶桂. *Chomei:* Hokei 寶桂. Kyowa through Bunsei (1801–1829). Wood. Figures.

247. Hokeisai 豐慶齋. *Uji:* Matsumoto 松本. *Na:* Toyojiro 豐次郎. Late. Wood. Masks.

248. Hokinsai 寶近齋. *Uji:* Suzuki 鈴木. *Na:* Masanao 正直. Middle and late. Lived in Tokyo. An excellent wood carver.

249. Hokoku 鳳谷. Middle. Wood. Figures.

250. Hokufu 北風. *Chomei:* Hokufu 北風. Late. Came from Ou. Was a rich man. Was a pupil of Toun (B 1247). Carved netsuke.

251. Hokusai 北哉. *Uji:* Ishida 石田. Currently living in Tokyo. Wood and ivory. Was a pupil of Mitsuaki Ishikawa (B 350). See mosha (No. 41).

252. Hokusui 北水. *Chomei:* Hokusui 北水. Early. Wood and ivory. Carving was very powerful.

253. Hokutei 北亭. *Chomei:* Hokutei 北亭. Middle. Excelled in wood carving. See mosha (No. 42).

254. Hokyu 保久. See Shoju X (B 1002).

255. Hokyudo 逢丘堂. See Itsumin (B 376).

256. Hokuzan 北山. Early. Wood and bamboo.

257. Homan 法満. Middle. Ivory.

258. Homan 寳満. Some netsuke bearing his signature are in existence.

259. Homei 法明. *Chomei:* Homei 法明. Kansei (1789–1800). Carved netsuke of figures and animals.

260. Homei 保明. *Uji:* Kodama 兒玉. *Chomei:* Homei 保明. Late. Ivory.

261. Homeisai 寳明齋. See Kogyoku (B 513).

262. Homin 芳民. *Uji:* Yasuda 安田. *Na:* Haruo 春男. Born in Osaka in 1909. Graduated from the wood-carving department of Tokyo Art School in 1932. Devoted himself to teaching wood carving and to promoting the use of wood for tea-ceremony articles. Occasionally carved netsuke. Was good at carving figures.

263. Homin 法民. *Uji:* Fukumoto 福本. Middle. Wood and ivory. Was a pupil of Hojitsu (B 243). See Fig. 151.

264. Homin 寳珉. *Chomei:* Homin 寳珉 or Homin and kakihan. Middle. Ivory. Figures. See mosha (No. 43).

265. Homin 寳眠. Ivory. May be the same artist as Homin (B 264).

266. Homin 鳳民. Late. Ivory.

267. Hompu 本布. Early. Ivory.

268. Horaku 寳樂. Middle. Wood. See Fig. 168.

269. Horyu 法龍. Late. Ivory. Hermits.

270. Hosai 芳齋. *Uji:* Oishi 大石. *Go:* Mitsutoshi 光壽. Meiji (1868–1911). Studied carving with Kobayashi 小林, who worked in horn and ivory. Amazed the public with his almost mysterious ability. Carved a watch out of ivory complete in every mechanical detail. Extremely versatile. Utilized a variety of carving techniques. Taught many pupils, but none reached his stature. Died in 1900 at the age of some 70 years.

271. Hosei 保正. Late. Ivory. Carved for export.

272. Hosei 法政. Late.

273. Hosetsu 芳雪. Middle. Wood inlays.

274. Hoshin 法眞. Early middle. Ivory. Figures. See Fig. 38.

275. Hoshin 奉眞. *Chomei:* Hoshin 奉眞. Lived in Kyoto before Temmei (1781–1788). Wood and ivory. Carved the palace of the Dragon King in a clam shell.

276. Hoshin 豐晋. Middle. Ivory.

277. Hoshinsai 法眞齋. Same as Hoshin (B 274).

278. Hoshinsai 寶眞齋. See Reigyoku (B 813).

279. Hoshunsai 寶春齋. See Masayuki (B 645).

280. Hoshunsai 寶舜齋. Late middle. Ivory.

281. Hosui 法水. *Chomei:* Hosui 法水. Tempo (1830–1843). Mostly wood.

282. Hotoku 保徳. *Na:* Hotoku 保徳. *Go:* Shoju 松壽. See Shoju XIII (B 1005).

283. Hotsueki 咄益. Middle. Wood.

284. Hou 法右. *Chomei:* Hou 法右. Middle. Wood and ivory. Was a pupil of Hojitsu (B 243).

285. Houn 法雲. Early middle.

286. Houn 鳳雲. *Uji:* Takahashi 高橋. *Na:* Seijiro 清次郎. *Go:* Shokosai 尚古齋. Born in 1824. Was a pupil of Kokei 幸慶, for whom he carved many netsuke. Carved a phoenix in the clouds which so impressed his master that Kokei gave him the *go* of Houn *(ho:* phoenix; *un:* clouds). Later established his own school at Kanda, Tokyo. The title of hogan was conferred on him for his sculpturing of Buddhist images. Was engaged for the modeling of the Five Hundred Rakan for the Kamakuraji-in. It is said that Houn carved the wooden molds and Seimin 整珉 cast the metal. Teacher of Toun Takamura (B 1246). Houn was one of the most respected and famous carvers of recent years.

法身十一翁
法橋寶山作

44. HOZAN

287. Hounsai 法雲齋. Same man as Houn (B 285).

(Hoyen: see Hoen.)

288. Hoyo 法與. *Uji:* Ishioka 石岡. Was a pupil of Hojitsu (B 243).

289. Hoyusai 豊勇齋. See Ishikawa Komei (B 350).

290. Hozan 寶山. *Uji:* Takahashi 高橋. *Na:* Kumakichi 熊吉. *Chomei:* Carved by 71-year-old Hokyo Hozan 行年七十一翁法橋寶山作. Middle. Came from Tokyo. Was an elder brother of Houn (B 286). Was a carver of Buddhist images for which he was awarded the artist title of hokyo. According to Koun Takamura (B 555), Hozan held a single hair which he tore into two strips with his thumb and index finger. He carved from a single block of wood multiple-armed Buddhas, each hand grasping a symbolic article. See Figs. 5 and 103. See mosha (No. 44).

291. Hozan 寶山. *Chomei:* Hozan 寶山. Middle. Wood.

292. Hozan 法山. *Uji:* Tanaka 田中. *Chomei:* Hozan 法山. Middle. Wood. Figures, birds, and insects. Was a pupil of Hojitsu (B 243).

293. Hozen 保全. *Tsusho:* Eiraku 永樂. *Mei:* Kahinshiryu *in* 河濱支流印. Was a famous ceramist of Kyoto. Made porcelain netsuke as a hobby.

–I–

294. Ichian 一庵. Middle. Wood.

295. Ichibi 一美. Middle. Wood.

296. Ichiboku 一木. Late. Wood and ivory. Lived at Tennoji, Osaka. Called himself Tajima 田島.

297. Ichibun 一文. Middle. Wood.

298. Ichidon 一鈍. Middle. Wood.

299. Ichieisai 一永齋. See Komin (B 531).

300. Ichigensai 一玄齋. Middle Wood.

301. Ichigyoku 一玉. Early. Wood.

302. Ichiju 一壽. Carved Nara dolls. Was a pupil of Shoju (B 993).

303. Ichijusai 一壽齋. See Kou (B 553).

304. Ichimin 一岷. *Chomei:* Ichimin 一岷. Bunsei (1818–1829). Wood. Animals, especially the animals of the zodiac.

305. Ichimin 一眠. Middle. Wood. May be the same carver as Ichimin (B 308).

306. Ichimin 一珉. Middle. Wood. May be the same carver as Ichimin (B 308).

307. Ichimin 一民. Middle. Wood.

308. Ichimin 一民. May be the same Ichimin described in B 306.

309. Ichiminsai 一眠齋. See Ichimin (B 305).

310. Ichiraku 一樂. Late. Wood. Cattle. Sometimes colored with lacquer. Signed this work with kao based on Ichiraku. See Fig. 111.

311. Ichiraku 一樂. Lived in Sakai prior to Temmei (1781–1788). Called himself Tsuchiya Botoken 土屋望籬軒. Made netsuke in the form of gourds and other objects from woven rattan and wisteria vines. Did not sign his work. See Figs. 27–28. See mosha (No. 45).

312. Ichiriki 一力. *Chomei:* Ichiriki 一力. Tempo through Keio (1830–1867). Carved excellent mushrooms in wood.

313. Ichirinsai 一輪齋. See Nobu-uji (B 776).

314. Ichirobei 市郎兵衛. *Uji:* Shibata 柴田. Lived in Horie, Osaka, before Temmei (1781–1788).

(Ichiyeisai: see Ichieisai.)

315. Ichiyosai 弌葉齋. See Rakumin (B 794).

316. Ichiyu 一友. Late. Did elaborate Shibayama-style inlay in wood. Carved his signature Ichiyu 一友 in a colored ivory plaque which he inlaid in the netsuke. See mosha (No. 46).

317. Ichiyusai 一遊齋. Late. Ivory.

318. Ichiyusai 一友齋. Late. Ivory.

319. Ichu 惟中. Middle. Wood. Masks.

320. Ihei 伊兵衛. Lived in Osaka prior to Temmei (1781–1788). Called himself Toshimaya 豐島屋. Made braided or woven netsuke similar to those of Ichiraku (B 311) but using silver and copper wire instead of rattan or vines. Also made ash-tray netsuke from woven metal ribbons. Did not sign his work. See Fig. 22.

321. Ikkan 一貫. *Chomei:* Ikkan 一貫 or Chofu Ikkan 張府一貫. Born in Nagoya. Carved figures and animals. Also insects decorated with *Prunus tomentosa*. The sleeping shojo carved during his prime and the rat carved in his later years reveal a divinely inspired skill. His carved okimono in cypress also

a   b

47. IKKAN   48. IKKEI   49. IKKO

demonstrate his artistry. See mosha (No. 47).

322. Ikkansai 一貫齋. Late. Ivory. Born in Tokyo.

323. Ikkasai 一華齋. Middle. Wood.

324. Ikkei 一俓. *Chomei:* Ikkei 一俓. Kansei (1789–1800). Figures and animals.

325. Ikkei 一溪. *Chomei:* Seikonsai Ikkei 青岑齋一溪. Middle. Wood. Called himself Seikonsai 青岑齋. See mosha (No. 48).

326. Ikkeisai 一鷄齋. See Hogyoku (B 238).

327. Ikki 一龜. Early.

328. Ikko 一孝. Late. Ivory. Figures.

329. Ikko 一幸. Late.

330. Ikko 一光. *Chomei:* Ikko 一光. Middle. Preferred wood but also carved in ivory. A brilliant artist. Probably taught Niko (B 759). See mosha (No. 49).

331. Ikko 一行. *Chomei:* Ikko 一行. Temmei and Kansei (1781–1800). Frequently carved oni.

332. Ikko 一口. Early. Wood.

333. Ikko 一虎. *Uji:* Hasegawa 長谷川. *Chomei:* Ikko 一虎; Ikko

Hasegawa *in* 一帚長谷川印; or date according to the zodiac calendar, place name, and Ikko. Kansei (1789–1800). Various opinions regarding his place of origin as Matsuzaka in Ise, Kyoto, and Tokyo. Carved unlacquered figures, animals, and other subjects. Also made netsuke representing sedge hats carved from bamboo and inlaid with stained ivory or foreign (Chinese) woods. An excellent artist. See mosha (No. 50).

334. Ikko 一江. Middle. Wood.

335. Ikkoku 一谷. Early. Ivory. Figures.

336. Ikkosai 一光齋. *Uji:* Saito 齋藤. *Na:* Itaro 伊太郎. *Kaimyo:* Bonshaku Junsei Shinshi. *Chomei:* Ikkosai 一光齋. Born in 1804. Lived in Osaka. Was an associate of Hojitsu (B 243). Made netsuke of fierce gods, figures, and animals. Died in 1876 at the age of 72. Cremated at Shinjo-ji.

337. Ikkosai 一光齋. See Toun (B 1248).

338. Ikkosai 一光齋. See Kojitsu (B 520).

339. Ikkosai 一孝齋. See Ikko (B 328).

340. Ikkosai 一固齋. Middle. Ivory.

a   b   c

50. IKKO

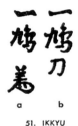

a   b

51. IKKYU

341. Ikkosai 一固齋. See Seimin (B 923).

(Ikkwan: see Ikkan.)

(Ikkwansai: see Ikkansai.)

(Ikkwasai: see Ikkasai.)

342. Ikkyu 一鳩. *Uji:* Hayashi 林. *Go:* Ikkyu 一鳩. *Chomei:* Ikkyu 一鳩 or Ikkyu *to* 一鳩刀. Born in 1914 on Cheju Island, Korea. Called himself Sounyo 宗雲用. Came to Osaka with his mother at the age of 12. Entered the school of Kyusai Hirai (B 576) as a private student in 1926. Was a diligent pupil. Studied carving during the day and attended school at night. Became independent in 1936 and was given the *go* of Ikkyu by his master. Made okimono, sash decorations (obikazari), and tea utensils. Excelled in carving wood, bamboo, dry lacquer, and ivory. When Kyusai was sick with stomach cancer, Ikkyu nursed him loyally, giving his blood for transfusions. Upon his death, Kyusai left everything to Ikkyu. See mosha (No. 51).

343. Ikkyu 一休. Early. Wood.

344. Ikkyu 一丘. Middle. Wood and ivory. See Fig. 175.

345. Insai 印齋. Prior to Temmei (1781–1788). Lived near Naniwa Bridge, Osaka. Called himself Futaya Dembei ふたや傳兵衛. Specialized in two netsuke designs which he carved in both wood and ivory. One is a standing man with a monkey on his shoulder; the other is an animal trainer asleep while a monkey steals his lunch. His work is unsigned.

346. Iotsu 爲乙. *Kundoku:* Tameoto. Early middle. Wood and ivory.

347. Ippachi 一八. Late. Wood.

348. Ippo 一寶. Middle. Wood.

349. Ipposai 一法齋. *Uji:* Ouchi 大内. *Na:* Kanzo 勘藏. *Kaimyo:* Bonshaku Gakuhojosei Shinshi. Born in 1829, although some say 1831. Lived in Asakusa, Tokyo. Called himself Jitsumin 實民. Was a pupil of Hojitsu (B 243). Was left-handed. Died in 1895. Cremated at the Ikko-in in Tokyo.

350. Ishikawa Komei 石川光明. *Uji:* Ishikawa 石川. *Go:* Juzan 壽山. *Kundoku:* Mitsuaki. Born in 1852. Learned carving from his master, Masamitsu Kikugawa (B 484). Carved pipes, flower vases, and okimono in ivory. His remarkable technique won him wide acclaim and finally he was recognized as the finest ivory artist of the Meiji period. Appointed a professor of the original Tokyo Art School and later rec-

a   b

52. ISSAN   53. ISSHI   54. ISSHINSAI

ommended as a member of the Imperial Household Art Committee. First studied painting with Kano Sosen 狩野素川 and was proficient at it. Used the *go* of Hoyusai 豐勇齋. See Fig. 167.

351. Isoji 磯次. Middle. Wood. Snakes.

352. Issai 一齋. Temmei (1781–1788). Called himself Ogasawara 小笠原 and lived in Wakayama. Carved in ivory and whale tooth. Was renowned as a fine craftsman even during his lifetime, and it was difficult to obtain examples of his work. Rarely are netsuke found that bear his signature. See Figs. 73, 80, and 82.

353. Issai 一哉. Early.

354. Issan 一山. *Chomei:* Issan. Early. Wood. Excellent carver. May be the same individual known as Hidari (left-handed) Issan. See Fig. 128. See mosha (No. 52).

355. Isseisai 一政齋. See Naomitsu (B 751).

356. Issen 一泉. Middle. Ivory.

357. Issen 一川. Middle. Wood. Called himself Ozawa 小澤.

358. Isshi 一止. Late. Ivory.

359. Isshi 一之. *Chomei:* Isshi 一之. Late. Carved in ivory and did inlay work in the Shibayama style. See mosha (No. 53).

360. Isshin 一眞. Middle. Wood.

361. Isshin 一心. Early. Wood. See Fig. 184.

362. Isshinsai 一心齋. *Chomei:* Isshinsai 一心齋. Wood. Left some fine carvings of Choryo. See mosha (No. 54).

363. Isshinsai 一心齋. See Masanao (B 611).

364. Isshinsai 一心齋. Middle. Called himself Yoshiyuki 美之.

365. Isshinsai 一心齋. See Gyokuzan (B 165).

366. Isshinsai 一信齋. Middle. Wood.

367. Isshosai 一照齋. See Hakumin (B 177).

368. Isshosai 一松齋. Early. Wood.

369. Isshu 一州. Middle. Wood.

370. Isshu 一舟. Middle. Wood.

371. Isshu 一周. Late. Carved in wood and in red lacquer.

372. Isshusai 一秀齋. Middle. Wood. See Fig. 152.

373. Issui 一水. Early. Wood.

374. Itchiku 一竹. Middle. Wood.

375. Itcho 一鳥. Middle. Wood.

376. Itsumin 逸民. *Chomei:* Itsumin 逸民. Tempo through Keio (1830–1867). Wood and ivory. Figures and animals. Called himself Hokyudo 逢丘堂.

377. Ittan 一旦. *Go:* Ittanfu 一旦夫 or Kyoryusai 競龍齋 *Chomei:* Ittan 一旦, Ittanfu 一旦夫, or Meifuka Kyoryusai 名府下競龍齋. Was a member of the Toba clan. Later lived in Nagoya and Gifu. Was an excellent wood carver. Preferred to carve figures and animals. Noted for his carvings of sleeping shojo. Habitually carried his current work, which he polished with his kimono sleeve. Died about 1877. See mosha (No. 55).

378. Ittanfu 一旦夫. Same as Ittan (B 377).

379. Ittei 一亭. Early. Wood.

380. Itten 一點. Middle. Wood.

381. Itto 一東. *Go:* Kakujuken 鶴壽軒. *Uji:* Ono 小野. *Na:* Benkichi 辨吉. Born in Kyoto but studied sculpturing in Nagasaki. Died in 1870 at the age of 74.

382. Iwao I 巖. See Tomiharu (B 1191).

383. Iwao II 巖. See Bunshojo (B 28).

384. Iwao III 巖. *Go:* Gansui 巖水. Was the son of Ogawa Yachiyo 小川八千代, a younger sister of Bunshojo (B 28). Died in 1848 at the age of 39. See Fig. 67.

385. Iwao Nagami 巖永見. *Uji:* Nagami 永見. Born in Nagahama. Ancestor of Fusazo Nagami, who presently lives in the village of Nagahama. Was a pupil of Tomiharu (B 1191). Originated the Nagahama ningyo.

-J-

386. Jigyoku 治玉. *Chomei:* Jigyoku 治玉. Kansei (1789–1800).

387. Jikkosai 實光齋. Some netsuke bearing his signature are in existence.

388. Jingetsu 刃月. Early. Wood.

389. Jirobei 次郎兵衞. Lived in Osaka before Temmei (1781–1788). Carved scabbards of horn. Also carved netsuke.

390. Jitokusai 自得齋. See Rakumin (B 795).

391. Jitsumin 實民. See Ipposai (B 349).

392. Jiyosai 慈羊齋. Early middle.

393. Jobun 如文. Early. Wood. Figures, animals, and masks.

394. Joko 上幸. Late. Ivory and tusk.

395. Joryu 如柳. *Chomei:* Joryu 如柳. Temmei and Kansei (1781–1800). Wood and ivory. Excelled in carving figures in netsuke. See Fig. 154.

396. Joryu 如龍. Early. Ivory.

397. Josensai 常川齋. Middle. Wood.

398. Josetsu 如雪. *Chomei:* Josetsu 如雪. Lived after Kaei (1848–1853). Ivory. Good at staining ivory. See mosha (No. 56).

399. Joshu 上秀. *Go:* Shunchiku-do 春竹堂. *Chomei:* Joshu 上秀. Tempo through Keio (1830–1867). Ivory.

400. Joso 如藻. *Uji:* Miyazaki 宮崎. *Na:* Seitaro 清太郎. *Kaimyo:* Shakufugaku Senshu Shinshi. *Chomei:* Joso 如藻. Born in Tokyo in 1855. Apprenticed to Kojitsu (B 520), the netsuke artist, at the age of 14. Won his independence at the age of 25. Took up residence at Asakusa, Tokyo. Excelled at carving small objects, including netsuke and pipes. His artistry was of a high order. Was a member of the Japan Art Association and one of the originators of the Tokyo Carvers' Association, for which he acted as examiner. Received several prizes for his works. Also honored and patronized by the Imperial Household. Joso worked with Koun (B 555), Kyuichi (B 575), and Mitsuaki (B 350) in 1888 in carving the ramma (transom decoration or frieze) in a bat design for the Imperial Library. Also interested in literature as the result of the influence of his relative, the aged Otsuki Nyoden. Joso wrote some excellent comic poetry and witty verse. Died in 1910 at the age of 56. Cremated at Kano-in in Shita-ya, Tokyo. Trained some fine pupils such as Soya (B 1115), Soko (B 1101), Gyokuso (B 160), and others. See Fig. 115.

401. Joso 如宗. *Chomei:* Joso 如宗. Late. Pupil of Ikkosai (B 336).

402. Josui 如水. Middle. Wood.

403. Jozan 如山. Late. Wood.

404. Jozan 城山. *Chomei:* Jozan 城山. Ansei (1854–1859). Mostly wood.

405. Ju 壽. Late. Ivory.

406. Jubi 重美. *Uji:* Hasegawa 長谷川. Gold lacquer netsuke bearing his signature are in existence.

407. Jugyoku 壽玉. *Go:* Chounsai 長雲齋. *Chomei:* Jugyoku 壽玉. Kaei (1848–1853). Was a pupil of

寿
玉

Ryukei (B 852). See mosha (No. 57).

408. Jugyoku 壽玉. *Uji:* Ueda 上田. *Na:* Naokichi 直吉. *Go:* Ryukosai 龍光齋. *Chomei:* Jugyoku or Ryukosai Jugyoku 龍光齋壽玉. Sometimes cut his mei or *in* on an inlaid ivory plaque. Lived in Higashi-Okubo, a suburb of Tokyo. Was a pupil of Keigyoku (B 468). Excellent carver in both wood and ivory. Most of his work was carved at the request of Tomigawa. One of his carvings is signed: "64 years old, Meiji 12." See Figs. 155 and 164. See mosha (No. 58).

409. Jujo 壽乘. Early.

410. Jukei 重敬. Early. Figure netsuke by this carver are in existence.

411. Juko 壽光. Early.

412. Jumin 壽民. Early.

413. Juraku 壽樂. Middle.

414. Jurakusai 壽樂齋. Same as Juraku (B 413).

415. Jusai 壽齋. Died 1776. Ivory.

416. Jusen 壽仙. Made netsuke in the design of children that bear his mei.

417. Juteini 壽貞尼. Died 1776. A woman whose family profession was the carving of objects from the cypress wood of Nara. Her husband, Shoju V (B 997), came from a Yamada family which dealt in Uji tea. Owing to her fear that the poor ability of her husband might injure the reputation of her family, she carved dolls in her husband's stead, becoming quite expert.

418. Juzan 壽山. See Ishikawa Komei (B 350).

419. Juzo 十藏. Lived in Wakayama during Temmei. Adopted the style of Issai (B 352).

–K–

420. Kagei 景井. Born in Osaka in 1850. Was the second son of Dosho (B 89). Called himself Kagei Ryojiro 景井兩治郎. Shibayama Yoshigoro 芝山芳五郎 of Tokyo visited Dosho on his return from China. Kagei became a pupil of Yoshigoro in Tokyo and returned to Osaka in 1874. Was proficient in the Shibayama style of inlay. Rendered great service in the export of art objects. Taught the carvers of Osaka the technique of the Shibayama inlay. Died in 1924.

421. Kagetoshi 景利. *Chomei:* Kagetoshi 景利. Middle. Wood and ivory. Famous for his minute carvings. Lived in Nagoya, though there

59. KAGETOSHI

is some opinion that he came from Kyoto. See Fig. 160. See mosha (No. 59).

422. Kagetsu 花月. Middle. Wood.

423. Kagetsu 霞月. *Chomei:* Kagetsu 霞月. Tempo (1830–1843). Wood.

424. Kagyokusai 花玉齋. Middle.

425. Kahei 嘉兵衛. Lived in Shimanouchi, Osaka, before Temmei (1781–1788). Called himself Omiya 近江屋.

426. Kahinshiryu 河濱支流. See Eiraku (B 98).

427. Kaho 香峰. *Uji:* Okazaki 岡崎. *Na:* Eizaburo 英三郎. Late. Lived at Morinomiya, Osaka. Was a pupil of Masaka (B 592).

428. Kaigyoku 懷玉 See Kaigyokusai (B 430).

429. Kaigyokudo 懷玉堂. See Kaigyokusai (B 430).

430. Kaigyokusai 懷玉齋. *Mei:* Masatsugu 正次, Kaigyokudo 懷玉堂, Kaigyoku 懷玉, Kaigyokusai 懷玉齋, Kaigyokusai *in* 懷玉齋印, Kaigyokusai Masatsugu *in* 懷玉齋正次印. *Kaimyo:* Tokuo Kaigyoku Zenjoman. Born September 13,

1813, the first son of Shimizu Kichibei 清水吉兵衛 of Sugishitadori, Osaka. In January 1829, he was adopted by Yasunaga Kichirobei 安永吉郎兵衛. After the death of his adoptive father, he succeeded to the name of Yasunaga. Had no teacher in the study of carving techniques. Made sketches from life. Carved in wood and ivory. Used the mei of Masatsugu 正次 until approximately his 20th year, Kaigyokudo 懷玉堂 until approximately his 30th year, Kaigyoku 懷玉 until about his 50th year, and Kaigyokusai 懷玉齋 thereafter. His output comprised mainly okimono and netsuke. About 70 or 80 percent of his work was exported to foreign countries.

Among his okimono masterpieces are "Scenes of Plowing," "Child and Shishi" (owned by the Sumitomo family), and "Takarazukushi" (a collection of symbols indicating wealth, happiness, comfort, and luxury). The "Takarazukushi" is in ivory and incorporates the Seven Lucky Gods. It is owned by a branch of the Imperial Family. Other okimono include the palace of the Dragon King carved in a clamshell and the happy old couple of Takasago carved in a pine cone. Kaigyokusai once fashioned a netsuke in the form

a b c
60. KAIGYOKUSAI

61. KAJIKAWA

of a mushroom basket. When some children who saw it were unable to identify the subject, he came to doubt the success of his effort, and he destroyed the netsuke without hesitation.

Kaigyokusai's work is extremely fine and beautiful. Using only the finest ivory material, he carefully polished and finished his work. At first he used the mei of Masatsugu. Although his skill at carving was excellent, his writing of his mei was criticized. Therefore he studied calligraphy until his ability to write was excellent. About 1887, he had many pupils. When they moved to Tokyo, he did not object but on the contrary suggested that carving in Tokyo would be improved by their presence and that they should become well known in Tokyo. Drank 2 or 3 liters of sakè every day, starting in the morning. Carved all night whenever he felt well. Died on January 21, 1892, at his residence in Osaka at the age of 80. Buried at the Hoju-in.

There are numerous carvings that bear the signature of Kaigyokusai, but many are forgeries. His grandson Seikei (Hidezo Yasunaga) presently lives in Osaka. See Figs. 32, 70, 74, 75, and 146. See mosha (No. 60).

431. Kaito 塊東. In his middle age he made a study of metal carving. Later became proficient in wood carving also. Created a new technique in which he combined metal work with wood carving.

432. Kajikawa 梶川. A famous gold-lacquer artist who made gold-lacquer netsuke. Died about 1887 at more than 70 years of age. See mosha (No. 61).

433. Kajun 可順. *Uji:* Kumoura 雲浦. Lived in Osaka prior to Temmei (1781–1788). Made uncolored netsuke representing mountain-dwelling ascetics in foreign (probably Dutch) dress.

434. Kakosai 可交齋. Some netsuke that bear his signature are in existence.

435. Kakuho 鶴峯. Middle. Wood. Came from Gifu. Was the father of Tessai Kano (B 1173).

436. Kakujuken 鶴壽軒. See Itto (B 381).

437. Kakushu 覺秀. Middle.

438. Kametomo 龜友. *Ondoku:* Kiyu 龜友. Early middle. Wood.

439. Kameya Higo 龜谷肥後. See Higo (B 221).

440. Kamman 貫滿. Born in Iwami. Was a pupil of Tomiharu

62. KANEYUKI

63. KANSHI

64. KASHU

(B 1191). Carved frog netsuke from ebony and shrimp netsuke from wild boar tusk. Signed: "Made by Kamman, living in Iwami 石見住 貫満作."

441. Kanchu 寛仲. Middle. Ivory. Goats.

442. Kanemichi 包道. Tempo (1830–1843). Ivory.

443. Kanetada 金忠. Early. Wood. Figures.

444. Kaneyoshi 周良. Middle. Ivory.

445. Kaneyuki 兼行. *Uji:* Matsuda 松田. Lived during middle and late. Carved netsuke from red sandalwood. Lived in Maruyama, Kofu. Signed: "Kofu Maruyama ju Matsuda Kaneyuki kao 江府丸山住松田兼行花押." See mosha (No. 62).

446. Kanji 寛治. *Go:* Kyozaido 橘材堂. *Chomei:* Kanji 寛治. Kaei (1848–1853). Mainly wood.

447. Kanjuro 勘十郎. Lived in Kyuhoji, Osaka, before Temmei (1781–1788). Was the master of Dembei of Tawaraya, a shop that produced straw rice bags. Made figure netsuke in ebony with face, hands, and legs inlaid in ivory.

448. Kanjusai 勘壽齋. Middle. Ivory.

449. Kansai 貫齋. Some netsuke bearing his signature are in existence. See Fig. 196.

450. Kanshi 觀子 or **Kan** 觀. See Ritsuo (B 826). See mosha (No. 63).

451. Kansui 閑水. Early middle. Wood.

452. Kanzo 勘蔵. *Uji:* Tatsuki 龍木. Lived in Temman, Osaka, prior to Temmei (1781–1788).

453. Karaku 可樂. *Uji:* Oga 大賀. Employed at the Osaka Museum about 1894 or 1895. Excelled in carving. Preferred figure netsuke.

454. Karaku 花樂. Early middle. Ivory.

455. Karyo 迦陵. Early. Wood and ivory.

456. Kasai 花齋. Some netsuke are found that bear his signature.

457. Kasen 嘉仙. Early. Wood and ivory.

458. Kashinsai 花信齋. See Miwa Zaiei (B 710).

459. Kashu 霞鶯. *Chomei:* Kashu 霞鶯. Before Temmei (1781–1788). A netsuke carver of no particular fame. See mosha (No. 64).

460. Kashun 花春. *Chomei:* Kashun 花春. Tempo (1830–1843). Ivory and wood.

65. KEIKOKU

461. Kawai Yoritake 河井賴武. See Yoritake (B 1287).

462. Kazumasa 一正. Early. Wood.

463. Kazumoto 一本. Early. Wood.

464. Kazushige 一重. *Chomei:* Kazushige 一重. Kansei (1789–1800). Carved netsuke of figures and animals.

465. Keifudo 溪風堂. Early. Wood. Masks.

466. Keigetsu 桂月. Middle. Wood.

467. Keigyoku 桂玉. Middle.

468. Keigyoku 珪玉. Middle. Lived in Fukagawa, Tokyo. Was the teacher of Jugyoku (B 408).

469. Keiju 慶壽. *Chomei:* Keiju 慶壽. Tempo (1830–1843). Wood.

470. Keikoku 溪谷. *Chomei:* Keikoku 溪谷. Late. Wood. Sometimes carved his mei in shell, which he inlaid in the carving. See mosha (No. 65).

471. Keimin 慶眠. Early. Ivory.

472. Keimin 桂民. *Uji:* Suwa 諏訪. *Na:* Kyuhachi 久八. Middle. A pupil of Rakumin (B 794).

473. Keiri 敬利. Late.

474. Keisai 珪齋. Late. Wood.

475. Keisai 桂哉. Keio (1865–1867). Mainly wood.

476. Keisai 溪哉. *Uji:* Matsushita 松下. *Na:* Ki-ichiro 喜一郎. *Chomei:* Keisai 溪哉. Was a pupil of Kyusai (B 576).

477. Keizan 慶山. Tempo (1830–1843). Wood.

478. Kensai 鎌齋. *Uji:* Arai 荒井. Late middle and late. Lived in Yunoshima, Hongo district, Tokyo. Carved netsuke and other small objects.

479. Kenya 乾也. A famous ceramist of Tokyo. Made porcelain netsuke. See Fig. 91.

480. Kichibei 吉兵衛. Before Temmei (1781–1788).

481. Kigyoku 龜玉. *Chomei:* Kigyoku 龜玉. Kansei through Bunsei (1789–1829). Wood. Made netsuke of figures, masks, and other subjects.

482. Kigyoku 貴玉. Middle. Ivory.

483. Kihodo 奇峰堂. See Masakazu (B 596) and Masaka (B 592). Both used go of Kihodo.

484. Kikugawa 菊川. *Chomei:* Kikugawa saku 菊川作 or kakihan.

Koka through Keio (1844–1867). Named Masamitsu 正光. Lived in Negishi, Tokyo. Learned ivory carving from Shobei 庄兵衛 until the age of 20. Devoted himself to carving netsuke. Made okimono after the opening of Yokohama to foreign trade. Was the teacher of Ishikawa Komei (B 350). See mosha (No. 66).

485. Kikugawa Masamitsu 菊川正光. See B 484. See mosha (No. 67).

486. Kikuo Kimioki 菊翁公興. Middle. Wood.

487. Kimeisai 喜明齋. See Ninraku (B 760).

488. Kinryusai 琴流齋. Bunsei (1818–1829). Called himself Tadatane 忠胤. Lived in Tokyo. Carved only netsuke.

489. Kintaro 金太郎. See Kogyoku Asami (B 512).

490. Kiryosai 貴凌齋. See Ekisei (B 102).

491. Kisai 龜齋. *Uji:* Arakawa 荒川. *Tsusho:* Shigenosuke 重之助. Died in 1897. Came from Izumo. His body was short and stumpy and his mind philosophical. His statue of the goddess Kushinada, which became one of the treasures of the Izumo Taisha Shrine, was exhibited at Chicago. It met with the same great reception accorded the white deer carved by Toen Morikawa (B 1177). Kisai made everything from small ojime to large houses. A house he built shook in the wind, turning a guest pale with fear. Kisai reassured the guest by saying that the houses he built were made to sway in the wind, which was the secret of their strength.

492. Kishosai 鬼笑齋. *Chomei:* Kishosai 鬼笑齋. Late. Ivory.

493. Kisui 淇水. Early. Ivory. Figures.

494. Kitei 龜亭. *Mei:* Kitei 龜亭 (yaki-in). A famous ceramist of Kyoto. Made porcelain netsuke as a hobby.

495. Kiyokatsu 清勝. *Chomei:* Kiyokatsu 清勝. Middle. Mostly ivory. Excelled at carving netsuke in the shape of shells and vegetables. Left some beautiful pieces. See mosha (No. 68).

496. Kiyomitsu 清光. *Chomei:* Kiyomitsu 清光. Bunkyu (1861–1863). Mainly wood.

497. Kiyozumi 清住. Early. Wood.

498. Kiyu 龜遊. *Go:* Chikusai 竹齋. Middle. Lived in Asakusa, Tokyo.

499. Kiyu 龜友. See Kametomo (B 438).

500. Kizan 龜山. *Chomei:* Kizan 龜山. Temmei and Kansei (1781–1800). Wood figures.

501. Kizan 希山. See Kizan (B 502).

502. Kizan 輝山. *Uji:* Kamibayashi 上林. *Na:* Zenshi 善士. *Chomei:* Kizan 輝山 or kakihan. Born in Tokyo in 1885. Interested in art from early childhood. Took spare time from school to study lacquering with Hashimoto Ichizo II 橋本市藏. Made a special study of kyushitsu (lacquering in a single coat with an antique effect) and kanshitsu (carved dry lacquer) as applied to Buddhist statues. Developed a new method for mixing and applying dry lacquer, which he used to produce some superb objects. Despite the complicated techniques and long hours required, Kizan enjoyed his work. His character was such that he had no desire for recognition or money. Neither exhibited his work nor sold to dealers but gave pieces away to those who were sincerely interested. Although he developed his special kanshitsu technique only after arduous labors and struggles, he made only a few original designs and destroyed most of them. Repeated only a small fraction of the original models. Also interested in the study of ancient art and chinaware. Moved to Osaka after the great earthquake of 1923. Most of his work consists of items of small size, some of which he signed or marked with his seal. For the most part, however, he did not sign his work. See mosha (No. 69).

503. Kobun 光文. Late.

504. Kochosai 光晁齋. Tempo (1830–1843). Ivory.

505. Koei 光瑛. Some netsuke bearing his signature are in existence.

506. Kogetsu 湖月. Early middle. Ivory.

507. Kogetsu 耕月. Middle. Wood and ivory.

508. Kogetsu 江月. Tempo (1830–1843). Mostly wood. His work is realistic and in good taste. Sometimes signed "77 years old" with his signature. In some instances he carved his signature on an inlaid plaque of black persimmon wood. See mosha (No. 70).

509. Kogetsusai 光月齋. *Go:* Naomasa 直正. *Chomei:* Kogetsusai Naomasa *in* 光月齋直正印. Kyowa through Bunsei (1801–1829).

虎溪 虎溪
a   b

71. KOKEI

Carved in ivory. Often made manju netsuke.

510. Kogyoku 孝玉. Late. Ivory.

511. Kogyoku 光玉. *Go:* Anraku-sai 安樂齋. Late. Carved netsuke of hermits and human figures.

512. Kogyoku 光玉. *Uji:* Asami 淺見. *Na:* Kintaro 金太郎. Middle and late. Son of Koun Asami (B 554). Lived in Asakusa, Tokyo.

513. Kogyoku 光玉 *Uji:* Nishino 西野. *Na:* Kyutaro 久太郎. *Go:* Homeisai 寶明齋. *Chomei:* Kogyo-ku 光玉. Born in 1775. Lived in Tokyo. A pupil of Gyokuhosai Ryuchin (B 843).

514. Kogyoku 幸玉. Carved ne-tsuke masks and figures of children.

515. Kogyokusai 光玉齋. Late. Ivory.

516. Kohosai 公鳳齋. *Uji:* Ueda 上田. *Chomei:* Kohosai 公鳳齋. Died about 1907. Lived at Kawara-machi, Osaka. Ivory. Left some fine carvings of chrysanthemums. See Fig. 163.

517. Ko-ichi 孝一. Some netsuke bearing his signature are in exist-ence.

518. Ko-ichi 光一. Late. Ivory.

519. Ko-ichi 公一. Some netsuke bearing his signature are in exist-ence.

520. Kojitsu 孝實. *Uji:* Saito 齋藤. *Na:* Yataro 彌太郎. *Kaimyo:* Bonshakuengyo Shinshi. Born in 1833. Was a son of Ikkosai (B 336). Succeeded Ikkosai II 一光齋二代. Entered the school of Hojitsu (B 243) in his middle years while living at Asakusa, Tokyo. Carved in ivory. Died on July 27, 1893. Buried at the Shinjo-ji. See Fig. 215.

521. Kojun 孝純. Early. Wood.

522. Kokaku 光角. *Chomei:* Ko-kaku 光角. Tempo (1830–1843).

523. Kokei 光慶. *Chomei:* Kokei 光慶. Ansei through Keio (1854–1867). Mostly wood.

524. Kokei 虎溪. *Chomei:* Kokei 虎溪. Temmei and Kansei (1781–1800). Wood. Animal netsuke. Excelled at carving tigers, a sub-ject for which he was famous. His animal netsuke reveal a great depth of feeling and beauty. Born in Ise. Studied carving in Kame-yama. Later lived in Kuwana. Desired to emulate Minko (B 661), whose style he adopted with realistic modifications. On results with which he was satisfied he carved a kakihan that was similar to Minko's. See Figs. 122 and 123. See mosha (No. 71).

a   b

72. KOKUSAI

73. KOMIN

525. Kokeisai 虎溪齋. See Sansho Wada (B 903).

526. Kokoku 光谷. Tempo through Keio (1830–1867). Mainly wooden netsuke.

527. Kokusai 谷齋. *Chomei:* Koku 谷 or Kokusai 谷齋. Bunkyu (1861–1863) through the first part of Meiji (1868–1911). Named Ozaki Sozo 尾崎惣藏 but also called himself Takeda 武田. At the age of 21 entered the school of Gyokuyosai Mitsuhina (B 163) and studied ivory carving for four years. Was extraordinarily clever at creating designs and developed a new carving technique.

His designs were Chinese in style but not slavish copies of the ancient days nor imitations of cloth patterns. His style is known as Kokusai-bori (Kokusai-style carving) and is extremely popular. Worked mainly in deer horn. Father of Koyo Ozaki, the great novelist. In order to secure the means for Koyo's education and career he became a professional jester and wore a red haori (topcoat), which earned him the nickname of Red Haori. His struggle was not futile, and at last Koyo established his greatness. See Figs. 20 and 26. See mosha (No. 72).

528. Kokusen 谷泉. *Chomei:* Ko-kusen 谷泉. Bunka (1804–1817). Wood.

529. Komei 好明. A metal artist.

530. Komin 光珉. Late. Ivory and wood. Came from Tokyo. Excelled at carving turtles. Some of his work is signed: "Made from the precious wood of the Sumida River 以角田川名木作." See Fig. 131. See mosha (No. 73).

531. Komin 孝民. *Go:* Ichieisai 一永齋. Middle. Ivory.

532. Kominsai 孝民齋. Middle. Ivory.

533. Konan 江南. *Uji:* Inoue 井上. *Na:* Kikutaro 菊太郎. Early Meiji (1868–1911). Lived at Kanasugi, Tokyo. Was a pupil of Uzawa Shungetsu (B 1066).

534. Korakusai 古樂齋. Early. Wood. Excelled at carving masks.

535. Koretaka 惟孝. See Shoju XII (B 1004).

536. Korin 孝林. *Go:* Ichieisai 一永齋. Carved mask netsuke.

537. Koryusai 光龍齋. *Chomei:* Naokazu 直一. See Naokazu (B 746).

538. Koryusai 江柳齋. See Shungetsu (B 1066).

539. Kosai 孝齋. *Uji:* Jujuboku 壽々木. Late. Ivory.

74. KOSEN

75. KOSETSU

540. Kosai 廣齋. *Uji:* Yugawa 湯川. *Na:* Masakichi 政吉. Meiji (1868–1911). Was a pupil of Hosai (B 270). Worked mainly in ivory and horn. Mostly animal subjects. Inclined towards pictorial representations. His work was much appreciated by foreigners, and most of it was exported. Thus there is practically none of his work to be found in Japan. Continued carving until about 1887.

541. Kosai 篁齋. Early. Ivory.

542. Kosai 江哉. Carved oni netsuke bearing the signature of Kosai.

543. Kosai 光齋. Second *go:* Moritoshi 守壽. Ansei through Meiji (1854–1911). Mostly ivory. Carved many mask netsuke. Has a beautiful style.

544. Koseki 光石. *Uji:* Naito 内藤. Late. Lived at Shimmonzen, Kyoto. At the request of foreigners, carved various objects which helped introduce Japanese carving abroad.

545. Kosen 光仙. *Uji:* Nishimoto 西本. *Chomei:* Kosen saku 光仙作. Late. Ivory. A pupil of Chokusai (B 55). Lived in Osaka. See mosha (No. 74).

546. Kosensai 光仙齋. See Nagamitsu (B 730).

547. Kosen 古泉. Middle. Ivory.

548. Kosetsu 光雪. *Uji:* Yamashita 山下. *Na:* Gijo 義城. *Chomei:* Kosetsu 光雪. Born in Takamatsu, Shikoku, in 1894. Entered the priesthood at 19 years of age. Studied lacquering with Ishii Keido 石井磐堂 of Takamatsu. During some time spent in the army practiced tsuishu, tsuikoku, and kokaryokuyo (a kind of Kamakurabori in red and green lacquer to represent flowers and leaves), at which he became very proficient. Came to Osaka in 1941 and became the chief priest of the Koetsu-ji at Takagamine, Kyoto. Revered Koetsu 光悦, whose style he studied. Produced many fine works of art including tea-ceremony articles, personal ornaments, and netsuke. He also made wood sculptures, flower vases, tea dippers, and other things in bamboo. See mosha (No. 75).

549. Koshin 公眞. Some netsuke bearing his signature are in existence.

550. Koshu 公州. There are some carvings of Daruma that bear his signature.

551. Koshu 光州. Some figure netsuke bearing his signature are in existence.

552. Kotei 皓亭. See Shoju XIII (B 1005).

553. Kou 光雨. *Go:* Ichijusai 一壽齋. Middle. Ivory.

554. Koun 光雲. *Uji:* Asami 淺見. Middle. Father of Kogyoku (B 512).

555. Koun 光雲. *Yomyo:* Nakajima Kozo 中島光藏. Born in Shitaya, Tokyo, on February 18, 1852. Was a clansman of the Daimyo of Inshu. Showed talent in handicraft as a child. At first intended to become an architect and agreed to become an apprentice. The plan failed, and instead he entered the school of Toun Takamura (B 1246), who was then the paragon of carving. Koun was 12 years old. Taught by Toun, he learned the fundamentals of carving. It is said that Koun's greatness today is due to this fortunate starting point. His first training was in cloisonné of kojimon (kana or letter form) designs and fretwork carving on flat boards, to which he devoted himself night and day. At the age of 17 his genius came into full play as he absorbed and applied the basic truths of carving. He was finally adopted as a son by Takamura.

Koun became a professor in the newly established Tokyo Art School and helped train and guide younger men. It is believed that Koun helped create a new era in the field of carving in our country. Some of his pupils are now themselves professors in art schools, and some are examiners for the Imperial Art Exhibitions. Koun was appointed a member of the Imperial Art Committee, in some measure as an act of appreciation for his help in creating a new art era.

Koun usually lived apart from worldly concerns and devoted himself to the art of creation. He had a long mustache and a friendly warmth which brought forth a response akin to worship from those who met him. Was the greatest authority on carving during Meiji, Taisho, and Showa. Died at his residence in Tokyo on October 10, 1934, at the great age of 83.

556. Kounsai 光雲齋. Some figure netsuke bearing his signature are in existence.

557. Koyoken 廣葉軒. See Yoshinaga (B 1303).

558. Koyu 好友. Early. Wood.

559. Kozan 光山. Early. Ivory.

560. Kozan 江山. Made figure netsuke bearing the signature Kozan.

76. KYOKUSAI   77. KYOKUSEI   78. KYOKUSEN

561. Kozan 古山. Middle through recent years. Wood and ivory.

562. Kunihiro 國弘. A rabbit netsuke bearing his signature is in existence.

563. Kurobei 九郎兵衛. See Shuzan (B 1093).

(Kwagetsu: see Kagetsu.)

(Kwagyokusai: see Kagyokusai.)

(Kwaigyoku: see Kaigyoku.)

(Kwaigyokudo: see Kaigyokudo.)

(Kwaigyokusai: see Kaigyokusai.)

(Kwaito: see Kaito.)

(Kwansai: see Kansai.)

(Kwanshi: see Kanshi.)

(Kwaraku: see Karaku.)

(Kwashinsai: see Kashinsai.)

(Kwashun: see Kashun.)

564. Kyogan 巨巖. Meiji (1868–1911). Born at Inno Island. Reputation based on his perforated carvings, but also good at carving bamboo. Died in late Meiji at the age of about 70.

565. Kyokusai 旭齋. *Chomei:* Kyokusai 旭齋. Late. Wood. Hermits, Kannon, and other figures. His work was pictorial but in fine taste. See Figs. 97 and 166. See mosha (No. 76).

566. Kyokusei 旭生. See Gyokuzan (B 164). See mosha (No. 77).

567. Kyokusen 旭扇. *Chomei:* Kyokusen 旭扇. Early middle. Good at carving figure netsuke. See mosha (No. 78).

568. Kyokuzan 旭山. Late. Wood. Good at carving frogs.

569. Kyomin 京民. Some netsuke bearing his signature are in existence.

570. Kyosui 京水. Some of his gold-lacquer netsuke are in existence.

571. Kyotei 狂亭. Late. Wood.

572. Kyoto 居當. Early.

573. Kyozaido 橋材堂. *Go:* Kanji 寛治. See Kanji (B 446).

574. Kyubei 久兵衛. Lived in Sakai. Studied the Chinese Ming gold and metal alloys. Using this type of material, cast netsuke by the lost-wax process in the shape of shells, pots, carapaces, dishes, cups, and gourds. Some serve as ash-tray netsuke. Some are perforated designs such as linked circles, arabesques, and hornless dragons (amaryu). Other designs are the phoenix, tiger, shishi, plum, chrysanthemum, and peach. Besides netsuke, he made Buddhist altar articles, sakè bottles, fire boxes, braziers, and incense burners. Some of his work is marked in the casting with the mei of Kyubei 久兵衛 or Tokyu 唐久 or "Kyubei living in Sakai, Izumi, a maker of Chinese articles in the style of Hsüan Tê of the Great Ming period 大明宣德年製泉刕堺住唐物師久兵衛作." His masterpiece is a lantern hanging at the tower gate of Sugahara Shrine at Sakai. The writing on a concave surface reads: "On this auspicious day of November of Kyoho 19 [1734] a metal artist living at Sakai of Senshu—Karamonoya Kyubei Tsunenobu made 享保十九卯寅年十一月吉日鑄工泉州堺住唐物屋久兵衛常信作." See Fig. 21.

575. Kyuichi 久一. Born on July 9, 1857. Called himself Takeuchi Kengoro 竹内兼五郎. Used the *go* of Shusai 州齋. Was the son of Tanaga, who owned a lantern shop in Asakusa, Tokyo. At 13 became a pupil of Ryusen Horiuchi (B 878), a netsuke carver. Ryusen died soon after, and Kyuichi entered the school of Shuraku Kawamoto (B 1077). At 22 he received from his master the artist name of Senshu 川洲, and became independent. Became friendly with Machida Hisanari 町田久成, the curator of

the Imperial Museum. Adopted the character *kyu* 久 and changed his given name to Kyuichi. Began using the *go* of Kyuen 久遠. In 1882, went to Nara. In 1887, when the Tokyo Art School was established, was appointed a professor in the sculpture department together with Kano Tessai 加納鐵哉. In 1890 exhibited a carving of the Emperor Jimmu which was widely acclaimed at the International Industrial Exhibit. Was an enthusiastic follower of the Nichiren sect of Buddhism. Made the original designs for the Nichiren bronze statue in Hakata and the statue of Nichiren in Nirvana found on the island of Ushigakubi in the Inland Sea. Became a member of the Imperial Art Committee in 1906. Was seven times an examiner of the Ministry of Education Exhibition. Died on September 24, 1916, at the age of 60. Starting his career as a netsuke artist, Kyuichi continuously wrote and lectured enthusiastically on the subject of netsuke. Was a true benefactor of the netsuke community.

576. Kyusai 汲哉. *Go:* Tetsugen 鐵玄, Tetsugendo 鐵玄堂, Kyusai 汲哉. *Chomei:* Kyusai 汲哉. Born in Osaka on March 29, 1879. Named Hirai Shin 平井新. Learned carving from his father Hansen 半仙. Called himself Tetsugen 鐵玄 or Tetsugendo 鐵玄堂 until he was 36 years old. Presented an incense case in the shape of a mokugyo (wooden gong) to Prince Songaku Konoe. Being very pleased, the prince took a character from the name of the Hankyu 斑鳩 Palace of the Chugu-ji, where he was then staying and conferred on Hirai the name of Kyusai, which he thereafter used as his *go*. In the autumn of 1927, he altered the characters of his *go* from 鳩齋 to 汲哉. Was requested by the Ministry of Commerce and Industry to enter the International Exhibition held at Paris in 1895. Kyusai entered a bamboo flower vase entitled "Goddess of Peace," for which he was awarded a bronze prize. Died on March 30, 1938, at the age of 60. Buried at the Hakugo-ji in Nara. Undoubtedly one of the great masters of recent years. See Figs. 54, 113, and 210. See mosha (No. 79).

577. Kyusai 鳩齋. *Chomei:* Kyusai 鳩齋 or Kyusai-in 鳩齋印. See Kyusai (B 576). See mosha (No. 80).

578. Kyusen 丘泉. *Go:* Rakushiken 樂之軒. Middle to late. Was a son of Gyuka (B 167). Was a tea master. Also carved Uji dolls.

Signed with a kakihan or *in*. See mosha (No. 81).

579. Kyuzan 久山. Middle. Wood. Figures.

–M–

580. Mampo 萬寶. Late. Came from Mino. Excelled at engraving seals.

581. Masa-aki 正明. *Chomei:* Masa-aki 正明. Temmei and Kansei (1781–1800). Wood. Animals.

582. Masabumi 正文. Middle Wood.

583. Masachika 正親. Late. Was adopted son of Kaigyokusai (B 430). Named Yasunaga Kichirobei 安永吉郎兵衛. Succeeded to the business of his natural father.

584. Masachika 政親. *Go:* Shoryusai 證龍齋. Late. Lived in Asakusa, Tokyo. Good at carving ivory.

585. Masafusa 正房. Middle. Wood and ivory. Signed: Masafusa. See mosha (No. 82).

586. Masaharu 正春. *Chomei:* Masaharu 正春. Kyowa through Bunsei (1801–1829). Mostly ivory. Carved netsuke of hermits, figures, animals, and masks.

587. Masahide 正秀. Early. Wood.

588. Masahide 正英. *Uji:* Kurokawa 黒川. *Chomei:* Sakiyo Kurokawa Masahide-in 崎陽黒川正英印. Early. Excelled at carving nuts and coconuts. Also good at carving mask netsuke.

589. Masahiro 正廣. Middle. Ivory. Called himself Ryuchokusai 龍直齋.

590. Masahiro 正弘. Middle. Wood. See Fig. 173.

591. Masajo 正女. Middle. Came from Nagoya. Wood. Sleeping shojo, shells, and other subjects. See mosha (No. 83).

592. Masaka 正香. *Uji:* Sawaki 澤木. *Na:* Risaburo 利三郎. *Go:* Kihodo 奇峰堂. *Chomei:* Masaka 正香 or Kihodo Masaka 奇峰堂正香. Born in Nagoya in 1868. Was a pupil of Masakazu (B 596), who later adopted him. Removed to Osaka in 1883 and there carved netsuke and small okimono. Especially good at carving rats. His entry in an exhibition held at Kobe in 1889 or 1890—a cake plate decorated with a bag of 100 rats—was purchased by the Emperor Meiji. Also sold, through the intermediary of Kiyosuke Ikeda, a carving representing a group of rats to Prince Komatsu, a carving of a Nio (Deva King) to Prince Arisugawa, and

other objects to other members of the royalty. Honored by Baron Kyuki with special permission to view the collection at the Shosoin. His style was pictorial and his techniques painstaking. See mosha (No. 84).

593. Masakata 正方. Middle. Wood.

594. Masakatsu 正勝. Was a son of Masanao (B 612). Work was fine and beautiful. Output very small because he was sickly. Examples of his work are rare. Died on January 4, 1899, at the age of 60. See Fig. 179.

595. Masakazu 正一. *Chomei:* Masakazu 正一 or Masanao 正直. Meiji (1868–1911). Lived in Ise Yamada. Called himself Chikuzenya. Operated an eel restaurant. Studied carving under Masanao (B 612). Became a proficient carver. Often used the signature of Masanao. Hence people referred to him as Chikuzenya Masanao. Died in late Meiji. See mosha (No. 85).

596. Masakazu 正一. *Uji:* Sawaki 澤木. *Na:* Manjiro 萬次郎. *Go:* Kihodo 奇峰堂 or Kihosai 奇峰齋. *Chomei:* Masakazu 正一. Meiji (1868–1911). Was a younger brother of Masatoshi (B 630). Came from Nagoya but later resided in Osaka.

Carved in ivory and wood. Made excellent netsuke of hermits, figures, animals, insects, and masks. Made many rat netsuke which were exported because they appealed to foreigners. Repeated the subject constantly. Died on January 28, 1891, at the age of 53. See Figs. 88 and 120. See mosha (No. 86).

597. Masakazu 昌一. Early middle. Wood.

598. Masakiyo 正清. *Uji:* Sakai 坂井. *Na:* Seizaburo 清三郎. *Chomei:* Masakiyo 正清. Was a pupil of Masakatsu (B 594). Lived in Uji Yamada but later moved to Akeno, a suburb. Carved mostly animals in wood. See Fig. 176.

599. Masakuni 正國. Early. Wood.

600. Masamaru 正丸. Early. Wood.

601. Masamichi 正道. Middle. Wood.

602. Masamichi 正路. Was a metal artist but also carved netsuke in wood.

603. Masamine 正峯. Middle. Excelled in carving ivory. Named Hidari.

604. Masamitsu 正光. *Uji:* Ejima 江島. *Na:* Kotaro 幸太郎. *Cho-mei:* Masamitsu 正光. Came from Takada, Echigo. Was a pupil of Masayoshi Ishikura (B 638), who later adopted him. Subsequently returned to his original family. Died in 1909 at the age of 73.

605. Masamitsu 正光. Called himself Hagiwara Kaiko 萩原塊光. Was a clansman of the family of Tatebayashi Akimoto of Joshu. Went to Tokyo and became a pupil of Kaneko Kaito 金子塊東, with whom he studied ivory and tusk carving. Excelled in carving tobacco pipes. His style was patterned after the carving methods of Kaito (B 431) and Kokusai (B 527). Died about 1902 at the age of 50 some years. See mosha (No. 87).

606. Masamitsu 正光. See Kikugawa (B 484).

607. Masamori 正守. Middle. Ivory.

608. Masanaga 正長. Early middle. Wood.

609. Masanao 正直. *Chomei:* Masanao 正直. Lived in Kyoto during Temmei and Kansei (1781–1800). Excelled in both wood and ivory carving. See Fig. 114. See mosha (No. 88).

610. Masanao 正直. See Hokinsai (B 248).

611. Masanao 正直. Early. Wood and ivory. Called himself Isshinsai 一心齋. See mosha (No. 89).

612. Masanao 正直. Born on August 12, 1815, in the village of Ugatamura in Ise. Named Suzuki Shinsuke but later changed to Suzuki Shinzaemon. Removed to Yamada. At first he was a metal craftsman but in his middle years studied carving with Ittan (B 377), who was a samurai of the Toba clan. Carved netsuke of toads, animals, landscapes, flowers, birds, and almost everything else. His animals are very fine. Much preferred to work in wood. Only a few of his netsuke in ivory are known. His carving is sensitive and strong. Usually utilized a convenient configuration in the netsuke itself for the attachment of the cord, thereby eliminating the himotoshi. Died on January 8, 1890. See Fig. 110. See mosha (No. 90).

613. Masanao 正直. *Chomei:* Masanao 正直. Masanao II was born on January 15, 1848, in Yamada. Named Miyake Chogoro 三宅長五郎. Was a pupil of Masanao (B 612), to whom he was related and was therefore permitted to adopt the signature of Masanao, becoming Masanao II. Good at carving. Like his teacher, excelled at carving toads and the animals of the zodiac. His style developed from the instructions of his teacher. Died on April 13, 1922. See Fig. 92.

614. Masanao 正直. *Chomei:* Masanao 正直. Born in March 1890 in Yamada. Was the son of Masanao II (B 613). Learned carving from his father. Named Miyake Kisaburo 三宅喜三郎. Became Masanao III. Was as able as his father in carving toads and the animals of the zodiac. Hashimoto Heihachi 橋本平八, Yamamoto Naomasa (B 749), Sakai Masahide (B 587), Sakuradani Naohiro 櫻谷直弘, and Nagai Masa-aki 永井正明 were all pupils of Masanao III.

615. Masanao 正直. *Chomei:* Masanao 正直. First lived in Yamada but later moved to Shawa, Sakamachi, Taki-gun, Ise. Called himself Yonehira 米平. Entered the school of Masanao I (B 612). Masanao I gave him a wood carving representing himself (Masanao). As a result, adopted the signature of Masanao. Hence people referred to him as Shawa Masanao 射和正直. See mosha (No. 91).

616. Masanobu 正信. *Uji:* Adachi 安達. *Na:* Tomoshichi 友七. Born in 1838. Was a pupil of Masayoshi (B 638). Was a samurai of the Owari clan.

正
忠

正
照

92. MASATADA

93. MASATERU

617. Masanori 正則. *Uji:* Kawakita 川北. Born in Ise but died in Kyoto. Learned carving from Masakazu (B 596), and his son Masaka (B 592).

618. Masanori 正度. Made mask netsuke.

619. Masasada 正貞. Late. Carved in ivory and wood.

620. Masashige 正重. Early. Wood. Figures.

621. Masatada 正忠. *Chomei:* Masatada 正忠. Early Meiji (1868–1911). Mainly wood. Was a pupil of Masanao (B 612). Carved many animal and insect netsuke. See mosha (No. 92).

622. Masatami 正民. *Chomei:* Masatami 正民. Kaei (1848–1853). Came from Nagoya but later moved to Osaka. Mainly ivory. Carved netsuke of figures, animals, and masks. Excelled in carving monkeys, which he made for export.

623. Masatami 正民. Died in 1928 at the age of 75. Lived his entire life in Nagoya. Called himself Moribe Fukuzo 森部福造. Was a pupil of Masakazu (B 596). Excelled in both wood and ivory carving. See Fig. 174.

624. Masatane 正種. Tempo (1830–1843). Ivory.

625. Masateru 正照. *Chomei:* Masateru 正照. Late. Son of Masachika (B 583) and a grandson of Kaigyokusai (B 430). Lived in Osaka. See mosha (No. 93).

626. Masatomi 正富. Some figure netsuke by him are in existence.

627. Masatomo 正友. *Chomei:* Masatomo 正友. Tempo through Kaei (1830–1853). Came from Ise. Carved netsuke of hermits, figures, animals, and insects.

628. Masatoshi 正壽. Early. Ivory.

629. Masatoshi 正年. Middle. Ivory.

630. Masatoshi 正利. *Go:* Unindo 雲烟堂, Takushijun 澤士淳, Chikukai Rojin 竹海老人, Usetsusai 雨雪齋, and others. *Mei:* Gekkin 月琴. *Chomei:* Masatoshi 正利. Died on August 5, 1884, at the age of 50. Called himself Sawaki Toshizo 澤木利造. Was the second son of Sawaki Risuke 澤木利助 of Nagoya and an elder brother of Masakazu (B 596). Excelled in carving and received a commission to work for the local clan. Commissioned by the Imperial Household Ministry to design the Great Seal in alabaster. Later moved to Osaka. In 1878, went to China to study for several years. Carved netsuke and tea-ceremony articles. Also made instruments for the playing of Chinese music of the Ming and Ch'ing periods. It is said that the moon guitar (gekkin) made by Masatoshi was superior to those made by the Chinese. See mosha (No. 94).

631. Masatoshi 正利. *Chomei:* Masatoshi 正利. Temmei and Kansei (1781–1800). Excelled in carving both wood and ivory. Carved netsuke of figures, animals, and masks.

632. Masatoshi 正利. *Chomei:* Masatoshi 正利. Late. Ivory and inlaid work.

633. Masatsugu 正次. See Kaigyokusai (B 430) and Fig. 39.

634. Masatsugu 正次. Called himself Hokutosai 北島斎.

635. Masaya 正也. A treasure boat (takarabune) netsuke bearing his signature is in existence.

636. Masayasu 正安. Carved netsuke of figures.

637. Masayasu 正保. Some netsuke are found bearing this signature.

638. Masayoshi 正義. *Azana:* Yaokichi 八百吉. *Chomei:* Masayoshi 正義. Died in 1848 at the age of

46. Had family names of Ishikura 石倉 and Goto 後藤, using them both. Came from Takada, Echigo. Excelled at carving many types of objects from childhood. Also carved netsuke. Was particularly good at carving shishi. See mosha (No. 95).

639. Masayoshi 政鑪. *Uji:* Iwama 岩間. Died in August 1837 at the age of 74. Entered the school of Chokuzui 直随 but was also taught by Seishin 誠信. At first called Kinzo 金蔵 but name later changed to Kinuemon 金右衛門. Was an expert metal artist of the Nara school. Especially good at carving figures, Noh masks, and animals. Created many original designs. Some of his work is as fine as that of Seizui (B 938), for which reason people nicknamed him Seizuibo (son of Seizui). Occasionally made gold kagamibuta netsuke. See mosha (No. 96).

640. Masayoshi 正吉. Middle. Ivory.

641. Masayoshi 正容. Carved figure netsuke.

642. Masayuki 正行. Middle. Ivory.

643. Masayuki 正幸. Some netsuke bearing his signature are found.

644. Masayuki 正之. *Uji:* Kato 加藤. *Chomei:* Masayuki 正之 or kakihan. Middle and late. Lived in Yotsuya, Tokyo. Studied medicine but later took up carving. Some of his fine ivory carvings of oni and Ofuku are to be found. See Fig. 87. See mosha (No. 97).

645. Masayuki 正之. *Chomei:* Hoshunsai 寶春齋 Masayuki *in.* Kyowa through Bunsei. Called himself Hoshunsai. Some say Hoshinsai, but this is not correct. Carved netsuke of figures and animals. See Fig. 183.

646. Masazane 正實. A netsuke carver of Edo.

647. Masazane 政實. Early. Wood.

648. Matagoro 又五郎. Family name was Yoshida 吉田, and his *go* was Kinko 金耕.

649. Mata-ichi 亦市. Figure netsuke bearing his signature are in existence.

650. Matauemon 又右衛門. *Chomei:* Kishu Matauemon *in* 又右衛門印. Lived in Kyushu prior to Temmei (1781–1788). Carved excellent netsuke. See mosha (No. 98).

651. Meido 明堂. *Uji:* Asahi 朝日. *Chomei:* Meido koku 明堂刻. In 1893, at the request of the Ministry of Agriculture and Commerce, exhibited some of his work at the Great Columbian Exposition in the United States. Was an expert carver in ivory.

652. Meigyoku 明玉. Figure netsuke with his signature are in existence.

653. Meijitsu 明實. *Chomei:* Meijitsu 明實. Tempo through Keio (1830–1867). Ivory. Was a pupil of Hojitsu (B 243).

654. Meikeisai 明鶏齋. See Hojitsu (B 243).

655. Meisei 明正. Mainly wood.

656. Meizan 明山. Some netsuke bearing his signature have been found.

657. Miki 三木. Some netsuke bearing his signature are in existence.

658. Mingyoku 民玉. *Go:* Seisei 青々. Early.

659. Min-ichi 珉一. *Chomei:* Min-ichi 珉一. Mainly wood.

660. Minjo 民乘. Late.

661. Minko 岷江. *Chomei:* Kakihan based on character min 岷 or based on Gose Minko 五瀨岷江. Sometimes carved Minko 岷江 on an inlaid ivory plaque. Born in Iga. Caught the attention of Marquis Todo while carving Buddhist household shrines. Marquis Todo took Minko and a group of ten others into his service. Minko moved to Tsu and took up residence in the home of Oumaba. Later Minko began carving netsuke and remarkable swords. He gave paramount consideration to original designs. It is said that he immediately dismissed any pupil who sketched from nature. For animal eyes he usually used metal. Made tonkotsu (tobacco cases) in wood with inlaid ivory and shell. It is reported that his work was widely forged even while he was alive. Also excelled at painting and at haiku poetry.

The following entry is found in the *Biographies of Ancient Sages of Mie Prefecture:* "Minko Tanaka was also known as Tadamitsu or Juntoku. His azana was Iwaemon. Minko is his *go*. He was born in Nakatsuge, Iga Province, in 1735. Was commissioned by the Tsu clan to do carving. His favorite materials were woods such as red sandalwood, ebony, boxwood, black persimmon, and others. Liked to carve animals and various fruits. Occasionally carved figures and various receptacles. He contrived a Daruma so cleverly that thumping his head

sent his eyes revolving in red and white colors and a walnut that when shaken revealed an insect protruding from a tiny aperture. Also devised a replica of the hanging bell of Dojo-ji in which the face of the priest Anchin is seen alternately flushed and pale as the bell hanger is turned. The design is surely enough to startle anyone.

"Also made smoking pipes, incense boxes, and writing-brush boxes on which he carved figures, horses, cloud dragons, and other designs. Also carved tobacco pouches from paulownia wood in which he inlaid ivory and foreign woods in various designs. He left many masterpieces. Was extremely bold in the use of his knife yet did not spare the minutest detail. His designs are often exquisite, vivid, and alive.

"Minko also excelled in painting and calligraphy, following the style of Shohaku Soga. Died on August 29, 1816, at the age of 82. Buried at the Rinsho-ji at his birthplace, Nakatsuge."

According to Nakae Sadanosuke, who inherited Minko's Buddhist mortuary tablet, 17 of his works of art, and Minko's articles of daily use, Minko was born in Tsugeuemachi, Mie Prefecture, in 1735. His tsusho was Sato Osamu. (According to the records of the Rin-sho-ji, his name was Sato Uemon, but this must be an error.) Since he was adopted by someone living in Nakatsuge, he might have changed his name to Tanaka Iwaemon. The gravestone at the Amida-ji in Tsu reads: "The grave of Tanaka Minko of Tsu, Sesshu Province. Died on August 29, Bun-ka 13 [1816]." The kaimyo shown there is Kitokuin Ganyo Ryumin Koji. The Gyofuku-ji, located at Kogo-ri, Kambe-mura, Naka-gun, Iga Province, was sustained by 40 bushels of rice from the Todo family. During Kansei (1789–1800) the present main temple was built. In the center of the temple's cross-beam the carving of a lion is seen and at its side the carving of an elephant. The carvings are dated Kansei 8 (1796) and marked: "Shintoku Minko designed and carved." The writing on a small tablet placed on the carving of a phoenix in front of the main temple reads: "Early winter of Boshin [1808—sexagenary cycle] made by Minko Shintoku, aged 72." These carvings are well known as master-pieces of Minko, but in view of various discrepancies and conflict-ing data further inquiry seems necessary. See Figs. 124 and 138. See mosha (No. 99).

662. Minko 珉江. A netsuke with his signature representing a badger is in existence.

663. Minko 眠江. *Chomei:* Minko 眠江. Temmei and Kansei (1781–1800). Carved netsuke of animals, insects, and other subjects.

664. Minko 珉虎. Late.

665. Minko 眠虎. Some figure ne-tsuke bearing his signature are in existence.

666. Minkoku 眠谷. Late. Ivory.

667. Minkoku 民谷. *Go:* Genryo-sai 玄了齋. *Chomei:* Minkoku 民谷. Kansei (1789–1800). Lived in To-kyo. Wood and Ivory. Excelled in carving figure netsuke. His superb technique accorded with his great fame. See Figs. 133, 185, and 186. See mosha (No. 100).

668. Minkoku 民谷. Succeeded Minkoku I (B 667). Was also well known.

669. Minkoku 民國. *Go:* Shokasai 松可齋. Late. Metal artist.

670. Minsei 岷正. *Mei:* Minsei 岷正. Carved wood in the style of Minko (B 661) but was more realis-tic. May have been a younger brother of Minko. Was an excellent carver.

民
正

101. MINSEI

102. MISHU

103. MITSUHARU

光
春
刀

671. Minsei 民正. *Chomei:* Minsei 民正. Middle. Ivory. See mosha (No. 101).

672. Minseki 民石. Middle. Some of his figure netsuke are in existence.

673. Minsetsu 眠雪. *Chomei:* Minsetsu 眠雪. Ansei (1854–1859). Mainly wood.

674. Minshu 岷秀. Late.

675. Minzan 珉山. Early. Ivory.

676. Minzan 民山. Middle. Wood.

677. Mishu みしう. *Chomei:* Mishu みしう. Late. Ivory. See mosha (No. 102).

678. Mitsuaki 光明. See Ishikawa Komei (B 350).

679. Mitsuchika 光親. Middle. Ivory.

680. Mitsuharu 光春. Prior to Temmei (1781–1788). Lived in Kyoto.

681. Mitsuharu 光春. *Chomei:* Mitsuharu 光春. Late. Tokyo. Metal artist. Made kagamibuta netsuke. See mosha (No. 103).

682. Mitsuharu 光晴. Late. Wood and ivory.

683. Mitsuhide 光秀. Middle. Wood.

684. Mitsuhina 光雛. See Gyoku-yosai (B 163).

685. Mitsuhiro 光廣. *Uji:* Ohara 大原. *Azana:* Gushi 愚子. *Go:* Tokurinsai 徳鄰齋 or Sessado Mitsuhiro 切磋堂光廣. *Kaimyo:* Sessado Mitsuhiro Shinshi. *Mei:* Mitsuhiro 光廣, Mitsuhiro kao, Mitsuhiro Ohara *in,* or Mitsu 光 *in* kao. Born in Onomichi in 1810. At the age of 17, went to Osaka, where he was apprenticed to a shop engaged in the production of plectrums for the samisen and in the sale of ivory. Learned carving by using ivory waste. As he progressed in ability, his name became well known in Osaka, Kyoto, and Tokyo. Was adopted by the master of the shop. Unfortunately he was in poor health, and in 1857, at the age of 48, he returned to his birthplace, Onomichi. Gradually recovered from his illness and again engaged in the profession of carving. Died on August 2, 1875, at the age of 66. Was buried at Tennei-ji (Zenshu sect) of Onomichi. The poem on his gravestone reads: "An unusual wind has blown against my body. Today is the day that I depart for the cool world."

A document inherited by his grandson, Hidezo Ohara, is entitled *Takarabukuro* (Bag of Treas-

a   b   c

104. MITSUHIRO

ures). It reads in part: "When I was a child I went to Naniwa [Osaka] in accordance with the instructions of my parents. I sought a preordained relationship, found my master, and learned my skills from him. This was my desire, to carve ivory, and to make it into forms and designs from my past experience: figures, animals, birds, fish, insects, flora, and even house furniture. It was only necessary that the design be interesting and in good taste. The carvings recorded in this document are few and inferior but whatever I carved I recorded herein. That is why I call this document *Takarabukuro.* Forgive the poorness of my work. Spring, Tempo 8 [1838], a man of Naniwa formerly residing in Onomichi, Ohara Mitsuhiro." The document contains about 300 titles of his carvings with short explanations. Following this biographical data is a record, the substance of which is practically the same as mentioned above. The last entry in the document reads: "Written September 23, Taisho 10 [1921], by Ohara Tosuke at the age of 79." Tosuke was a son of Mitsuhiro, and it was he who erected his father's gravestone. Mitsuhiro liked waka poems and while living in Osaka was given the name of Daishotei Gagan by Shosho, the famous poet and tea-ceremony master. This fact is entered in the document as an addition. Besides the *Takarabukuro,* the Ohara family has a tobacco pouch that Mitsuhiro made in Keio 1 (1865) at the age of 56. On the front he inlaid an ivory piece in the design of a skull and a gravestone and wrote: "The autumn wind blows. Oh! Look at the eyes!" On the reverse he inlaid pampas grass. The ojime is inlaid with buffalo horn in the design of a crown and scepter and is inscribed: "It must not be Ono no Komachi, since pampas grass grows there." The netsuke is in ivory and represents a stray bit of wood and the moulted shell of a cicada. The mei on the netsuke reads: "Winter, Keio 1 [1865], old man Mitsuhiro Sessado-in." He also signed Mitsuhiro on the ojime and on the reverse decoration of the pouch placed the mei Sessado Shujin. This design originates from the old story of the poetess Ono no Komachi as it is preserved in the chants accompanying the Noh play *Sotoba Komachi,* which pictures her in pitiful old age. In May, 1934, Mitsuhiro was posthumously honored as a master netsuke artist by the Osaka Prefectural Arts and Crafts Association. See Figs. 100 and 106. See mosha (No. 104).

105. MITSUNOBU

光
典

106. MITSUOKI

686. Mitsuhiro 光裕. See Mitsu-toshi (B 707).

687. Mitsuhisa 光久. *Chomei:* Mitsuhisa 光久. Tempo (1830–1843). Mostly ivory.

688. Mitsukiyo 滿清. Middle. Wood.

689. Mitsukiyo 光清. Middle. Wood.

690. Mitsukuni 光國. Early. Ivory.

691. Mitsukuni 光邦. Late. Ivory.

692. Mitsumasa 光政. Late. Ivory.

693. Mitsumasa 光正. Came from Edo.

694. Mitsumasa 光昌. *Go:* Gotoke Kyudai Teijo 後藤家九代程乘. Metal artist: the ninth generation of the Goto line of metal artists.

695. Mitsunaga 光長. *Uji:* Ogura 小倉. *Na:* Koemon 幸右衛門. Middle and late. Lived in Kanda, Tokyo.

696. Mitsunao 光直. Middle.

697. Mitsunao 滿猶. Late. Mask netsuke of his are in existence.

698. Mitsunobu 光信. *Chomei:* Mitsunobu 光信. Middle. Wood. See mosha (No. 105).

699. Mitsunori 光則. Middle. Wood.

700. Mitsuo 光雄. Late. Wood.

701. Mitsuoki 光興. *Uji:* Otsuki 大月. *Mei:* Ryusai 龍齋. Was a metal artist. During Kyowa (1801–1803) visited Edo, later returning there again. Excelled at drawing scenic designs on poetry cards. Had many pupils who became masters. Carved netsuke in boxwood as a hobby. His work is extraordinarily refined. Also made kagamibuta netsuke on which he placed his mei Mitsuoki. See mosha (No. 106).

702. Mitsusada 光定. *Uji:* Ohara 大原. Kyowa through Bunsei (1801–1829). Made figure and mask netsuke. Skillful carver. See Fig. 187.

703. Mitsushige 光重. *Chomei:* Mitsushige 光重. Kyowa through Bunsei (1801–1829). Carved netsuke of figures, masks, and other subjects.

704. Mitsutada 光忠. Middle. Ivory.

705. Mitsutomo 光友. Early. Ivory.

706. Mitsutoshi 光壽. See Hosai (B 270).

三
輪
圖

707. Mitsutoshi 光利. *Chomei:* Mitsutoshi 光利. Late. Ivory. Lived in Asakusa, Tokyo. Named Otani Koga. See Fig. 188.

708. Mitsutsugu 光次. Late. Ivory.

709. Mitsuyoshi 光好. Middle. Ivory.

710. Miwa 三輪. There may have been three or even four carvers who used the signature Miwa. First there was Miwa Yukan 三輪勇閑, whose family name was Hiromori 廣森. Called himself Kinokuniya Shozaemon 紀伊國屋庄左衛門 and lived in Sekiguchi, Tokyo. Was a man of high principles. Made netsuke as a hobby but is regarded as the originator of the Edo-style netsuke. Drew his subject matter and designs from the familiar Japanese scene. Before his time, cypress and cedar were usually used in carving netsuke. Since these materials were easily defaced, Miwa used cherry wood and toboku. Did not polish or lacquer his carvings. Lined the cord holes with yellow-tinted ivory or tusk, employing some secret method to accomplish this. Did not carve ivory. Was a most skillful and original artist. Lived during Temmei. Signed Miwa or Miwa in a seal form. See Figs. 3, 68, 71.

There was also Miwa Zaiei 三輪 在榮. His *go* was Kashinsai 花信齋. Excelled in drawing monkeys and in carving. Died on July 7, 1789. Cremated at the Zenkei-ji in Yotsuya, Tokyo. The *Remarks on Old Paintings* contains an entry similar to the above, and states that the data is quoted from the *History of Remains*. However, in view of the identity of names and period, and other similarities, it may be that he is the same individual as Miwa Yukan. The third person is Miwa Rikan 三輪利寛, whose biography is unknown. See mosha (No. 107).

711. Miyashiro 宮代. Given name was Chokichi (B 53).

712. Mokubei 木米. Was a famous Kyoto ceramist. Also made porcelain netsuke.

713. Mokusui 黙睡. Early. Figure netsuke of his are in existence.

714. Mondo 主水. *Go:* Tanaka Minosuke Ryukei 田中巳之助立慶. *Kaimyo:* Kogenjoami Anzen. Born January 22, 1857, in Osaka. He is Jocho Ho-in XXXII, the great sculptor of Buddhist images. (Ho-in is a title limited usually to painters and sculptors.) Although the imperial restoration in 1868 caused his family profession to suffer, with resulting difficulties in

先
代
作
主
水
彩

108. MONDO

meeting the daily necessities of life, nevertheless studied carving from his father, Yasumichi 康道. When he grew older, he carved many Buddhist images. Machida Kyusei 町田久成 gave him the artist name of Kobusshi 弘佛師. Studied the art objects of old shrines and temples with his teacher, Fukuta Junyu of Toto. This research proved very beneficial. Exhibited statues of the goddess of mercy and Prince Shotoku at the Third and Fourth National Industrial Exhibitions. Produced a considerable number of netsuke. Occasionally made Shuzan-style netsuke. Almost all the netsuke exported abroad as Shuzan netsuke are his work. Was high-spirited, waggish, and unconventional. Carved the wooden images of Jizo, the guardian saint of children, of Kiyoshi Kojin, and the White-Robed Kannon found at the Three Famous Beauty Spots of Japan. Liked to draw Buddhist images. Was extraordinarily artistic in coloring his work. Died on March 10, 1917, at the age of 61.

715. Mondo 主水. *Chomei:* Mondo kakihan. Called himself Jokei Tanaka. Until March 1917, he used the mei Tekisui. Succeeded Mondo (B 714) as Mondo XXXIII. Was taught carving by his master from childhood. Later entered the Kyoto Arts and Crafts School, from which he graduated with an excellent record and commendations. After graduating, he devoted himself to the study of ancient sculpture to his great improvement. When the empress visited Osaka, he presented her with a wood carving of a doll, for which the mayor of Osaka commended him in a letter. Many of his great works and masterpieces are found. Carved netsuke as a hobby. Is living today south of Sumiyoshi Shrine. See mosha (No. 108).

716. Morikane 盛周. Middle.

717. Morikazu 守一. *Chomei:* Morikazu 守一. Tempo (1830–1843). Mostly wood.

718. Morimitsu 守光. Middle.

719. Morinobu 守信. Late.

720. Morinobu 守延. Some netsuke bearing his signature are found.

721. Moritoshi 守壽. See Kosai (B 543).

722. Moritsugu 守次. Early middle. Wood.

723. Motochika 元親. Some netsuke bearing his signature are found.

724. Motonobu 元信. Early.

725. Mugai 夢外. Early middle. Wood.

726. Muhachi 夢八. Middle.

727. Munechika 宗親. Late. Wood.

728. Myochin 明珍. A metal artist.

729. Myogaya Seishichi 茗荷屋 清七. See Seishichi (B 930).

–N–

730. Nagamitsu 長光. *Go:* Ko-sensai 光仙齋. Middle.

731. Nagamitsu 永光. *Chomei:* Nagamitsu 永光. Early. Mostly wood. See Fig. 96.

732. Nagao Ta-ichiro 長尾太市 郎. See Ta-ichiro (B 1152).

733. Nagasada 永貞. Middle. Wood.

734. Nagasada 長貞. Late.

735. Nagataka 長孝. Named Ko-ami 幸阿彌. Made gold-lacquer netsuke.

736. Nagatsugu 永次. Middle. Ivory.

737. Nagayoshi 永吉. *Chomei:* Nagayoshi 永吉. Keio (1865–1867). Wood and ivory.

738. Nagayuki 長行. *Chomei:* Nagayuki 長行. Ansei (1854–1859). Usually worked in wood.

739. Namboku 南木. Early middle. Wood and ivory.

740. Namichika 浪近. Some netsuke bearing his signature are found.

741. Nansai 南齋. Late. Some figure netsuke of his are found.

742. Naoharu 直春. *Go:* Onkokan 温古観. *Yomyo:* Benzo 辨藏. *Chomei:* kakihan based on Yanagawa Naoharu. Kansei through Bunka (1789–1817). Lived in Kanda, Edo. Son of the metal artist Yana-gawa Naoyue 柳川直故. Usually called Koheiji 小平治, which he later changed to Sanzaemon 三左 衛門. His technique was much superior to that of his grandfather Naomasa 直政. Trained many pupils, among whom Kono Shum-mei 河野春明 was one of the best. Occasionally made kagamibuta netsuke. See mosha (No. 109).

743. Naohide 直秀. Late. Wood and ivory.

744. Naokata 直方. *Chomei:* Nao-kata 直方. Tempo (1830–1843). Mainly wood.

745. Naokazu 直一. Late. Mostly wood. Came from Nagoya. Good at carving netsuke in the design of small-change coppers.

746. Naokazu 直一. *Go:* Koryusai 光龍齋. *Chomei:* Naokazu 直一 or kakihan based on Koryusai Naokazu. Tempo (1830–1843). Wood and ivory. Mainly figures. See mosha (No. 110).

747. Naomasa 直政. Late. Wood.

748. Naomasa 直正. See Kogetsusai (B 509).

749. Naomasa 直正. *Uji:* Yamamoto 山本. *Na:* Yasuhira 安平. *Chomei:* Naomasa 直正. Born on July 20, 1908, in Yamada, Ise. Apprenticed to a kitchenware shop in Fukiage. Entered the school of Masanao III (B 614). Carved netsuke of animals and figures. Preferred to use the boxwood found in Asakuma Mountain. See mosha (No. 111).

750. Naomitsu 直光. *Go:* Baihosai 貝實齋. Early middle.

751. Naomitsu 直光. *Uji:* Murata 村田. *Na:* Masajiro 政次郎. *Go:* Isseisai 一政齋. Born in December 1867 at Osaka. Became a pupil of Ichiyusai Naoharu (B 317) of Tokyo and studied carving. First carved in coral, later in wood and ivory, making many netsuke. Died on February 22, 1931, at the age of 65. Buried at the Seiren-in, Tennoji, Osaka.

752. Naosada 直貞. Early. Some netsuke are found that bear his signature.

753. Naoshige 直茂. Early middle. Ivory.

754. Naoyuki 直雪. Early. Wood. Called himself Shibayama 芝山.

755. Naoyuki 尚行. See Ritsuo (B 826).

756. Naoyuki 直行. *Chomei:* Naoyuki 直行. Late. Lived in Osaka until his middle years, when he moved to Nara. Carved netsuke and other objects. Excelled at carving deer. See mosha (No. 112).

757. Natsuo 夏雄. *Uji:* Fushimi 伏見. *Na:* Jisaburo 治三郎. *Chomei:* Natsuo in hiragana (cursive form of Japanese syllabary). Born April 11, 1828, in Yamagi Province. Was adopted by Jisuke Kano. In 1840, entered the school of Koju Ikeda, a metal artist of the Otsuki school. Natsuo adopted the *go* of Juro 壽郎. Made great progress in metalcraft. Taught by Koju for three years. Subsequently applied the realistic style of the Shijo Maruyama school to his art. Studied fine examples of the various schools of metal art. Finally originated his own school. Learned calligraphy from Tanematsu Tanemori and painting from Raisho Nakajima. At the age of 25 went to Edo and changed his name to Natsuo. At that time metal artists were not in favor, and it is said that he had difficulty in earning a livelihood. During the early part of Meiji, was commissioned to create designs for gold coins. Also commissioned by the Imperial Household Department to carve the decorations for the emperor's sword. Was an examiner for various exhibitions. In 1890, became a professor at the Tokyo Art School. Occasionally carved kagamibuta netsuke. Died on February 3, 1898, at the age of 71. See Fig. 10. See mosha (No. 113).

758. Negoro Soshichi 根來宗七. Many wood carvings using a combination of red and black lacquer are to be found. See Fig. 172.

759. Niko 二光. Made splendid wood carvings in the style of Kaigyoku (B 428). May have been a pupil of Ikko (B 330).

760. Ninraku 仁樂. Born in 1843. Called himself Naito Kimeisai 内藤喜明齋.

761. Ninsei 仁清. Was a famous Kyoto ceramist. Made porcelain netsuke that bear his signature. See Fig. 36.

762. Nisai 二哉. *Chomei:* Nisai 二哉. Born in 1880 in Yamatoshimmachi. Called himself Yoshimoto Yahei 吉本彌平. Was adopted at the age of six by Gyokusen Yoshimoto (B 157), a pupil of Reigyoku Tanaka (B 813). Learned the Shibayama style of inlay from his father. Went to Tokyo at the age of 18 to become a pupil of Reigyoku Tanaka, his father's teacher. Later resided in Kyoto and Osaka. After the age of 50 he devoted himself to carving netsuke and tea-ceremony articles out of boxwood. See mosha (No. 114).

763. Nobuaki 延秋. Late. Wood.

764. Nobuchika 信親. Late. Wood.

765. Nobuhide 信英. Early. Wood.

766. Nobuhisa 信久. Early. Wood.

767. Nobukatsu 信勝. Middle. Wood.

768. Nobukazu 信一. Early. Wood.

769. Nobukazu 信壽. See Hattori (B 199).

770. Nobukiyo 信清. Early. Wood.

771. Nobumasa 信正. Middle. Wood and ivory. See Fig. 189.

772. Nobumitsu 信光. Late. Excelled in wood carving.

773. Nobumoto 宣元. Lived before Temmei (1781–1788).

774. Nobunao 信直. *Uji:* Kobayashi 小林. Late.

775. Nobuteru 信照. Late. Some netsuke that bear his signature are in existence.

776. Nobu-uji 信氏. *Go:* Ichirinsai 一輪齋. Middle.

777. Nobuyoshi 信義. *Chomei:* Nobuyoshi 信義. Keio (1865–1867). Wood.

778. Nobuyuki 信行. Middle. Wood.

779. Nonoguchi Ryuho 野々口立圃. *Uji:* Nonoguchi 野々口. *Na:* Chikashige 親重. *Go:* Sho-o 松翁. Died on September 30, 1669, at the age of 75. Called himself Shozaemon 庄左衛門 of Beniya. Came from Hozu, Tanaba. Studied drawing with Tanyu. Developed an appreciation of Sotatsu, whose style influenced his work. Also studied haiku with Teitoku, waka with Mitsuhiro, and calligraphy with Prince Takatomo. Was proficient in carving and made netsuke. His designs and technique surpassed ordinary artistry. Also made Hina dolls, which he sold, thereby earning the popular name of Hinaya (doll maker).

780. Norikazu 則一. *Uji:* Katayama 片山. *Na:* Sennosuke 專之助. Late. Was a pupil of Masaka (B 592). Lived in Kyoto. Was a carver of rosary beads (juzu). Carved netsuke in his spare time.

781. Norishige 則重. Tempo (1830–1843), but in the opinion of Kyuichi Takeuchi he worked from Anei through Temmei (1772–1788). Wood and ivory. His designs are unusual and in fine taste. Came from Edo.

–O–

782. Ogasawara Issai 小笠原一齋. See Issai (B 352).

783. Okakoto 岡言. Tempo (1830–1843). Came from Kyoto. Was a pupil of Okatomo (B 784). Excelled at carving animals. There is a netsuke of Okakoto signed: "80 years old."

784. Okatomo 岡友. *Uji:* Yamaguchi 山口. *Chomei:* Okatomo 岡友. Before Temmei (1781–1788). Lived in Higashiyama, Kyoto. Carved netsuke of flowers and of small living things. Excelled at carving monkeys and quail on millet. His designs and technique are excellent. Preferred ivory and Japanese oak (isu) as his material. See Fig. 206. See mosha (No. 115).

785. Okatori 岡隹. *Chomei:* Okatori 岡隹. Temmei through Kansei (1781–1800). Born in Kyoto. Was a younger brother of Okatomo (B 784). Studied carving with Okatomo. Carved in ivory. Was good at carving animals. See mosha (No. 116).

786. Okinatei 翁亭. Middle. Ivory.

787. Osai 翁齋. May be the same artist as Okinatei (B 786).

788. Otoman 音滿. *Chomei:* Otoman 音滿. Middle. Came from Hakata, Kyushu. Ivory and wood. Was a dealer in obi but at last secured fame as a carver. Excelled at carving tigers. See Figs. 190 and 218.

789. Oto-o 音雄. Early. Some of his animal netsuke are in existence.

– R –

790. Raku 樂. Early. Ivory.

791. Raku 樂. Member of a family of ceramists named Raku. As his hobby, made netsuke in Rakuyaki (hand-molded earthenware).

792. Rakueisai 樂永齋. Late. Ivory.

793. Rakuhyo Rojin 樂8老人. *Chomei:* Rakuhyo Rojin. Keio (1865–1867). Wood.

794. Rakumin 樂民. *Go:* Ichiyosai 弌葉齋. Ansei (1854–1859). See Fig. 204.

795. Rakumin 樂眠. *Go:* Jitokusai 自得齋. Koka (1844–1847). Came from Tsuchiura. Granted title of hogan.

796. Rakuosai 樂王齋. *Chomei:* Rakuosai 樂王齋. Kyowa through Bunsei (1801–1829). Ivory and wood. Carved netsuke of figures, animals, and other subjects.

797. Rakushiken 樂只軒. See Gyuka I (B 167).

798. Rakushiken 樂之軒. See Kyusen (B 578).

(Rakuyeisai: see Rakueisai.)

799. Rakuyu 樂雄. Late.

800. Rakuzan 樂山. Carved Uji dolls. Occasionally used camellia wood.

801. Rammei 蘭明. Early middle. Ivory.

802. Rangyoku 蘭玉. Early. Ivory.

803. Ran-ichi 蘭一. *Chomei:* Ran-ichi 蘭一. Kansei (1789–1800). Ivory. Made excellent animal netsuke. Was a pupil of Rantei (B 812).

804. Ranju 蘭重. Middle. Ivory.

805. Ranko 蘭光. Early middle. Ivory.

806. Ranrinsai 蘭輪齋. See Shuzan (B 1094).

807. Ranseki 蘭石. Early middle. Ivory.

808. Ransen 蘭川. *Chomei:* Ransen 蘭川. Middle. Ivory. Was a pupil of Rantei (B 812). Mainly carved animal netsuke. See mosha (No. 117).

809. Ranshi 蘭之. Middle. Mainly ivory.

810. Ranshu 蘭秀. *Chomei:* Ranshu 蘭秀. Tempo through Keio (1830–1867). Wood and ivory.

811. Ransui 蘭水. Early late. Ivory.

812. Rantei 蘭亭. *Uji:* Nagai 長井. *Chomei:* Rantei 蘭亭. Kansei (1789–1800). Came from Izumo Province but lived in Kyoto. Mainly ivory. Was an openhearted character. Regarded as an expert carver. His work reached perfection. Carved netsuke of animals, flowers, birds, landscapes, and other subjects, but was best at figure carving. At the request of Prince Ninnaji, made a nut carving of 1,000 monkeys so tiny that the individual monkeys could not be seen with the unaided eye. Was at last awarded the title of hokyo. See Figs. 102 and 104. See mosha (No. 118).

813. Reigyoku 嶺玉. *Uji:* Tanaka 田中. *Go:* Hoshinsai 寶眞齋. Late. Ivory. Lived in Nippori, Tokyo.

814. Rekisai レキサイ. Middle. There are netsuke that bear his signature.

815. Rekizan 歷山. *Uji:* Yoda 譽田. *Na:* Jimbei 仁兵衛. *Yomyo:* Senkichi 仙吉. *Go:* Rekizan 歷山. *Go:* Kingendo 金鉉堂. Died on November 7, 1908, at the age of 69. Liked painting from childhood and was good at it. Also composed excellent waka, using the name of Shigeki. Loved carving more than anything else. Mainly carved small pots and netsuke. His family was in the tool business, and he had only his spare time for painting, poetry, and carving as his hobbies.

蓮
哉

京
刀

119. RENSAI　　　　　　　　　　120. RYO

816. Ren 蓮. See Rensai (B 818).

817. Rendo 蓮堂. *Uji:* Kurauchi 倉内. Late. Came from Shizuoka but removed to Asakusa, Tokyo.

818. Rensai 蓮齋. *Uji:* Ishikawa 石川. *Chomei:* Rensai 蓮齋. Renounced the headship of his family in 1876. Wood, ivory, and horn. See Fig. 78. See mosha (No. 119).

819. Rensai 蓮齋. *Uji:* Ishikawa 石川. *Na:* Kakujiro 角次郎. Was a son of Rensai (B 818). Lived in Asakusa, Tokyo.

820. Rikan 利寛. *Go:* Miwa 三輪. Early. Wood.

821. Rikyo 梨喬. Late. Wood.

822. Rimu 梨夢. Middle.

823. Rinji 輪次. Early.

824. Risui 里水. Early. Wood.

825. Rito 籬桃. See Tomiharu (B 1191).

826. Ritsuo 笠翁. *Go:* Ogawa Haritsu 小川破笠, Kanshi 觀子, Naoyuki 尚行, and others. *Chomei:* Haritsu makie 破笠蒔繪 or kan-in on an inlaid ceramic plaque. Early. Was a famous carver and gold lacquer artist. Excelled at ceramic inlays.

(Riusai: see Ryusai.)

827. Riyo 李楊. Middle.

828. Rosetsu 蘆雪. Middle. Wood.

829. Roshu 蘆舟. Middle. Lived in Asakusa, Tokyo. Called himself Seiryu-un 星龍雲. Excelled at carving tsuishu lacquer.

830. Ryo 凉. *Uji:* Kawahara 河原. *Chomei:* Ryo to 凉刀. Late. Mainly ivory. Came from Tokyo. Was an excellent carver. See Fig. 192. See mosha (No. 120).

831. Ryogyoku 亮玉. Middle. Wood.

832. Ryo-ichi 亮一. Middle. Wood.

833. Ryo-ichi 良一. Middle. Wood.

834. Ryoji 凌次. *Uji:* Ono 小埜. Middle. Wood, ivory, and horn.

835. Ryoko 凌光. Late. Ivory.

836. Ryoko 凌廣. Middle. Ivory.

837. Ryomin 陵民. *Uji:* Ono 小野. Late. Ivory. See Figs. 18 and 213.

838. Ryomin 凌珉. Late. See Fig. 208.

839. Ryomin 寮民. Middle. Ivory.

840. Ryosai 良齋. Middle. Ivory.

841. Ryoun 凌雲. Late. Ivory.

842. Ryozan 良山. *Uji:* Matsumoto 松本. *Na:* Kimbei 金兵衛. Ansei (1854–1859) through early Meiji (1868–1911). Lived in Kanda, Tokyo. Was a carver of Buddhist images. Ryozan habitually attended at the ceremonials and exhibits of the Narita Temple in order to view the famous statue of Fudo-myo-o (God of Fire). Carved images of Fudo-myo-o all his life. Was therefore often called Fudo Kimbei. Granted the title of hokyo.

843. Ryuchin or **Ryuchinsai** 龍珍 or 龍珍齋. *Go:* Gyokuhosai 玉寶齋. Keio through Meiji (1865–1911). Full name was Yamada Bunjiro 山田文次郎 though there is another opinion that his name was Ganjiro 元治郎. Was the pupil of Ryukei (B 852) and the teacher of Kogyoku (B 513).

844. Ryuchokusai 龍直齋. See Masahiro (B 589).

845. Ryuei 龍榮. Late. Ivory.

846. Ryugyoku 龍玉. Kansei through Bunsei (1789–1829). Carved netsuke of figures, subjects indicating thunder and lightning, masks, and other subjects.

847. Ryugyokusai 柳玉齋. Late.

848. Ryuheisai 隆平齋. *Uji:* Asada 淺田. Late. Ivory and tsuishu. Lived in Kyoto.

849. Ryuho 立法. Late. Wood.

850. Ryuho 立圃. See Nonoguchi Ryuho (B 779).

851. Ryuho 柳甫. Some netsuke bearing his signature are in existence.

852. Ryukei 龍珪. *Chomei:* Ryukei 龍珪. Koka through Keio (1844–1867). Came from Kyoto but later moved to Tokyo. Learned ivory carving from Hokei (B 245) and decided to become a professional netsuke carver. Used the *go* of Shinshisai 神子齋, but some people incorrectly say Shinryosai 神了齋. Studied the tinting of ivory, which he adapted for netsuke carving. Made both small and large netsuke. His designs are unusual, and his carving is sharp. Taught many pupils. Awarded the title of hokyo.

853. Ryukei 龍珪. Lived in Edo. Gold-lacquered his wood carvings.

854. Ryukei 隆桂. Late. Wood.

855. Ryukei 龍桂. Late. Some netsuke are found that bear his signature.

856. Ryukoku 龍谷. Late. Ivory.

857. Ryukoku 流谷. *Uji:* Kikugawa 菊川. Middle. Mainly horn. Carved figure netsuke.

858. Ryukosai 龍光齋. Middle. Ivory.

859. Ryukosai 龍光齋. See Jugyoku (B 408).

860. Ryukosai 龍光齋. *Uji:* Sasa 佐正. Middle. See Fig. 200.

861. Ryumin 龍珉. *Uji:* Ono 小野. *Na:* Mataemon 又右衛門. Late. Was a pupil of Rakumin (B 794). There is some opinion that he is the same man as Ryumin (B 863). See Fig. 15.

862. Ryumin 龍民. See Ryumin (B 861).

863. Ryumin 龍眠. *Uji:* Kimura 木村. *Na:* Kinroku 金六. Was a pupil of Ryukei (B 852). Also did metal carving. There is some opinion that he is the same man as Ryumin (B 861).

864. Ryumin 龍岷. Middle. Made netsuke of figures, masks and other subjects. See Fig. 94.

865. Ryumin 隆民. Late.

866. Ryumin 立民. *Chomei:* Ryumin kao 立民花押. Late. Tokyo. Metal artist. Made kagamibuta netsuke. See mosha (No. 121).

867. Ryuo 龍王. Early middle.

868. Ryuosai 龍王齋. Middle.

869. Ryuraku 龍樂. *Chomei:* Ryuraku 龍樂. Early. Carved small mask netsuke and other subjects. See mosha (No. 122).

870. Ryusa 龍左. Before Temmei (1781–1788). Lived in Edo. Was a lathe worker. Produced netsuke that could be used as ash trays.

871. Ryusa 龍佐. *Go:* Gyokugasai 玉賀齋. Middle. There is a netsuke of his signed: "71 years old."

872. Ryusai 笠齋. Middle. Wood. Masks.

873. Ryusai 龍齋. Early.

874. Ryusai 龍齋. *Uji:* Otsuki 大月. *Na:* Mitsuoki 光興. *Chomei:* Ryusai 龍齋. Kyowa (1801–1803). Was a metal artist. Visited Edo but later returned to Kyoto. Was an excellent painter and was considered an expert in decorating poem cards (tanzaku). Had many pupils. Carved superb boxwood netsuke as a hobby.

875. Ryusai 立齋. *Uji:* Sano 佐野. *Na:* Tokuemon 德右衛門. Died in early Meiji (1868–1911) when still young. Carved ivory, wood, horn, and bamboo. At one time studied under Hosai Oishi (B 270) but later resorted to copying masterpieces and made great technical progress. Excelled in relief carving. Had a graceful and distinctive style.

876. Ryusei 龍生. Early. Wood.

877. Ryusen 立川. Early. Wood.

878. Ryusen 龍仙. *Uji:* Horiuchi 堀内. Died in early Meiji (1868–1911). Was the teacher of Kyuichi Takeuchi (B 575).

879. Ryushatei 龍車亭. Carved figure netsuke. Came from Tamba but lived in Edo and Kyoto.

880. Ryushinshi 柳心子. Early. Metal artist.

881. Ryusho 柳處. Some netsuke bearing his signature are found.

882. Ryusho 龍昇. Middle. Ivory.

883. Ryu-un 龍雲. See Roshu (B 829).

884. Ryuzan 龍山. Late. Ivory.

–S–

885. Sada-aki 貞明. Late. Wood.

886. Sadakazu 定一. *Chomei:* Sadakazu 定一. Keio (1865–1867). Painted his carvings.

887. Sadanaga 定長. Early.

888. Sadatoshi 貞利. *Chomei:* Sadatoshi 貞利. Tempo (1830–1843). Mostly wood.

889. Sadatsugu 定次. Early. Ivory.

890. Sadayoshi 定由. Early middle. Wood and ivory.

891. Saigyoku 齋玉. *Chomei:* Saigyoku 齋玉. Tempo (1830–1843). Mainly wood.

892. Saishi 才之. Early. Wood.

893. Sako 左光. Early. Ivory.

894. Sancho 山鳥. Early. Wood.

895. Sandai 三代. Early.

896. Saneo 眞雄. Late.

897. Sangetsu 盞月. Early. Wood. Carved large-size netsuke.

898. Sangoku 三國. *Go:* Sessai 雪齋. Middle. Wood.

899. Sanko 三小. Before Temmei (1781–1788). Lived in Osaka. Was an excellent carver. Called himself Kohei.

900. Sanko 三光. *Chomei:* Sanko 三光. Anei through Temmei (1772–1788). Carved figure netsuke. Was particularly good at portraying Benkei.

901. Sanraku 山樂. Early and middle. Wood and ivory.

902. Sansha 三車. Early.

903. Sansho 三笑. *Uji:* Wada 和田. *Go:* Kokeisai 虎溪齋. *Chomei:* Sansho 三笑 or Kokeisai Sansho 虎溪齋三笑. Born on November 6,

1871, in Minami-ku, Osaka. Original given name was Genjiro 源治郎, which he later changed to Yataro 彌太郎. Was a pupil of Dosho (B 89). Carved in wood and ivory and also did Shibayama-style mosaic. Died on July 20, 1936. See Fig. 105. See mosha (No. 123).

904. Sansui 山水. Late. Ivory.

905. Sari 左里. *Chomei:* Sari 左里. Temmei and Kansei (1781–1800). Wood. Excelled at carving toads and molluscs but also carved other animals and shells.

906. Seibei 清兵衛. Before Temmei (1781–1788). Lived in Kyoto. Did excellent wood carving. His work was referred to as Seibei carvings. Since his work was famous, there were many forgeries.

907. Seiboku 正卜. *Chomei:* Seiboku 正卜. Middle. There are fox netsuke in wood bearing his signature.

908. Seifushun 清富春. See Tomiharu (B 1191).

909. Seiga 清我. Middle. Wood.

910. Seigyoku 晴玉. Late. Some of his netsuke of children are in existence.

911. Seigyoku 清玉. Late. Wood.

912. Seigyu 青牛. *Uji:* Sagano 相野. Late. Lived in Osaka. Carved mask netsuke but rarely signed them.

913. Sei-ichi 清一. Middle. Ivory.

914. Seiju 成壽. Some netsuke that bear his signature are found.

915. Seikei 正慶. *Uji:* Kojima 小島. *Na:* Kuwajiro 鍬二郎. *Chomei:* Seikei 正慶. Born about 1877. Came from Nagoya. Learned carving as a pupil of Masakazu (B 596) and Masaka (B 592). See mosha (No. 124).

916. Seiko 青江. Early.

917. Seiko 静虎. *Uji:* Matsu-ura 松浦. Late. Mainly ivory. Came from Osaka. Was a pupil of Naomitsu Murata (B 751).

918. Seiko 正光. See Kikugawa (B 484).

919. Seiku 晴空. Late.

920. Seikyo 清虚. Some netsuke are found that bear his signature.

921. Seimin 清民. Middle. Ivory.

922. Seimin 政民. Late. Ivory.

923. Seimin 静民. *Uji:* Okawa 大川. *Na:* Mankichi 萬吉. *Go:* Ikkosai 一固齋. Middle. Lived in Honjo, Tokyo. Was a pupil of Rakumin (B 794).

924. Seimin 晴民. *Chomei:* Seimin 晴民. *Azana:* Kaeru Seimin 蛙晴民. Early Meiji (1868–1911). Ivory. Lived at Yotsuya, Tokyo. Especially good at carving red frogs, which is the reason that he was nicknamed Kaeru (frog) Seimin. (Some people write his name 晴珉.)

925. Seimin 晴民. *Go:* Chounsai 長雲齋. Tempo through Keio (1830–1867). Was a good carver.

926. Seimin 晴珉. Same as Seimin (B 925).

927. Seisei 青々. See Mingyoku (B 658).

928. Seisetsu 正接. See Chogetsu (B 51).

929. Seishi 静之. Middle. Ivory.

930. Seishichi 清七. *Uji:* Myogaya 茗荷屋. Before Temmei (1781–1788). Lived near the Nishihongan-ji in Osaka. Was a frieze carver. Also carved netsuke. Liked to do elaborate carving but also did simple carvings which were excellent.

931. Seishinsai 青岑齋. *Go:* Ikkei 一溪. *Chomei:* Seishinsai Ikkei 青岑齋一溪. Early. Wooden netsuke of hermits that bear his signature are found.

932. Seishu 正州. *Chomei:* Seishu 正州. Tempo (1830–1843). Mainly wood.

933. Seisui 清水. Early. Wood. Figure netsuke.

934. Seiun 清雲. Middle.

935. Seiyodo 青陽堂. Tomiharu (B 1191) was the first of this line. There were three generations of the Seiyodo family. Some pupils also adopted the name of Seiyodo.

936. Seizan 晴山. Late. Ivory.

937. Seizan 静山. Late. Ivory.

938. Seizui 政隨. *Uji:* Hamano 濱野. *Chomei:* Seizui 政隨. Died on October 26, 1769, at the age of 74. Was a metal artist, a pupil of Toshihisa Nara 利壽. Developed a new and refreshing carving style incorporating powerful use of engraving tools. In turn, various branches stemmed from Seizui's style. Also carved netsuke in wood as a hobby. His designs are original, and the carving indicates a thorough training and refinement.

939. Sekiho 石峯. *Go:* Yukodo 幽篁堂. Tempo (1830–1843). Mainly ivory. Lived in Honjo, Tokyo. Was good at carving in the round and at perforated or openwork carving.

940. Sekiho 石峯. *Chomei:* Sekiho in 石峯印. Was a pupil of Sekisen

125. SEKISAI

126. SENTSU

(B 947). Studied the ancient masks at Nara. Made pottery mask netsuke in Onko ware.

941. Sekiju 石壽. Early.

942. Sekio 石翁. Early.

943. Sekio 石應. Some netsuke bearing his signature are found.

944. Sekiran 石蘭. Middle. Ivory.

945. Sekiran 石欒. Died in early Meiji (1868–1911). Came from Minato, Mito. Carved shrines and netsuke. The statue of Inari, the god of the rice harvest, owned by Monzaburo Kasama in Hitachi, is his work.

946. Sekisai 石齋. *Mei:* Sekisai 石齋. Late. Made Rakuyaki (earthenware) netsuke. See mosha (No. 125).

947. Sekisen 石仙. *Chomei:* Sekisen *in* 石仙印. Engaged in the production of Onko ware at Akasaka, Mino. Also made porcelain mask netsuke.

948. Sekishu 石舟. Early middle.

949. Sekka 雪阿. *Uji:* Shima 島. Meiji (1868–1911). Was a son of Sessai (B 955). Came from Echizen. Was a carpenter. So captivated by the sight of some carvings of Masakazu (B 596) in 1888 or 1889 that he immediately entered the school of Masakazu, where he studied until the death of his teacher. Carved a figure okimono which was exhibited at Chicago. Died shortly thereafter in Osaka. His work is rarely found but is excellent.

950. Sen-ichi 專一. Middle. Ivory.

951. Sento 船橙. *Uji:* Yoshioka 吉岡. *Na:* Kosaburo 小三郎. Middle.

952. Sentsu 仙通. *Chomei:* Sentsu 仙通. Bunsei (1818–1829). Wood. See mosha (No. 126).

953. Senzo 專藏. See Senzo (B 954).

954. Senzo 仙藏. Anei (1772–1780). Named Onogi Senzo 大野木專藏. Was a farmer at Shibayama, Shimofusa-no-kuni. During Anei he developed the mosaic technique of inlaying shells and pearl. Later added coral, ivory, and other materials in addition to shells and pearl. The technique he created is now widely known as Shibayama-bori (Shibayama carving). Senzo moved to Edo and changed his name to Shibayama Senzo 芝山仙藏. See Fig. 69.

955. Sessai 雪齋. *Uji:* Shima 島. *Chomei:* Sessai 雪齋 or Hokyo Sessai 法橋雪齋. Died in 1879 or 1880 at the age of 59. Came from Mikuni,

雪
斎

127. SESSAI

Echizen. Served the lord of the Echizen clan. Granted title of hokyo. An excellent carver who excelled in carving snakes. See mosha (No. 127).

956. Sessai 雪齋. See Sangoku (B 898).

957. Setsu 雪. May be an abbreviated name or the name of a female carver. The true facts are uncertain.

958. Setsuju 雪壽. Early. Wood.

959. Setsutei 雪亭. *Uji:* Sasaki 佐々木. Late. Was a pupil of Sessai (B 955).

960. Setsutei 雪亭. *Uji:* Nakanishi 中西. *Go:* Rokko 六甲. Carved in ivory for export. Was a pupil of Sekka Shima (B 949). Lived in Nakayama but later moved to Ashiya. Was a teacher of the Ohara school of flower arrangement.

961. Shibayama 芝山. The name Shibayama developed into a generic term applied to the technique of encrusting a carving with various materials in a mosaic pattern. The technique was developed by Senzo Shibayama (B 954). Nevertheless, the word is still used as though it were a family name. See Fig. 69.

962. Shigechika 重親. *Chomei:*

Shigechika 重親. Tempo through Keio (1830–1867). Mainly wood. Carved animal netsuke.

963. Shigehide 重秀. Early. Wood. Figure netsuke.

964. Shigehiro 重廣. Late. Ivory. Figure netsuke.

965. Shigekado 重門. Middle. Wood. Animal netsuke.

966. Shigekatsu 重勝. Early middle. Carved netsuke in wood representing long-nosed tengu (demons).

967. Shigekazu 茂一. Some netsuke that bear his signature are found.

968. Shigemasa 重正. Kyowa through Bunsei (1801–1829). Wood and ivory. Carved netsuke of figures, animals, and other subjects. Excelled at carving snails. See Fig. 195.

969. Shigemitsu 重光. *Mei:* Deme 出目. Early middle. Carved mask netsuke. Signed the mei of Deme 出目.

970. Shigenaga 重永. Early.

971. Shigeru 茂. Some netsuke bearing his signature are found. May be an abbreviated mei.

972. Shigetsugu 重次. Middle. Ivory.

128. SHOGEN

129. SHOHOSAI

973. Shigeyoshi 重義. Early middle. Wood.

974. Shigeyuki 重幸. *Uji:* Saito 齋藤. *Na:* Kintaro 金太郎. Late. Lived at Shitaya, Tokyo. Was a pupil of Harushige (B 196). Good at carving flowers and insects.

975. Shigyoku 芝玉. Middle. Some netsuke that bear his signature are in existence.

976. Shikotsu 子骨. There are some netsuke that bear his signature.

977. Shin-ichi 眞一. Middle. Wood.

978. Shinke'sai 眞敬齋. *Chomei:* Shinkeisai 眞敬齋. Tempo through Keio (1830–1867). Wood and ivory. Usually carved figure netsuke.

979. Shinsai 眞齋. Middle. Ivory.

980. Shinsai 眞哉. Late. Wood.

981. Shinshisai 神子齋. *Chomei:* Shinshisai 神子齋. See Ryukei (B 852).

982. Shitoku 子得. *Chomei:* Shitoku 子得. Middle. Carved some boxwood netsuke of lotus leaves and turtles.

983. Shitsu-ichi 叱一. Some netsuke are found that bear this signature.

984. Shiyu 士友. Late. Carved some figure netsuke.

985. Sho 昇. Some netsuke bearing his signature are in existence. May be an abbreviated mei.

986. Shogen 正玄. *Chomei:* Shogen yaki-in 正玄燒印. Was a bamboo craftsman of Kyoto. His family held one of the seven positions in the Senke school of the tea ceremony for several generations. Mainly carved tea-ceremony articles but also bamboo netsuke. See mosha (No. 128).

987. Shogetsu 勝月. Middle. Ivory. Carved oni netsuke.

988. Shogetsu 松月. *Chomei:* Shogetsu 松月. Bunsei through Tempo (1818–1843). Staghorn animal netsuke. See Fig. 52.

989. Shogyoku 正玉. *Chomei:* Shogyoku 正玉. Kansei (1789–1800). Ivory. Figures and oni.

990. Shohosai 正鳳齋. *Chomei:* Shohosai 正鳳齋. Late. Ivory. See mosha (No. 129).

991. Shojosai 猩々齋. See Shuraku (B 1077).

992. Shoju 松樹. Middle. Nuts. Carved Daruma netsuke.

993. Shoju I 松壽初代. *Uji:* Okano 岡野. *Na:* Heiuemon 平右衛

松
壽

門. Died on August 10, 1708. Lived in Nara. Carved objects from cypress of Iyasuga.

994. Shoju II 松壽二代. Succeeded Heiuemon Okano (B 993). Died on October 2, 1734.

995. Shoju III 松壽三代. Succeeded to the name as the third generation. Was an excellent carver. Died on October 9, 1738.

996. Shoju IV 松壽四代. Succeeded to the name. Date of his death is uncertain.

997. Shoju V 松壽五代. Succeeded to the name. His wife, Juteini, was an excellent carver and carried on the family profession for her husband. Died on November 14, 1760.

998. Shoju VI 松壽六代. Succeeded to the name. His true na was Manzoku. Died on October 3, 1769.

999. Shoju VII 松壽七代. Succeeded to the name. Was a younger brother of Manzoku (B 998). Died on October 25, 1779.

1000. Shoju VIII 松壽八代. Succeeded to the name. Although he became Shoju VIII, his true uji was Yamada. Died on November 10, 1797.

1001. Shoju IX 松壽九代. *Chomei:* Shoju 松壽. Full name was Okano Heizaburo 岡野平三郎, but true na was Hohaku. Was a younger brother of Shoju VIII (B 1000). Made improvements in the carving of Nara dolls. In addition carved incense boxes in the design of deer. Died on September 10, 1824, at the age of 71. See mosha (No. 130).

1002. Shoju X 松壽十代. *Chomei:* Hokyu 保久. Full name was Okano Mampei 岡野萬平, but true na was Hokyu. Became an adopted child of Hohaku (Shoju IX) and excelled among the members of the Okano family in carving. Died on December 28, 1825, at the age of 58. It is written somewhere that Hokyu carved the word "shame" on his works but the author of this statement must have confused his work with the work of Toen (B 1177).

1003. Shoju XI. 松壽十一代 Full name was Okano Mampei but true na was Tsunenori. Was the first son of Hokyu (Shoju X). Remained single all his life. Died on October 5, 1843, at the age of 42.

1004. Shoju XII 松壽十二代. Full name was Okano Mampei but

true na was Koretaka. Was the last child of Hokyu (Shoju X). Died on August 22, 1884, at the age of 61.

1005. Shoju XIII 松壽十三代. Full name was Okano Heizaburo but true na was Hotoku. Was first son of Koretaka (Shoju XII). Used another *go* of Kotei 皓亭.

1006. Shokasai 松可齋. Middle. Wood, horn, and ivory. Animal netsuke.

1007. Shokasai 松可齋. See Minkoku (B 669).

1008. Shokin 松琴. Late. Wood.

1009. Shoko 昇己. *Uji:* Nishino 西野. *Na:* Shotaro 昇太郎. *Chomei:* Shoko 昇己. Born in 1915 at Senju, Tokyo. Named Nishino Shotaro. In 1930, entered the school of Soko Morita (B 1101), becoming his star pupil. Developed in the style of his master. Became independent in May, 1943, and is engaged in carving in Tokyo. See mosha (No. 131).

1010. Shoko 尚古. Middle. Some netsuke bearing his signature are in existence. See Figs. 81 and 199.

1011. Shokosai 尚古齋. See Houn (B 286).

1012. Shokosai II 尚古齋. *Uji:* Hayakawa 早川. *Chomei:* Shokosai tsukuru 尚古齋造. Lived in Minami-ku, Osaka. Pre-eminent in fashioning bamboo baskets. Also made bamboo netsuke. At present Shokosai IV is succeeding him. See mosha (No. 132).

1013. Shokyusai 正久齋. *Chomei:* Shokyusai 正久齋. Kyowa through Bunsei (1801–1829). Ivory. Figures, birds, and animals.

1014. Shomin 升民. Born in 1841. Lived in Yuraku-cho, Tokyo. Was a son of Shounsai (B 1032).

1015. Shomin 勝民. *Go:* Hokyusai 鳳久齋. Some netsuke bearing his signature are in existence.

1016. Shomin 勝珉. Late. A famous metal artist. See Fig. 1.

1017. Shominsai 松民齋. See Chikamasa (B 30).

1018. Shominsai 松眠齋. See Chikamasa (B 30).

1019. Sho-o 松翁. See Ryuho Nonoguchi (B 779).

1020. Shoraku 正樂. Early middle. Ivory.

1021. Shoraku 笑樂. Late. Ivory.

1022. Shorinsai 松隣齋. Middle. Ivory.

1023. Shoryusai 證龍齋. See Masachika (B 584).

1024. Shosai 笑齋. *Uji:* Tsuda 津田. *Chomei:* Shosai *to* 笑齋刀. Born on August 25, 1878, in Osaka. Lived in Tsurumachi, Osaka. Learned carving from Naomitsu (B 751). Mainly carved netsuke. Usually used ivory. Excelled at carving skulls and prawns. His pupils, among whom were Hatanaka Shoroku 畑中笑六 and Nishida Shoju 西田笑壽, rendered great assistance to Shosai, for which they were commended by the Osaka Prefectural Government. It is said that after the death of Shosai in 1928 at the age of 50, his pupil Shoroku moved close to his master's house in order to assist his widow. See mosha (No. 133).

1025. Shoseki 蕉石. Late. Wood.

1026. Shoso 正祖. Middle. Wood.

1027. Shoto 松濤. Tempo (1830–1843). Carved many netsuke of kappa (water imps). His technique was highly unconventional and unusual.

1028. Shoun 松雲. *Uji:* Yamamoto 山本. *Na:* Takejiro 武次郎. *Go:* Hokunsai 報君齋 or Shoun 松雲. *Chomei:* Shoun 松雲 or kakihan based on Shoun. Born on January 23, 1913, at Shimofukagusa, Kyoto. His father was a gardener. At 16 years of age became a pupil of Komin Tsuji—a man from Uji, although there are no netsuke that bear his mei—with whom he studied for about one year. Later studied carving for about one year with Ryuheisai Asada (B 848), a man who lived in Kyoto and carved netsuke in ivory or tsuishu. Was drafted for the war between Japan and China. Returned to Kyoto on the termination of his enlistment. Carved in ivory. In 1940 began to carve in wood also and changed his *go* to Shoun. Strove to attain the perfection of Kaigyokusai (B 430). Carved netsuke, okimono, and other objects. See mosha (No. 134).

1029. Shoun 松雲 or **Shoundo** 松雲堂. See Hakuryu (B 181).

1030. Shoundo 正雲堂. Early. Wood.

1031. Shounsai 松雲齋. See Shoun (B 1028).

1032. Shounsai 升雲齋. *Uji:* Maeda 前田. Middle.

1033. Shoyusai 正友齋. Early.

1034. Shozan 正山. *Chomei:* Shozan 正山. Tempo through Keio (1830–1867). Wood. Carved netsuke of Jurojin, animals, and other objects. Some of his work is excellent. See mosha (No. 135).

136. SHU

137. SHUCHI

1035. Shozan 松山. Early. Some of his figure netsuke are in existence.

1036. Shu 會. *Uji:* Hirakata 平舘. *Na:* Shujiro 會次郎. *Chomei:* Shu 會 or Makie Shu 蒔絵會. Born in 1897 into the family of a Shinto priest in Kyoto. Presently is a priest of Sannomiya Shrine, Higashiyama, Kyoto, and a director of the Shinto Priests' Association in Kyoto. Graduated from the Lacquer Department of the Kyoto Arts and Crafts School. Subsequently became a pupil of Kimura Hideo 木村秀雄. Excelled at gold lacquering, in which he originated a new technique as a result of his experiments, for which he was honored by the Imperial Art Council. Has served as a professor at Kyoto Prefectural Arts and Crafts School since 1930. On numerous occasions he was elected as an examiner for the art exhibitions sponsored by Kyoto Prefecture and Kyoto City. In 1942, he was honored by the empress, who made a purchase of his work. Occasionally carv d netsuke as a hobby. Lacquered his netsuke to enhance their effect. See mosha (No. 136).

1037. Shuchi 舟知. *Chomei:* Shuchi 舟知. Temmei through Kansei

(1781–1800). Was a pupil of Shugetsu I (B 1042). Was a priest living in Sakai.

1038. Shuchi 秋冶. *Chomei:* Shuchi 秋冶. Early middle. Carved figure netsuke in wood. See mosha (No. 137).

1039. Shuetsu 周悦. Middle. Wood.

1040. Shuetsu 秀悦. Late. Some oni netsuke are found that bear his signature.

1041. Shugasai 集雅齋. Some netsuke bearing his signature are found.

1042. Shugetsu 舟月. *Uji:* Higuchi 樋口 or Hara 原. *Chomei:* kakihan based on Shugetsu. Meiwa (1764–1771). Lived in Shimanouchi, Osaka. Enjoyed painting, perfecting himself in the style of the Kano school and earning the title of hogan. Also skillfully carved netsuke of unusual elegance. His netsuke were held in high esteem by the public. Moved to Edo, where he opened a Hina doll shop in Jikkemmise and eventually became quite prosperous. Originally created Hina dolls in designs suggesting the Shishinden Hall (of the Imperial Palace) by the inclusion of mandarin orange trees and cherry trees. For the offense of portraying sacred objects he was made to face the magistrate and was thrown into jail. Later he was deported from Edo. He returned to Osaka and continued producing mask netsuke as he had done prior to his misadventure in creating Hina dolls. The mask of Ofuku was his forte. See Fig. 4.

1043. Shugetsu II 舟月. Shugetsu II was the son of a lumber dealer who lived alongside the Maruta River in Kanda, Tokyo. When he was 13 he saw his elder brother at the Kanda Festival in fine circumstances while he, as a younger brother, had to work as an apprentice eating cold rice and wearing straw sandals. Being discontent, he rebelled and quit his master's house. Idly wandered into Shugetsu's house in Jikkemmise, where he watched him carve, utterly fascinated. Under Shugetsu's urging, a master-apprentice contract was made, and he entered Shugetsu's school. Eagerly studied methods and made great progress. Shugetsu liked the boy and gave him his name as Shugetsu II. When Shugetsu II was about 17 or 18, his master was deported from Edo. Shugetsu II wanted to share his punishment, but the main family interfered. However, Shugetsu II accompanied his master to Osaka, and at parting assured him that he would welcome him back to Edo whenever he should be able to make arrangements for his return. When he was 23, Shugetsu II traveled to Osaka to keep his promise but sadly found his master deceased. He brought back to Edo his master's widow and nephews, Shiro and Goro. It is said that the widow died with her head on the knee-pillow of Shugetsu II on the occasion of the celebration of her 61st anniversary.

Shugetsu II used the *go* of Shizan on his paintings. Also made Hina dolls and helmeted dolls (kabuto ningyo), as well as festival carriages for dolls. Occasionally made netsuke which were of excellent quality. It is said that the Cock of Renko (a drum placed before government buildings, according to Chinese tradition, to summon officials to hear suggestions, complaints, or petitions) at Odemmacho and the Shoki at Kanda are examples of his work.

1044. Shugetsu III 舟月. Shugetsu III was born to a very poor family in Jikkemmise. Because his father died when he was barely 13, Shugetsu III lost the opportunity to study his father's craft. However,

舟
民

138. SHUMIN

when his father was close to death he called Shugetsu III to his bedside and carved animals of the zodiac as an example for his son to follow. In this way the son had some opportunity to follow in his father's path. Soon after, the father died in his sleep. It is said that his sister devoted herself to the development and success of Shugetsu III until she was some 60 years old and never married.

1045. Shugetsu IV 舟月. Meiji (1868–1911). Shugetsu IV was named Hara Kingoro 原金五郎. Learned carving from his father. Carved Hina dolls, netsuke, and other objects. Beginning in Meiji 5, carved mostly okimono in ivory and in Chinese woods for export. It is said that Kyuichi Takeuchi (B 575) taught him the techniques.

1046. Shugo 舟吾. Middle. Was a pupil of Shugetsu (B 1042).

1047. Shugyoku 秀玉 or Shugyokusai 秀玉齋. Early middle. Ivory.

1048. Shugyokusai 集玉齋. Middle. Ivory.

1049. Shu-ichi 秀一. See Hidekazu (B 209).

1050. Shu-ichi 舟一. Carved mask netsuke. Most likely was a pupil of Shugetsu (B 1042).

1051. Shuji 舟司. Early middle. Wood.

1052. Shuji 舟二. Late. Carved wooden netsuke decorated with ivory.

1053. Shuko 周光. Late. Wood.

1054. Shuko 秀興. Some netsuke bearing his signature are in existence.

1055. Shuko 周江. Middle. Carved netsuke in painted wood.

1056. Shukoku 舟谷. Late. Wood.

1057. Shukosai 周公齋. Early. Wood.

1058. Shumemaru 院幣丸. Before Temmei (1781–1788). Lived in Kanijima, Osaka. Called himself Unjudo 雲樹洞. Was a Shintoist. Carved netsuke only when specially requested. Therefore few of his carvings are found. Did mostly rough, simple carvings but occasionally colored his netsuke. See Fig. 59.

1059. Shumin 舟民. *Uji:* Hara 原. Kansei (1789–1800). Wooden masks and figures. Was a pupil of Shuzan (B 1090) or Shugetsu II (B 1043). In most cases he sheathed the himotoshi in ivory. See mosha (No. 138).

1060. Shumin 舟珉. *Na:* Masa 政.

Chomei: Shumin 舟珉. Died about 1875. Mostly wood. Was a pupil of Shugetsu III (B 1044). Carved figures, birds, animals, and other subjects.

1061. Shumin 秀珉. Early. Wood.

1062. Shumin 秀民. Middle. Was a metal artist. Some netsuke bearing his signature are found.

1063. Shumpo 春浦. *Go:* Haku-zan 白山. *Chomei:* Shumpo 春浦. Died in late Taisho (1912–1925). Came from Sakai. Dealt in plasters and ointments. Carved netsuke in bamboo in his spare time. See mo-sha (No. 139).

1064. Shunchikudo 春竹堂. See Joshu (B 399).

1065. Shunchosai 春長齋. Middle. Wood.

1066. Shungetsu 春月. *Uji:* U-zawa 鵜澤. *Na:* Koryusai 江柳齋. *Chomei:* Shungetsu 春月. Born in Tempo (1830–1843). Middle and late. Lived in Shitaya. Was a pupil of Chogetsu Yamada (B 51). Was the teacher of Inoue Kikutaro 井上菊太郎, Kawakami Teijiro 川上貞次郎, and others. Carved netsuke and okimono for export after the opening of our ports for trade.

1067. Shungyoku 春玉. Late. Specialized in shell inlay on wood carvings.

1068. Shunkosai 春光齋. *Chomei:* Shunkosai 春光齋. Temmei and Kansei (1781–1800). Mostly wood. Carved netsuke of figures and animals.

1069. Shunkosai 春江齋. See Chogetsu (B 51).

1070. Shunsai 春齋. Early middle. Called himself Chikuyuken 竹友軒.

1071. Shunzan 春山. *Uji:* Tanaka 田中. *Na:* Katsutaro 勝太郎. Late. Came from Osaka.

1072. Shunzan 春山. Early middle. Wood.

1073. Shuo 秀翁 or **Shuosai** 秀翁齋. Middle. Ivory. See Figs. 203 and 205.

1074. Shuraku 秀樂. See Shuraku (B 1077).

1075. Shuraku 秀樂. Middle. Was a metal artist. Made the metal plaques for kagamibuta netsuke.

1076. Shuraku 周樂. Some netsuke bearing his signature are in existence.

1077. Shuraku 州樂. *Uji:* Kawa-moto 川本. *Na:* Tetsujiro 鐵次郎. *Go:* Shojosai 猩々齋. Early Meiji

SHUGETSU IV—SHURAKU · **289**

舟
山

(1868–1911). Wrote his mei (Shuraku) variously 洲良久 or 舟樂 or 秀樂. Entered the school of Hara Shugetsu III (B 1044) and after ten years of apprenticeship became independent. Excelled in wood carving but, following the example of Asahi Gyokuzan (B 164), began to work in ivory. Carved netsuke and okimono. Kyuichi Takeuchi (B 575) was also a graduate of the school of Hara Shugetsu III.

1078. Shuraku 舟樂. Early.

1079. Shuraku 舟樂. See Shuraku (B 1077).

1080. Shurakusai 秀樂齋. Middle. Wood.

1081. Shuryo 周良. Middle. Ivory.

1082. Shusai 周齋. Late. Wood.

1083. Shusai 秀齋. Late. Wood.

1084. Shusai 州齋. See Kyuichi (B 575).

1085. Shusen 舟仙. Early Middle.

1086. Shusen 周川. Middle. Wood.

1087. Shu-un 秋雲. Middle. Wood.

1088. Shu-unsai 舟雲齋. Late.

(Shuyetsu: see Shuetsu.)

1089. Shuyo 秀予. Early. Wood.

1090. Shuzan 舟山. *Chomei:* Shuzan 舟山. Early. Was good at carving mask netsuke of Okame in wood. Judging from his style he was probably a pupil of Shugetsu (B 1042). See mosha (No. 140).

1091. Shuzan 秋山. *Chomei:* Shuzan 秋山. Temmei and Kansei (1781–1800). Lived near Echigo. Carved netsuke of figures, animals of the zodiac, masks, and other subjects. Was a good carver but somewhat lacking in refinement.

1092. Shuzan 周山. *Yomyo:* Mitsuoki 充興. *Tsusho:* Shujiro 周次郎. *Go:* Tansenso 探僊叟. Died in 1776. Name was Yoshimura Shuzan 吉村 周山. Came from Shimanouchi, Osaka. Studied painting with Mitsunobu Sagakawa. Was a credit to the school and earned the title of hogan. Enjoyed carving netsuke. There are many designs associated with Shuzan which he made into netsuke from the weird and fantastic illustrations of the *Sankaikyo* and the *Ressenden*. Colored his carvings beautifully. Used mainly cypress for his netsuke, which he did not sign. His work has been widely forged. Those ignorant of the technique of painting could never hope to approach the level of his art.

Buried at the Komyo-ji, Tennoji-ku, Osaka. Shuzan exerted an

a   b

a   b

enormous influence in originating the Osaka style of netsuke carving. Many carvers devoted themselves to making Shuzan-style netsuke from Anei through Meiji and Taisho (1772–1925). It is said that copies of Shuzan netsuke made by several carvers for the purpose of practicing carving and coloring were exported to foreign countries.

1093. Shuzan 周山. *Chomei:* Shuzan 周山 or kakihan based on character *shu* 周. Lived in Nagamachi, Osaka. Named Kurobei 九郎兵衛. Called himself the successor of Shuzan Yoshimura (B 1092) and carved Shuzan-style netsuke. However, he used boxwood and invariably carved his signature. People referred to him as Shuzan Nagamachi to distinguish him from Shuzan Hogan, since Nagamachi was the slum area where he lived. His subjects were usually hermits and figures. All his carvings are colored. See Fig. 60. See mosha (No. 141).

1094. Shuzan 周山. *Go:* Ranrinsai 蘭輪齋. Middle.

1095. Soen 莊園. Late. Was a pupil of Toen (B 1177). Carved painted wood netsuke.

1096. So-ichi 宗一. Called himself Shibayama So-ichi 芝山惣一. Was

taught inlay technique by Ekisei (B 102) and became excellent.

1097. Soju 宗壽. Some netsuke are found that bear his signature.

1098. Soju 藻壽. *Uji:* Fukai 深井. *Na:* Motohisa 基壽. *Chomei:* Soju 藻壽. Born in 1918 in Ogata-gun, Nagano. In 1937, became a special student of Soko Morita (B 1101) and absorbed his master's style. See mosha (No. 142).

1099. Soka 草花. See Heishiro (B 201).

1100. Soko 藻晃. *Uji:* Toshiyama 利山. *Na:* Yonejiro 米次郎. *Chomei:* Soko 藻晃 or Soko-in-koku 藻晃印刻. Born in Kanazawa City in 1868. In 1880, he came to reside in Osaka in the neighborhood of Kinya 琴谷, who was one of the best pupils of Gyokkin Iida (B 133). Kinya taught carving to Soko for about three years. Subsequently studied carving methods with Mondo Tanaka (B 714) and also learned a great deal by careful observation of the work of Tessai Kano (B 1173). Soko hired many employees in 1887 and engaged in the business of producing wooden smoking pipes, since they had become very popular. The business failed, as did his venture into the metal-casting business in 1905 or 1906. There-

143. SOKO

after devoted himself to carving. Mostly carved in wood but occasionally made colored netsuke. Excelled at carving historical subjects. Also good at metal engraving and at painting. Died on October 3, 1935. See Fig. 99. See mosha (No. 143).

1101. Soko 藻己. *Uji:* Morita 森田. *Na:* Kisaburo 喜三郎. *Chomei:* Soko *to* 藻己刀, Soko koku 藻己刻, or Soko 藻己. Born in December, 1879, at Hongo-ku, Tokyo. His father, Masatoshi, was a metal artist but died when Soko was 5 years old. In January of his 15th year became a special pupil of Joso Miyazaki (B 400) and applied himself very diligently. Became independent in 1907 at the age of 29. Lived in Asakusa but later moved to Oji. Mainly worked in wood but occasionally ivory. Usually did not color his work but sometimes made colored obidome, okimono, and other objects. Recently also carved Buddhist images. His style is realistic and indicates some influence from Hojitsu (B 243) and Kaigyokusai (B 430) in addition to that of his master, Joso. His work is delicate and reveals extreme care with each movement of his knife. It is beautiful and highly refined. His recent Kannon of Eleven Faces is a microscopic carving only 9/10 of an inch in height. It is so tiny that the smallest face of Kannon at the top of the carving can hardly be seen with the naked eye. His work has been exhibited at the Tokyo Craftsmen's Association, Japan Art Association, Great Japan Marine and Art Association, the Admirers of Prince Shotoku, and others. On about 15 occasions Soko was awarded prizes. In 1931, was an examiner for the Japan Art Association and for the Great Japan Marine and Art Association. Was also a director of the latter and vice-chairman of the Group for the Expansion of Ivory Carving. Is the leader of the current netsuke carvers. Has several pupils. His principle is to start pupils with mask carving as a foundation for the carving of the faces in figure netsuke. Is extremely careful in the selection of materials. Uses honen for animal eyes, yellow mother-of-pearl for the eyes of frogs, and umi-matsu for the pupils.

His method of staining is to boil the completed carving for 24 hours in an earthenware pot containing a mixture of *Alnus firma* and Cape jasmine. After the piece is cooled, it is thoroughly washed and polished with the leaves of *Aphananthe aspera*. It is then boiled in man-

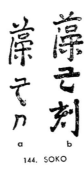

a   b

144. SOKO

145. SOKOKU

drake bark for about 10 hours, after which it is again washed and polished. Soko would not put his signature on a piece if there was any aspect of the carving that did not fully satisfy his artistic demands. It is said that there are several hundred which, though almost completed, never found their way into the hands of the public. See Fig. 198. See mosha (No. 144).

1102. Sokoku 藻谷. Middle. Wood. Lived in Kyomachibori, Osaka. Was a famous carver.

1103. Sokoku 藻谷. *Uji:* Egawa 江川. *Na:* Asa-ichi 淺一. Born in 1920 in Shizuoka Prefecture. Entered the school of Soko Morita (B 1101) in 1934 and developed in accordance with his master's standards.

1104. Sokoku 宗谷. *Chomei:* Sokoku *to* 宗谷刀. Middle. Ivory and horn. See mosha (No. 145).

1105. Sokyu 宗休. *Uji:* Negi 根來. Before Temmei (1781–1788). Lived in Kyomachibori, Osaka. Was an expert maker of artificial teeth. Also carved excellent netsuke.

1106. Somin 宗民. Late. Some figure netsuke bearing his signature are found.

1107. Somin 宗珉. A famous metal artist. See Figs. 1 and 62.

1108. Sosei 宗政. Middle.

1109. Soshichi 宗七. *Uji:* Satake 佐竹. Lived in Uchimoto-cho, O-saka. Was a frieze carver but carved colored netsuke as an avocation. Was good at both wood and ivory carving.

1110. Sosho 宗章. Middle. Wood and ivory.

1111. Sosui 藻水. *Uji:* Ouchi 大内. *Na:* Jiro 次郎. *Chomei:* Sosui 藻水. Born in 1911 in Asakusa. Eldest son of Gyokuso (B 160). Immediately after his graduation, became a pupil of Soko (B 1101), with whom he studied for ten years. Presently lives in Itabashi-ku, Tokyo with his father, Gyokuso. Carves okimono as well as netsuke. His work was selected for exhibition by the Japan Art Association, Tokyo Art Work Exhibition, Japan Marine Art and Crafts Exhibition, and others. Received awards on several occasions since 1932.

1112. Sosui 素水. *Uji:* Okochi 大河内. *Na:* Tsunematsu 恒松. *Chomei:* Sosui 素水 or Sosui *to* 素水刀. Liked to carve. Became a member of the Craftsman's Association organized by Kyusai Hirai (B 576), which he finally completely controlled. As a hobby carved in the round and engraved seals. Also carved tea-ceremony articles. Lived in Omino, Minami Kochi-gun. See mosha (No. 146).

1113. Soun 宗雲. Late. Ivory.

1114. Sowa 宗和. *Uji:* Kanamori 金森. *Na:* Shigechika 重近. *Go:* Sowa 宗和. Died in 1656 at the age of 73. Became Daimyo of Hida but later entered the priesthood. Used the *go* of Sowa. After retirement lived in a suburb of Uji. Was well known as tea-ceremony master. In his spare time, carved figures of local women tea pickers in the wood of the tea bush. His technique was elegant, and his carvings came to be known as Uji ningyo (Uji dolls).

1115. Soya 藻也. *Uji:* Nakano 中野. *Na:* Genshiro 源四郎. Lives and works in Kawasaki City. Was a pupil of Joso (B 400).

1116. Soyo 藻與. Late. Mostly mask netsuke.

1117. Soyo 宗與. Was a famous metal artist.

(Soyen: see Soen.)

1118. Sozan 叟山. Early middle. Wood.

1119. Sozan 宗山. Tempo (1830–1843). Ivory. Those of his netsuke which are found are excellent.

1120. Suginoya 杉之舎. See Chikayuki (B 33).

1121. Suikoku 翠谷. Probably middle. Nut netsuke bearing his signature are found.

1122. Suiseki 翠石. Late.

1123. Sukemasa 佐正. See Ryukosai (B 860).

1124. Sukenaga 亮長. *Uji:* Matsuda 松田. *Chomei:* Sukenaga 亮長. Bunsei (1818–1829). Came from Takayama, Hida. Family was engaged in the business of making chopsticks. During his childhood, studied carving with Suketomo Yoshida (B 1128) and became proficient. Sukenaga regretted the loss of power in the carving of Nara dolls because of the veiling effects of the paint. He studied the problem and hit upon a solution in the use of the wood of the yew tree, which has natural reddish and whitish bands and produces the effect of Nara dolls without the disadvantage of coloring. He is regarded as the originator of the ittobori (carving with a single knife) style of carving characteristic of Hida. Embarked enthusiastically on the carving of ittobori, which is regarded as one of the noted products of the district.

See Figs. 126, 127, and 219. See mosha (No. 147).

1125. Sukenao 亮直. Middle. Boxwood. Carved netsuke of figures and skulls.

1126. Sukesada 亮貞. Late. Yew. Carved rabbits and other animals.

1127. Suketada 亮忠. Early. Wood. Carved netsuke of figures and masks. Was an excellent carver.

1128. Suketomo 亮朝. *Uji:* Yoshida 吉田. Was the teacher of Sukenaga (B 1124). Wood. Carved figure netsuke.

1129. Suketoshi 亮俊. Was the son of Sukeyuki Izumi (B 1133), who taught him carving. Carved netsuke, okimono, and other objects.

1130. Suketsune 亮常. Early. Wood. Figure netsuke.

1131. Sukeyoshi 亮芳. *Chomei:* Sukeyoshi 亮芳. Late. Yew. Came from Takayama, Hida. See mosha (No. 148).

1132. Sukeyuki 亮之. *Chomei:* Sukeyuki 亮之. Middle and late. Came from Takayama, Hida. Carved netsuke of figures and other subjects using wood of the yew tree. See mosha (No. 149).

1133. Sukeyuki 亮之. *Uji:* Izumi 泉. Middle and early late. Came from Bamba, Omi. Was a maker of household Buddhist shrines. Good at carving frogs. Preferred Japanese oak as his material.

–T–

1134. Tadachika 忠親. *Chomei:* Tadachika 忠親. Bunkyu (1861–1863), although some opinions date him from Kyowa through Bunsei (1801–1829). Carved figure netsuke in ivory. Was a pupil of Tomochika (B 1195).

1135. Tadahide 寔秀. Early. Wood.

1136. Tadahiro 忠廣. *Chomei:* Tadahiro 忠廣. Middle. Ivory. See mosha (No. 150).

1137. Tadahisa たゞひさ. Early. Wood.

1138. Tadakatsu 忠勝. Late. Wood. Turtles.

1139. Tadakuni 忠國. Late. Wood. Also lacquer carvings.

1140. Tadamichi 忠道. *Chomei:* Tadamichi 忠道. Middle. Wood. See mosha (No. 151).

1141. Tadamitsu 忠光. *Mei:* Tenka-ichi 天下一. Early middle. Ivory. Animals.

1142. Tadamune 忠宗. Late. Ivory.

1143. Tadanari 忠成. *Chomei:* Tadanari. 忠成. Middle and late. Came from Hakushu. Carved gargoyle netsuke in black persimmon wood. See mosha (No. 152).

1144. Tadanori 忠則. Specialized in carving excellent shishi heads.

1145. Tadatane 忠胤. *Go:* Kinryusai 琴流齋. *Chomei:* Tadatane 忠胤. Late. Ivory.

1146. Tadatoshi 忠利. *Chomei:* Tadatoshi 忠利 in embossed characters. Temmei through Kansei (1781–1800). Came from Nagoya. Was a famous carver. Carved excellent netsuke of figures, birds, animals, fish, shells, masks, and other subjects. See Figs. 116, 121, and 130. See mosha (No. 153).

1147. Tadatsugu 忠次. Early. Wood.

1148. Tadayoshi 忠義. *Uji:* Morishita 森下. *Na:* Heizo 兵藏. Middle and late. Lived in Shiba Kotohiracho, Tokyo.

1149. Tadayoshi 忠義. *Chomei:* Tadayoshi 忠義 or Hogan Tadayoshi 法眼忠義. Tempo through Keio (1830–1867). Came from Nagoya. Earned the title of hogan. Excelled at carving shells, animals,

and other subjects. See Fig. 223. See mosha (No. 154).

1150. Tadayoshi 忠吉. Early. Wood.

1151. Tadayuki 忠之. Tempo (1830–1843). Wood. Mermaid netsuke. Used elaborate designs.

1152. Ta-ichiro 太市郎. *Uji:* Nagao 長尾. Was a pupil of Issai Ogasawara (B 352). Was also a member of the resident group of the castle guard. Excelled in delicate carving.

1153. Taishin 泰眞. *Uji:* Ikeda 池田. *Mei:* Taishin 泰眞. Born in 1825. In 1835, at the age of 11, entered the lacquer school of Zeshin Shibata (B 1337). Because of his diligence and application, became the best lacquerer among Zeshin's pupils. After Zeshin's death, was recommended as a member of the Imperial Art Committee. Occasionally made gold-lacquer netsuke. See mosha (No. 155).

1154. Takugyoku 琢玉. Early. Wood.

1155. Takusai 琢齋. *Na:* Tomitane 富種. *Tsusho:* Senshiro 専四郎. *Go:* Takusai 琢齋. *Chomei:* Takusai 琢齋. Died in 1888 at the age of 72. Came from Suwa-gun, Shinshu. Was the second son of Tomimasa 富昌. His grandfather Tomimune

156. TAKUSAI   157. TAMETAKA   158. TANEKIYO

富棟 came to Edo and entered the school of Tachikawa Mohei 立川茂平 to study carving. Later Tomimune returned to his own town, where he exercised his profession and taught carving to his descendants. Tomimasa died in 1856 at the age of 74. Takusai's son Yoshikiyo 義清 succeeded to his father's profession.

1156. Takusai 啄齋. *Chomei:* Takusai 啄齋. Early middle. Wood. See mosha (No. 156).

1157. Takushijun 澤士淳. See Masatoshi (B 630).

1158. Tameoto 爲乙. *Ondoku:* I-otsu. Early middle. Wood and ivory.

1159. Tametaka 爲隆. *Uji:* Kita 喜多. *Na:* Kiuemon 喜右衞門 *Chomei:* Tametaka 爲隆. Before Temmei (1781–1788). Lived in Hommachi, Nagoya. Carved figure netsuke in wood. Originated the technique of carving raised designs and crests on kimono, giving the appearance of embossing. This accounts for the prevalence of the technique in the Nagoya area. It is said that he was a heavy drinker and quite eccentric. See Fig. 142. See mosha (No. 157).

1160. Tametomo 爲友. Middle. Ivory.

1161. Tanekiyo 種清. *Chomei:* Tanekiyo 種清. Middle. Wood. See mosha (No. 158).

1162. Tansai 丹齋. *Go:* Tansai 丹齋 or Bairindo 梅林堂. *Chomei:* Tansai 丹齋. Late Tokugawa (1601–1867). Family name is unknown. Bairindo signifies a garden of bamboo and plum trees and was probably adopted out of his love for fine old plum trees which he grew in his garden. Lived in Tsu. First apprenticed to Kamaya Gorosaburo, a maker of iron pots in Kyoto, a trade in which Tansai improved his skill over several years. Returned to Tsu and received commissions from the Tsu clan. Tansai fashioned the bronze seals of the Daimyo of Tsu, Todo Takatora, and of the Yuzokan school of the Tsu clan. Preferred bronze as his material. Liked to portray the subjects of the Four Wise Men and to illustrate in inlaid designs the stories and poems written by Tsuzaka Toyo, the Confucianist. Some of his work is found with designs of snails carved from touchwood. Since he was a superior draftsman, his carvings also tended to be of excellent technique. Maeda, the Daimyo of Kashu, presented the Daimyo of Fujido with a Daruma 12 feet in height. The latter was so pleased with his gift that in re-

159. TEMMIN

turn he commissioned Tansai to make a bronze sakè cup, 3 feet in diameter and decorated with a raised design of dragons and clouds. The dragons seemed to breathe and the clouds to drift. The Daimyo of Kashu was most pleased and treasured the gift. It is said that the very same sakè cup is in use today at the water fountain in Kenroku Park. Tansai also excelled in painting and in haiku poetry. While his netsuke are not rare, they are scarce.

1163. Tanso 坦叟. Was a metal artist.

1164. Tatsuki Kanzo 龍木勘藏 See Kanzo (B 452).

1165. Tatsuo 龍雄. *Uji:* Kaneda 金田. *Na:* Kanejiro 兼次郎. Meiji (1868–1911). Rendered considerable service in the interest of carving during Meiji. Also carved netsuke.

1166. Teiji 貞二. Late. Wood.

1167. Teimin 貞珉. Middle. Wood.

1168. Teimin 貞民. *Uji:* Nakayama 中山. *Na:* Teijiro 貞次郎. Called himself Gosokusai 吾速齋. Did inlay work.

1169. Teizan 禎山. Late.

1170. Teizui 定隨. Middle. Wood.

1171. Temmin 天民. *Chomei:* kakihan based on Temmin. Tempo (1830–1843). Was a metal artist of Edo. Called himself Shojo Temmin. Shuraku (B 1075) was a pupil in his school. Made kagamibuta netsuke. See mosha (No. 159).

1172. Tenko 天工. Early middle. Wood.

1173. Tessai 鐵哉. *Uji:* Kano 加納. *Na:* Kotaro 光太郎. *Go:* Tessai 鐵哉. *Chomei:* kakihan based on the character 光 or Tessai *to* and kakihan based on the character 光. Born on February 15, 1845, at Hommachi, Gifu. Father's name was Jinzaemon Kano. Family originally engaged in sakè brewing but later changed to dealing in cloth. All members of the family were interested in painting, and some of them supported their families by brush painting or carving. Tessai entered the priesthood at the age of 12, studying carving and the painting of Buddhist subjects by himself. As Jinzaemon died when Tessai was 23, Tessai returned to secular life as the head of his family household. Established himself as a professional painter and sculptor. In the winter of his 30th year, took up residence in Surugadai, Tokyo, and devoted himself to carving as his chief interest. At 38

a   b

160. TESSAI

鋒玄

161. TETSUGEN

moved to Nara, where he made a further study of painting and carving. At 41 was appointed by the minister of education as a member of the committee for the study and research of the ancient arts. In this connection visited the shrines and temples of the Five Provinces—Yamato, Yanagi, Settsu, Kii, and Omi—in order to study their art treasures. At 45 was appointed a professor of the Tokyo Art School but later again removed to Nara, where he studied the sacred treasures of various temples and rendered great service in copying many of them. Thereafter he lived successively at Gojo Temple, Yamato, Jisei Temple, Takatsu, Osaka, and other places. Once returned to Tokyo, but in 1917 again moved to Nara, where he built a small shack which he called Saishoshoja and in which he carved almost daily. Originated teppitsu-bori, a technique of engraving landscapes, figures, or other subjects on a flat surface such as wood or metal. The paintings and brush writings which were his hobby won him a great public reputation. Died on October 28, 1925. See mosha (No. 160).

1174. Tetsugen 鐵玄. *Chomei:* Tetsugen 鐵玄. See Kyusai (B 576). See mosha (No. 161).

1175. Tetsugendo 鐵玄堂. Same carver as Tetsugen. See Kyusai (B 576).

1176. Toei 東英. Late. Wood.

1177. Toen 杜園. *Uji:* Morikawa 森川. *Yomyo:* Tomokichi 友吉. *Go:* Toen 杜園. *Chomei:* Toen 杜園, Toen saku 杜園作, or kakihan based on Toen. Born on June 26, 1820, at Inoue-cho, Nara. Studied painting with Kien. His work was admired by the Daimyo of Tosa, Kajino, who was the magistrate of Nara. As a mark of his esteem, the magistrate awarded Toen the na of Fuso and the *go* of Toen—names derived from Japanese mythology. At 17, he began to study Noh comedy in the school of Yamada Hachiemon and mastered it. In March, 1854, the emperor saw a play in which Toen acted. Studied carving in the school of Hohaku (B 240) at the age of 18 and rapidly became proficient. His work was entered in the First National Industrial Exhibition, held in 1877, and he was awarded the Phoenix Prize. On numerous occasions was awarded prizes at various art exhibits. Was patronized by the Imperial Household, from which he received many orders. At the request of the Imperial Museum, made copies of ancient Nara carvings which were a b c

162. TOEN   163. TOKIMINCHO   164. TOKOKU   165. TOKUSEI

identical in appearance with the originals. The deer okimono exhibited at the Chicago World's Fair in 1892 was his last masterpiece and is presently seen at the Imperial Museum. He was the paragon of the great master carvers of Nara ningyo. Died at Nara on July 15, 1894, at the age of 75. See Figs. 29 and 40. See mosha (No. 162).

1178. Togen 桃源. *Uji:* Setani 瀬谷. *Na:* Gennosuke 源之助; later changed to Kajizo 梶藏. *Go:* Togen 桃源. *Chomei:* Togen 桃源. Born on November 3, 1844, in Koriyama. Succeeded to his father Jinzo's *go* of Togen. Was a clansman but carved Nara ningyo.

1179. Togetsu 都月. Late. Carved netsuke of butterflies in ebony.

1180. Togyoku 都玉. Late.

1181. Togyokusai 東玉齋 See Tomomasa (B 1207).

1182. Toju 東珠. Early middle. Wood.

1183. Tokimincho 鴇民晁. *Chomei:* Tokimincho 鴇民晁, Rakumin Toki Hogan 樂民鴇法眼, or kakihan based on Toki Hogan. Koka through Keio (1844–1867). Made netsuke in wood and ivory. See mosha (No. 163).

1184. Tokoku 東谷. *Uji:* Suzuki 鈴木. *Na:* Tetsugoro 鐵五郎. *Chomei:* Tokoku 東谷 or Tokoku *to* 東谷刀, sometimes in a metal plaque inlaid in the carving. Lived in Tokyo. Enjoyed carving and was self-taught. Never served as an apprentice. In 1862 opened his own school. Carved netsuke which were highly prized and valued. Equally proficient in carving ivory, horn, metal, wood, and stone. At present his school is represented by Tokoku III. See Figs. 50 and 76. See mosha (No. 164).

1185. Tokosai 東光齋. Early. Ivory.

1186. Tokujutei 徳壽亭. Middle. Wood. Some of his work bears the mei: "74 years old."

1187. Tokuryo 篤良. Early middle. Carved ojime and other small objects.

1188. Tokusai 得哉. *Chomei:* Tokusai 得哉. Keio (1865–1867). Mainly wood.

1189. Tokusei 徳清. *Chomei:* Tokusei 徳清. Early middle. Wood. Tigers. See mosha (No. 165).

1190. Toman 東滿. *Chomei:* Toman 東滿. Early middle. Wood. Excellent craftsman. See mosha (No. 166).

166. TOMAN 　　　 167. TOMIHARU 　　　 168. TOMOCHIKA I 　　　 169. TOMOCHIKA II

1191. Tomiharu 富春. *Uji:* Shimizu 清水. *Chomei:* Sekiyohako Seiyodo cho 石陽波江青陽堂彫. *Chomei:* Seifushun of Seiyodo of Kawaigawa, Iwami Province, carved at the age of 62 in the summer of Kansei 6 石見國可愛河青陽堂清富春享年六十二歳而彫刻之干時寛政甲寅夏也. *Chomei:* Tomiharu Seiyodo of Kawaigawa, Sekishu, carved at the age of 58 on July 24, Kansei 2 石州可愛河青陽堂富春享年五十八歳而彫刻之干時寛政二庚戌七月二十四日也. *Go:* Seifushun 清富春, Shunyodo 春陽堂, Seiyodo 青陽堂, Rito 籬桃, and others. Born in 1723 in Tamatsukuri, Izumo. Was Iwao I. Since his name was Tomiharu, he used the Chinese reading to compose his *go* of Seifushun. In 1745, at the age of 13, he entered the priesthood at the Choei-ji, Iruma, Jizeki-gun, Hata-mura. Liked carving and later journeyed to Edo to study. Returning to his home province of Izumo, he finally settled in Naka-gun, where he abandoned the world of Buddhism and married a local woman. Lived there continuously until his death. Was quite a good haiku poet. Used many artist names such as Shunyodo, Seiyodo, Rito, and others. Since his home was situated near the Kawai River, he used the name of Kawaigawa on some of his carvings. Died on October 23, 1811, at the age of 88. See Fig. 139. See mosha (No. 167).

1192. Tomin 東岷. *Chomei:* Tomin 東岷. Temmei through Kansei (1781–1800). Wood. Figures and devils.

1193. Tomin 東民. Late. Wood.

1194. Tomoaki 友明. *Uji:* Inagawa 稲川. Middle. Ivory.

1195. Tomochika I 友親初代. *Go:* Yamaguchi Chikuyosai 山口竹陽齋. *Chomei:* Tomochika 友親. Born in Edo in 1800. Was a younger brother of Shominsai Chikamasa (B 30), from whom he learned carving and became a professional. Lived in Sugamo, Tokyo. Carved mainly in ivory. Carved Ashinaga, Tenaga, animals, shells, and many subjects taken from Hokusai's *Manga*. Efforts were concentrated on designs rather than on refinement. The years of his productivity cover Bunsei and Tempo. Died in 1873 at the age of 74. Taught many pupils. See Figs. 79 and 137. See mosha (No. 168).

1196. Tomochika II 友親二代. Was a grandson of Tomochika I (B 1195), whom he succeeded as Tomochika II. See mosha (No. 169).

1197. Tomochika III 友親三代. *Uji:* Yamaguchi 山口. *Na:* Chinnosuke 鎮之助. *Go:* Chikuyosai 竹陽齋. *Chomei:* Tomochika 友親 or Chikuyosai 竹陽齋. Born in 1842. Lived in Sugamo, Tokyo. In 1863, succeeded Tomochika and became Tomochika III. Carved netsuke. Also made okimono for export. See Fig. 220. See mosha (No. 170).

1198. Tomochika 友近. *Chomei:* Tomochika 友近. Bunsei (1818–1829). Carved in wood, ivory, and horn. Was a pupil of Tomotada (B 1215). Later moved to Edo. See mosha (No. 171).

1199. Tomofusa 友房. *Uji:* Hata 畑. Lived in Tsuyama, Saku-shu. Carved lacquer netsuke. Was called Lacquerer Kambei. Also carved in ivory.

1200. Tomoharu 友春. Middle.

1201. Tomohide 友秀. Middle. Ivory.

1202. Tomohisa 友久. Middle. Wood.

1203. Tomohisa 知久. Middle. Ivory.

1204. Tomoji 友二. Middle. Wood.

1205. Tomokado 友門. Middle. Wood.

1206. Tomokazu 友一. *Uji:* Kano 加納. *Chomei:* Tomokazu 友一. Born in Kajimachi, Gifu. When 17 years of age, went to work for a reputable family named Shibata 柴田. Liked carving and devoted all his spare time to the use of the carving knife or the writing brush. One day his master scolded him for spending his time in this manner. Thereafter he waited until his master and fellow workers were asleep and then assiduously practiced carving, making great progress. One day his master happened to see his work and was lost in admiration. Thereafter the master gave Tomokazu his full support. Specialized in carving netsuke. Later went to Kyoto, where his name became well known. Upon his return to Gifu, planted two cherry trees near the Kannondo Temple at Mokuyama, near the foot of Kinkazan Mountain. The two trees formed the gateway to the hermitage he built—a place where he lived in celibacy for the rest of his life. In the hermitage were no furnishings other than books, knives, and a table. Once, wishing to carve a deer netsuke, he left his house unguarded for three days while he went to Shiro Mountain, where he sketched living deer, so enthusiastic and diligent was he in

a   b

172. TOMOKAZU

173. TOMOTADA

carving. His work is admired by many people. The time of his death is uncertain, but it was probably during Tempo, when it is said that he was over 70 years of age. The figure of Kannon enshrined in the rest hut of the present Moku-yama Temple is attributed to To-mokazu. Excelled at carving netsuke of turtles and monkeys. See Fig. 136. See mosha (No. 172).

1207. Tomomasa 友政. *Uji:* Kato 加藤. *Na:* Masajiro 政次郎. *Go:* Togyokusai 東玉齋. Middle. Was a pupil of Tomochika (B 1195).

1208. Tomomasa 友正. *Chomei:* Tomomasa 友正. Middle. Ivory.

1209. Tomomitsu 友光. Middle. Ivory.

1210. Tomonaga 友長. Middle.

1211. Tomonobu 友信. *Chomei:* Tomonobu 友信. Temmei and Kansei (1781–1800). Carved netsuke of figures, animals, and insects.

1212. Tomonobu 朝信. Early. Wood.

1213. Tomosada 友定. Early. Wood.

1214. Tomoshichi 友七. See Masanobu (B 616).

1215. Tomotada 友忠. Middle. Called himself Eirakusai 永樂齋.

Lived in Edo. Was the teacher of Ninraku (B 760).

1216. Tomotada 友忠. *Uji:* Izumiya 和泉屋. *Na:* Shichiemon 七右衛門. *Chomei:* Tomotada 友忠. Prior to Temmei (1781–1800). Lived in Kyoto. Was extraordinarily skillful in carving cattle in either ivory or wood. His work became widely known as "Tomotada cattle." Even during his lifetime, forgeries of his work were common. His carvings were so alive and vivid that reportedly only a glance was necessary to determine their authenticity. Signed Tomotada 友忠. (I was shown a netsuke in the form of a tiger accompanied by a letter purportedly written by Tomotada to a man named Tsukuno. The letter is dated 1602. It thanks Tsukuno for the kindness he showed when Tomotada was ill and in appreciation presents him with the accompanying tiger netsuke. Whether or not Tomotada was alive at such an early date and whether so elegant a carving was already made, I do not know. I merely repeat this as indicative of someone's opinion.) See Fig 108. See mosha (No. 173).

1217. Tomotada 伴忠. *Uji:* Yanagawa 柳川. *Na:* Zenzo 善藏. *Chomei:* Tomotada 伴忠 in em-

174. TOMOTADA

175. TOSHI

bossed characters. Tempo (1830–1843). Learned metal work from Tanabe Tomomasa 田邊伴正, the founder of the Tanabe branch of the Yokoya school of metal artists. As a hobby he carved inro, netsuke, and other objects in wood. His technique was exquisite. See mosha (No. 174).

1218. Tomotaka 友高. Bunkyu (1861–1863). Was a pupil of Tomochika (B 1195).

1219. Tomotane 友胤. *Chomei:* Tomotane 友胤. Temmei and Kansei (1781–1800). Lived in Kyoto. Carved netsuke of angels, human figures, and animals.

1220. Tomotoshi 友利. Early. Ivory.

1221. Tomotsugu 友次. Early. Ivory.

1222. Tomotsune 友常. Early middle. Wood.

1223. Tomotsune 共常. Some mask netsuke bearing his signature are found.

1224. Tomoyoshi 友由. Middle. Wood.

1225. Tomoyoshi 友佳. Middle. Wood.

1226. Tomoyoshi 友善. Early middle. Called himself Ichiryu (—柳). Was a maker of sword decorations but also carved netsuke.

1227. Tomoyuki 知行. Early. Ivory, wood, and bone.

1228. Tomoyuki 知之. Early.

1229. Tomoyuki 友之. Bunkyu (1861–1863). Was a pupil of Tomochika (B 1195).

1230. Toryu 屠龍. Early. Ivory.

1231. Toshi 桃枝. Middle. Was a pupil of Toyo (B 1252). Made gold-lacquer netsuke. See mosha (No. 175).

1232. Toshichika 俊親. Late. Ivory.

1233. Toshiharu 利治. *Go:* Bokugyuken 牧牛軒. Middle.

1234. Toshihiro 利廣. Middle. Wood.

1235. Toshikazu 利一. Early middle. Wood.

1236. Toshikazu 年一. Late. Wood.

1237. Toshikazu 壽一. Late. Ivory.

1238. Toshimasa 利正. Early. Wood.

1239. Toshimune 壽宗. Early. Wood.

304 · INDEX OF NETSUKE CARVERS

豊一

1240. Toshinaga 壽永. *Uji:* Kojima 小島. Middle. Was the master of Sento (B 951).

1241. Toshinori 壽則. Middle. Wood.

1242. Toshiyuki 壽之. Early. Wood.

1243. Totenko 東天紅. Came from Kazusa.

1244. Tou 東雨. *Chomei:* Tou Gisaku 東雨戲作. Tou is another *go* of Tsuchiya Yasuchika I, who was known as one of the three great metal artists of Nara. Carved netsuke in wood or bamboo as a hobby. His work is roughly carved yet powerful and graceful.

1245. Touemon 藤右衛門. Before Temmei (1781–1788). Lived in Goyo Sayamachi, Kyoto. Called himself Daikokuya 大黒屋.

1246. Toun 東雲. Died on September 23, 1910, at the age of 64. Lived in Asakusa, Tokyo. Was a pupil of Houn (B 286). Was granted the title of hogan for his sculpture of Buddhist images. Was the teacher of Koun Takamura (B 555).

1247. Toun 東雲. Came from Oshu. Was a sculptor of household shrines. Also carved netsuke.

1248. Toun 東雲. *Go:* Ikkosai 一光齋, used only in his later years. Tempo (1830–1843). Principally carved netsuke in elaborate designs. See Fig. 129.

1249. Toun 渡雲. Middle. Some netsuke bearing his signature are found.

1250. Tounsai 東雲齋. Early middle. Wood.

(Toyei: see Toei.)

(Toyen: see Toen.)

1251. Toyo 東洋. Late. Wood.

1252. Toyo 桃葉. Early. Was a famous gold-lacquer artist.

1253. Toyokazu 豊一. *Chomei:* Toyokazu 豊一. Middle. Wood. Was a pupil of Toyomasa (B 1254). See mosha (No. 176).

1254. Toyomasa 豊昌. *Uji:* Naito 内藤. *Na:* Sensuke 専助. *Chomei:* Toyomasa 豊昌. Born in 1773 into a farming family of Taki-gun, Tamba Province. The *go* of his family was Fujiya 藤屋. During Kansei engaged in the profession of carving seals. In addition to his profession, he made wood carvings and made decorations for women's carved swords (koshimotobori). His work was original and refined. Excelled at decorating koshimoto-

豊
昌

bori to suit soft and feminine taste. Before beginning work he worshipped Dainichi Buddha and then entered a paper-covered bamboo cubicle just large enough for him to squeeze into. Utilizing a narrow beam of light entering through a small hole in the roof, he did his carving. Was an excellent composer of haiku and waka poems. Also arranged flowers in the style of the Enshu school, using the *go* of Shunshoan for this purpose. Aoyama Tadasuke, the lord of Shinoyama Castle, liked Toyomasa and commissioned him to do various carvings, giving him the mei of Toyomasa. When a relative of the lord, Aoyama Yamato-no-kami, requested Toyomasa to make him an okimono, Toyomasa carved the subject of a snake and a precious stone. On the bottom of the okimono Toyomasa wrote: "By commission at Shinoyama, Toyomasa, aged 73 and his son, a left-handed carver aged 35, made in January, Koka 2 [1845]." Died in November, 1856, at the age of 84. Buried at the Kannon-ji, Shinoyama-machi. See Fig. 86. See mosha (No. 177).

1255. Toyoyasu 豊客. Born in 1810. Died in September, 1883. Was a son of Toyomasa (B 1254). Was left-handed and hence commonly known as Hidari Toyomasa 左豊昌. Buried at the Kannon-ji, Shinoyama-machi.

1256. Toyozane 豊實. Middle. Wood.

1257. Tozan 東山. Late. Inlay work.

1258. Tsuji 辻. Before Temmei (1781–1788). Wood. Was an excellent carver.

1259. Tsunemasa 恒正. Late. Ivory.

1260. Tsunemasa 常政. Early. Ivory.

1261. Tsunenori 恒徳. See Shoju XI (B 1003).

1262. Tsurigane 鐘. Middle. Ivory.

1263. Tsuzen 通全. Middle. Carved in bone.

–U–

1264. Umboku 雲卜. Early. Wood.

1265. Umehara 梅原. *Ondoku:* Baigen. See Baigen (B 4).

1266. Umon 禹門. Meiji (1868–1911). Carved mask netsuke in colored wood.

1267. Umpo 雲鳳. Middle. Called Ogura Kouemon. Was a pupil of Tomochika (B 1195).

1268. Umpo 雲浦. See Kajun (B 433).

1269. Unjudo 雲樹洞. See Shumemaru (B 1058).

1270. Unkai 雲開. Early. Figure netsuke.

1271. Unkyo 雲橋. *Chomei:* Unkyo 雲橋. Tempo (1830–1843). Mainly wood.

1272. Unsei 雲青. Middle.

1273. Unshodo 雲松堂. *Chomei:* Unshodo 雲松堂. Early. Black persimmon wood. Animals. See mosha (No. 178).

1274. Unzan 雲山. Middle.

1275. Uwasa 宇和左. Late. Carved in wood, which he lacquered.

– W –

1276. Waryu 和流. Before Temmei (1781–1788). Lived in Edo. Carved in the style of Miwa (B 710) and was probably his pupil.

1277. Washiro 和四郎. Prior to and during Tempo (1830–1843). Came from Suwa. His main vocation was the carving of household shrines. Also carved netsuke and okimono of fine quality.

1278. Washoin 和性院. Before Temmei (1781–1788). Lived in Kami-machi, Osaka. Was a mountain-dwelling ascetic. Did colored carving in the style of Umpo (B 1267).

– Y –

1279. Yamatojo 大和女. Before Temmei (1781–1788). Lived in Edo. Called himself Nakayama. Excelled at delicate carving such as the minute representation of animal hair in ivory ash-tray netsuke.

1280. Yasuchika 安親. *Uji:* Otogawa 音川. Middle through Late. Was a pupil of Tomochika (B 1197).

1281. Yasuchika 安親. See Tou (B 1244).

1282. Yasuhei 彌須平. Before Temmei (1781–1788). Lived in Wakayama. Carved colored netsuke.

1283. Yasuhide 康秀. Middle. Wood and ivory. Figure netsuke.

1284. Yasutada 安忠. Early. Wood. Animal netsuke.

(Yekisei: see Ekisei.)

1285. Yomin 庸民. Middle. Wood.

1286. Yo-o 陽鳳. *Uji:* Niwa 丹羽. *Na:* Akira 章. *Chomei:* Yo-o 陽鳳. Late. Mainly wood. Lived at Tennoji, Osaka.

1287. Yoritake 賴武. *Uji:* Kawai 河井. Before Temmei (1781–1788). Lived in Kyoto. Was a sculptor of Buddhist images. Carved netsuke as a hobby. His carvings are extremely beautiful and executed in a rare style. Established his own school.

1288. Yoshiaki 義明. See Goto Yataro (B 128).

1289. Yoshiaki 義明. Middle. Lived in Tokyo.

1290. Yoshihide 吉秀. Middle. Wood. Mask netsuke.

1291. Yoshihisa 義久. Middle. Wood.

1292. Yoshikane 美兼. *Chomei:* Yoshikane 美兼. Keio (1865–1867). Mainly wood.

1293. Yoshikazu 義一. Late.

1294. Yoshikazu 吉一. Early. Wood.

1295. Yoshikazu 善量. Some netsuke are found that bear his signature.

1296. Yoshimasa 吉政. Early. Wood. Called himself Deme 出目.

1297. Yoshimasa 良昌. Early. Wood.

1298. Yoshimasa 義昌. Middle. Ivory. Called himself Seiyodo 青陽堂. Was most probably a member of the Tomiharu school.

1299. Yoshimasa 吉昌. Some netsuke bearing his signature are in existence.

1300. Yoshimasa 吉正. *Chomei:* Yoshimasa 吉正. Kansei through Bunsei (1789–1829). Ivory. Figure netsuke. See Fig. 194.

1301. Yoshimoto 宜元. Before Temmei (1781–1788).

1302. Yoshinaga 吉長. *Chomei:* Yoshinaga 吉長. Before Temmei (1781–1788). Lived in Kyoto. Called himself Koyoken 廣葉軒. See Figs. 109 and 224. See mosha (No. 179).

1303. Yoshinaga 吉永. Late. Ivory.

1304. Yoshinao 義直. *Chomei:* Yoshinao 義直. Tempo (1830–1843). Wood.

1305. Yoshinobu 芳信. Early middle. Wood.

1306. Yoshinori 美徳. *Uji:* Kagei 景井. *Na:* Hidetaro 秀太郎. *Go:* Kosho 高笑, but later changed to Yoshinori 美徳. Born in 1848 in Osaka. Was the first son of Dosho (B 89) and, like his father, specialized in ivory. Also excelled in inlay work. Lived at Tennoji, Osaka. Carved mostly netsuke, okimono, and other small objects. His hobby was composing waka poems and painting in the Japanese style. Also interested in tea ceremony and ancient court music (Bugaku). Died in 1906. Buried at the Yuko-ji Fujisawa, Sagami Province.

1307. Yoshioki 良興. Early. Wood.

1308. Yoshiro 與四郎. *Chomei:* Yoshi *in* 與四印. Was a famous ceramist of Yamashina, Kyoto. Also made ceramic netsuke. See mosha (No. 180).

1309. Yoshitada 義忠. Middle. Wood.

1310. Yoshitada 吉忠. Late. Ivory.

1311. Yoshitaka 義孝. Middle. Ivory.

1312. Yoshitomo 吉友. Early middle. Ivory.

1313. Yoshitoshi 敬利. *Ondoku:* Keiri. See Keiri (B 473).

1314. Yoshitsugu 芳繼. Early. Was a samurai of the Yanagawa clan. Excelled at carving hannya masks.

1315. Yoshitsugu 義次. Early. Wood. Mask netsuke.

1316. Yoshiyuki 芳之. *Chomei:* kakihan based on Yoshiyuki. Late. Did beautiful work in ivory. See mosha (No. 181).

1317. Yoshiyuki 由之. Early. Carved figure netsuke.

1318. Yoshiyuki 義之. *Go:* Isshin-sai 一心齋. Middle.

1319. Yoyusai 羊遊齋. Was a famous gold-lacquer artist. Also made gold-lacquer netsuke.

1320. Yugetsu 友月. *Uji:* Takeda 武田. *Na:* Nobuoki 信興. *Azana:* Hidehira 秀平. Bunsei (1818–1829). Was placed in charge of the handiwork of the Maeda family of Kanazawa. Later was put in charge of repair and construction, for which he received 500 koku (about 2,500 bushels) of rice. Excelled in elaborate wood carving. During Bunsei constructed the Minzan ceramic kiln at Kasugayama and made porcelain. Died on September 13, 1844.

1321. Yugyokusai 友玉齋. Middle. Ivory.

1322. Yugyokusai 遊玉齋. Middle. Ivory.

1323. Yukimune 之宗. *Chomei:* Yukimune 之宗. Lived subsequent to Kaei (1848–1853). Some of his ivory mask netsuke are found.

1324. Yukodo 幽皇堂. See Sekiho (B 939).

1325. Yukoku 幽谷. Late. Wood. See Fig. 66.

1326. Yumehachi 夢八. *Ondoku:* Muhachi. See Muhachi (B 726).

1327. Yumin 友民. Middle. Wood.

1328. Yusai 友齋. Early middle. Was a gold-lacquer artist but also made netsuke.

1329. Yusai 友哉. Middle. Was a gold-lacquer craftsman.

1330. Yusai 幽齋. *Chomei:* Yusai 幽齋. Late. Carved netsuke representing mushrooms in a basket so cleverly that the mushrooms, although mobile, do not fall free. See mosha (No. 182).

1331. Yusen 友仙. Middle. Ivory.

1332. Yusen 有仙. Middle. Wood.

1333. Yushu 遊舟. Middle. Wood.

1334. Yuzan 友山. Middle. Wood.

– Z –

1335. Zemin 是民. Some netsuke with his signature are found.

1336. Zeraku 是樂. Lived near Sanjukken-bori, Edo.

1337. Zeshin 是眞. *Yomyo:* Shibata Kametaro 柴田龜太郎, but later changed to Shibata Junzo 柴田順藏. *Go:* Reisai 令哉 or Zeshin 是眞. *Chomei:* Zeshin 是眞 or Makie Zeshin 蒔繪是眞. Meiji (1868–1911). Called himself Tairyukyo 對柳居. Studied gold lacquering with Koma Kansai 古滿寛哉 and painting with Suzuki Nanrei 鈴木南嶺. Later went to Kyoto and entered the school of Okamoto Toyohiko 岡本豊彦. Associated with Kagawa Keiki 香川景樹, Rai Sanyo 賴山陽, and others, from whom he learned a great deal. Visited the Sansei-ji of the Tofuku-ji complex to sketch the 16 Rakan (Buddhas) made by Ryumin Ri. Subsequently overcame innumerable obstacles in order to buy the 16 Rakan, a story that is repeated to this day with undiminished admiration. Made a detailed study of gold-lacquer painting in order to retain the qualities of sumi-e (ink paintings) in this medium. Developed painting in lacquer and other original ideas. Rendered great service during

183. ZESHIN   184. ZOROKU   185. ZUISHO

the Meiji era to the field of lacquer. Was an examiner for various exhibitions and in 1890 was elected to membership in the Imperial Art Committee. Died on July 13, 1891, at the age of 85. Occasionally made gold-lacquer netsuke and even carved netsuke. See Fig. 197. See mosha (No. 183).

(Zingetsu: see Jingetsu.)

1338. Zokoku 象谷. *Uji:* Fujikawa 藤川. *Na:* Isan 爲參. *Tsusho:* Keizo 敬造. *Go:* Zokoku 象谷. *Chomei:* Zokoku 象谷. Born on October 4, 1806. Lived east of the Fujimori Kojinja, Takamatsu City, Sanuki Province. Used an alias of Shisei 子成. Also used a family name of Tamakaji 玉楮, which some people say was given him by the daimyo of the clan, but this opinion is incorrect. He composed the name of Tamakaji of his own volition, using two characters from a famous saying of Resshi (Lieh-tsu), a Chinese Taoist, about a man who uses precious stones to make paper from mulberry leaves. His family business was that of selling lacquer and painting scabbards. He excelled in colored lacquer, tsuishu, and tsuikoku. Greatly respected by the

people of his district as a genius in lacquer and in carving. Zokoku served the various daimyo of the Takamatsu clan—Matsudaira Raien, Yoritane, and Yorifusa—and at their orders created fine carvings. As a result he rose to samurai status. In addition to carving, was good at waka poetry. Occasionally worked in porcelain and called his work Fuigo pottery.

1339. Zoroku 藏六. *Chomei:* Zoroku 藏六. Was a famous ceramist of Kyoto. Also made ceramic netsuke. See mosha (No. 184).

1340. Zuigyoku 瑞玉. *Chomei:* Zuigyoku 瑞玉. Koka through Keio (1844–1867). Ivory.

1341. Zuikoku 隨谷. Late. Ivory.

1342. Zuisho 瑞松. *Uji:* Hotta 堀田. *Chomei:* Zuisho 瑞松. Born in 1835. Came from Tajima (Hyogo Prefecture) but later moved to Tokyo. Studied painting with Taizan (泰山) and made carvings in the Taizan style. Excelled in carving wood and bamboo. Originated the Hotta type of lacquer for lacquering. Died on September 8, 1916, at the age of 80. See mosha (No. 185).

Bibliography

Akamatsu, Keifuku: "Tamakaji Zokoku O" (Old Man Tamakaji Zokoku), *Shoga Kotto Zasshi* (Magazine of Calligraphy, Painting, and Curios), No. 299, May 1, 1933

Brockhaus, Albert: *Netsuke* (English edition), 1924

——: *Netsuke* (German edition), 1905

Dillon, Edward: *The Arts of Japan* (3rd edition), 1911

Edo, Seisai: *Kotto Shu* (Collection of Curios), 1804–1817

Fukuda, Yasuzo: *Tabako no Hanashi* (The Story of Tobacco), 1933

Gempuan, Shujin: "Netsuke ni Tsuite" (On Netsuke), *Shoga Kotto Zasshi* (Magazine of Calligraphy, Painting, and Curios), Nos. 243–246, September 1, 1928

Gonse, Louis: *L'Art Japonais,* 1883

Hayashi, Yonosuke: *Makieshi Den Nurishi Den* (History of Lacquerers and Gold Lacquer Craftsmen), 1927

Hokusai, Katsushika: *Banshoku Zuko* (Illustrations of Multitudinous Occupations), 1835–1850

——: *Hokusai Manga* (Caricatures by Hokusai), 15 vols., 1814–1878

Ido, Fumihito: *Fukuromono* (History of Japanese Bags), 1919

Iizuka, Beiu: "Examination of Netsuke," *Shoga Kotto Zasshi* (Magazine of Calligraphy, Painting, and Curios), No. 237, March 1, 1928

Imperial Household Museum: *Brief History of the Art of Imperial Japan,* 1916

——: *Compendium of Artistic Crafts,* 1921

Inaba, Tsuryu: *Soken Kisho* (Appreciation of Superior Sword Furnishings), 1781

Isai, Katsushika: *Bambutsu Zukai Isai Gashiki* (Isai's Designs for Everything), 1864

——: *Kacho Sansui Zushiki* (Illustrations of Flowers, Birds, Mountains, and Rivers), date unknown

Japan Society of London: *Transactions and Proceedings,* Vol. III (Fourth Session), 1894–1895

Kiuchi, Hango: "History of Ivory Sculpture," *Shoga Kotto Zasshi* (Magazine of Calligraphy, Painting, and Sculpture), No. 65, November 10, 1913
Kogetsu, Ro-o: *Sakasuikoshu* (Brief Biographies of Old Tea Masters), 1852
Kuwabara, Yojiro: *Zoho Kokin Soken Kinko Ichiran* (Supplementary List of Swords and Goldsmiths of Ancient and Modern Times), 1927
Matsumura, Shofu: *Sketches of Recent Famous Artists,* 1924
Mondo, Jokei: *Mondo Shokei* (Life Sketch of Mondo), 1917
Naito, Masamune: *Tokyo Chokokai Shi* (History of the Tokyo Society of Carvers), 1927
Niryu, Sensei: *Choko Hinagata* (Designs of Art Craftsmen), 1827
Ohara, Mitsuhiro: *Takarabukuro* (Bag of Treasures), 1837
Ono, Gemmyo: *Summary of Buddhist Art,* 1925
Osaka Prefectural Arts and Crafts Association: *Kyodo Meiko narabi ni Jocho Shorei Korosha Shoden* (History of Famous Folk Artists Who Have Encouraged and Promoted Artcrafts), 1931
——: *Osaka-fu Kogei Kyokai Kai-in Meibo* (List of Members of the Osaka Prefectural Artcrafts Society), 1930
Sasaki, Chujiro: *Nihon no Netsuke* (The Netsuke of Japan), 1936
Sasaki, Kosei: *Sculpture of Japan,* 1922
Shisui, Rokkaku: *Shikko Shi* (History of Lacquerers), date unknown
Takamura, Koun: *Koun Kaikodan* (Reminiscences of Koun), 1929
Takeda, Denuemon: *Bijutsu Chokoku Gafu* (Art of Sculpture Illustrated), 1892
Takeuchi, Kyuichi: Articles on netsuke in *Shoga Kotto Zasshi* (Magazine of Calligraphy, Painting, and Curios), Nos. 68–70, February 1, 1914
——: "Hashi-ichi, a Lacquer Artist," *Shoga Kotto Zasshi* (Magazine of Calligraphy, Painting, and Curios), No. 72, June 1, 1914
——: "Netsuke," *Encyclopedia of Japan,* 1919
Tamai, Kyujiro: *Morikawa Toen Shoden* (Sketch of the Life of Morikawa Toen), 1931
Tokyo Art Academy Alumni Association: *Kinkozotetsu,* 1898
Tokyo Meibo Kenshokai (Tokyo Association for Honoring Famous Gravestones): *Zasshi Sotai* (Magazine of Moss Cleanings), date unknown
Ueda, Reikichi: *Shumi no Netsuke* (Netsuke as a Hobby), 1934
Yokoi, Tokifuyu: *Kogeisho* (Crafts and Reflections), 1927

Addenda

Barbanson, Adrienne: *Fables in Ivory,* 1961
Lanfranchi, G. V.: *Il Netsuke, Un' Arte Giapponese,* 1962
Meinertzhagen, Frederick: *The Art of the Netsuke Carver,* 1956
Okada, Yuzuru: *Netsuke, A Miniature Art of Japan,* 1951
Roth, Steg: *Netsuke* (in Swedish and English), 1933
Ryerson, Egerton: *The Netsuke of Japan,* 1958
Tollner, Madeline R.: Netsuke, *The Life and Legend of Japan in Miniature,* 1954
Volker, T: *The Animal in Far Eastern Art,* 1950

Glossary-Index

abacus *(soroban)* netsuke, 66
agate *(meno)* netsuke, 77
ama, see diving girl
amagatsu, see good-luck doll
amber *(kohaku)* netsuke, 77, 145 (Fig. 146)
anabori (cavern carving), 96 (Fig. 96), 110
Anchin (priest of Dojo-ji), 110
Anraku Shukosai, 52 (Fig. 55)
apricot stone *(anzu no tane)* netsuke, 74
Ariomaru, 150 (Fig. 155)
Arts of Japan (Dillon), 203
Asahina Saburo, 184 (Fig. 190)
Asakusa dolls, 114
Ashikaga era, use of netsuke in, 61
Ashinaga (Longlegs), 109
ash-tray *(kurawa)* netsuke, 36 (Fig. 21), 37 (Fig. 24), 56, 66, 76
asobinin (gamblers and drifters), 109
Asuka era, sculpture of, 24
azana (nickname), 213

bakemono (demons and fiends), 47 (Fig. 46), 141 (Fig. 136)
bamboo *(take)* netsuke, 44 (Fig. 38), 77, 151 (Fig. 157), 200 (Fig. 225)
bamboo root *(chikkon)* netsuke, 77, 200 (Fig. 225)
Bambutsu Zukai Isai Gashiki (Isai's Designs for Everything), 108, 203
Bandoyaki netsuke, 76
Banshoku Zuko (Illustrations of Multitudinous Occupations), 108, 203
Basho, 170
Bazan, 128, 134 (Fig. 125)
bearded *sennin,* 139 (Fig. 133); see also *sennin*
Beisai, 130

bekko, see tortoise shell
Bijutsu Chokoku Gafu (Art of Sculpture Illustrated), 108, 203
black coral *(umimatsu)* netsuke, 47 (Fig. 46), 77, 102 (Fig. 108)
black lacquer *(tsuikoku)* netsuke, 77, 188 (Fig. 197)
black persimmon wood *(kurokaki)* netsuke, 74
boar tusk *(inoshishi no kiba)* netsuke, 75, 82 (Fig. 67)
Bokuzan, 127
bone *(hone)* netsuke, 39 (Fig. 30), 77
boxwood *(tsuge)* netsuke, 54 (Fig. 59), 73–74, 126–27
brass wire *(shinchu harigane)* netsuke, 76
Brief Accounts of Visits to Osaka Gravestones, 208
Brockhaus, Albert *(Netsuke),* 203; see also collectors and collections
Buaku mask, 29 (Fig. 5)
Buddhist gong *(mokugyo)* netsuke, 151 (Fig. 157), 162, 195 (Fig. 210)
Bugaku dance, 24 (fn), 137 (Fig. 130)
Bukan Zenshi, 54 (Fig. 59)
"Bumbuku Chagama" (The Miraculous Teakettle), 100 (Fig. 106)
Bunka and Bunsei periods, use of netsuke in, 63, 164
Bunshojo, 129, 140 (Fig. 135)
butterfly dance *(kocho no mai),* 149 (Fig. 153)
byakudan, see sandalwood

camellia wood *(tsubaki)* netsuke, 74
camphorwood *(kusunoki)* netsuke, 74
cane *(to)* netsuke, 38 (Fig. 27), 77, 123
carved dry lacquer *(kanshitsu)* netsuke, 77

carving characteristics of materials, 73–78
carving styles, 74–77, 110, 122, 125–26, 129, 171; see also *anabori, ittobori, Kamakura-bori, Kokusai-bori, saishoku, subori*
cast metal *(imono)* netsuke, 36 (Fig. 21), 76
cavern carving, see *anabori*
cha, see tea wood
Character Sketches of Osaka Citizens, 208
cherry wood *(sakura)* netsuke, 28 (Fig. 3), 74
Chikamasa Shominsai, 171
Chikayuki Fukushima, 114
chikkon, see bamboo root
Chikuden Tanomura, 171
Chiku-unsai, 152 (Fig. 158)
Chinai, 40 (Fig. 31)
Chinese subjects and influences, 62, 169, 201
Chohi, 31 (Fig. 9), 50 (Fig. 52)
Choka, 90 (Fig. 84)
Chokaro Sennin, 194 (Fig. 208)
chokoku (sculptured), 215
Chokwa, *see* Choka
Chokwaro, *see* Chokaro
chomei (carved signature), 213
Chomin, 47 (Fig. 46), 152 (Fig. 159)
chonin (tradesmen), 85 (Fig. 73), 124, 136 (Fig. 129)
Chuichi, 168
Chukyo area, netsuke produced in, 126–29
classification of netsuke, 55–57
cloisonné *(shippoyaki)* netsuke, 66, 80 (Fig. 63)
collectors and collections, 26, 165, 168, 174, 203–4; Baron Go, 204; Brockhaus, 203; Ejima, 204; Fujii, 204; Tokyo Imperial Household Museum, 168, 204; Jonas, 203; LePage, 204; Sasaki, 204; Tanigawa, 204; Taniguchi, 204; Yamaguchi, 204; Yasuda, 204
Complete History of Osaka, 208
copper wire *(dosei harigane)* netsuke, 36 (Fig. 22), 76
coral *(sango)* netsuke, 77, 106 (Fig. 117)
cypress *(hinoki)* netsuke, 73, 74, 109, 119, 125

dagger netsuke, 53 (Fig. 58), 66
Daikoku, 35 (Fig. 19), 71, 79 (Fig. 60)
Daisen, 36 (Fig. 23)

dances portrayed in netsuke, *see* Bugaku dance, butterfly dance, Gigaku dance, lion dance, Noh dance, Okina dance, *shojo* dance
Daruma, 45 (Fig. 40), 87 (Fig. 76), 105 (Fig. 115), 109, 110, 136 (Fig. 128)
Deme family, 110, 114, 118, 162
Deme Joman, 45 (Fig. 41), 114
Deme Saman, 114
Deme Uman, 114, 125
designs and subjects of netsuke, 55–57, 62, 70–71, 107–12, 115–16, 159–62, 169–72, 174; Chinese influences on, 62, 169, 201; limitations on, 107–8; mechanical secrets of, 161; related to poetry, 170; related to ukiyo-e, 171; source books for, 108–9, 119, 125, 169, 203
Dillon, Edward *(Arts of Japan),* 203
diving girl *(ama),* 82 (Fig. 66), 87 (Fig. 77), 133 (Fig. 123), 140 (Fig. 134)
Dohachi Niami, 115
Dojo-ji, 105 (Fig. 116), 110
doll *(ningyo)* netsuke, 56, 114; *see also* Asakusa dolls, good-luck doll, monkey doll, Nara dolls, Noh dolls, Uji dolls
Doraku Anrakusai 51 (Fig. 53), 179 (Fig. 181), 207
Dorakusai, *see* Doraku Anrakusai
Doshaku (Drawings of Saints of Buddhism and Taoism), 169
Dosho Kagei, 101 (Fig. 107), 119, 122, 197 (Fig. 216), 207

ebony *(kokutan)* netsuke, frontispiece (Fig. 1), 74, 185 (Fig. 191)
Echigo district, netsuke produced in, 129–30
Echizen district, netsuke produced in, 129–30
Edo area, netsuke produced in, 124–26
Edo era, *see* Tokugawa era
Ehon Makuzugahara (Picture Book of Makuzugahara), 69
Eisai, 32 (Fig. 13)
Ejima Shojiro, *see* collectors and collections
Enshi, 190 (Fig. 200)
erotic netsuke, 111–12
export of netsuke, 162, 166–68, 172, 174

fables illustrated in netsuke, *see* "Bumbuku Chagama," "Shitakiri Suzume"

Fenollosa, Ernest F., 173
filial piety, see Nijushiko
flint bag *(hiuchi-bukuro)*, 58–59
forgeries, 111, 116, 120, 162, 168; *see also* signatures and seals
fossil wood *(umoregi)* netsuke, 77
fuchi (pommel), frontispiece (Fig. 1), 30 (Fig. 8); *see also* sword furnishings
fuchigashira (pommels), frontispiece (Fig. 1), 30 (Fig. 8), 76; *see also* sword furnishings
Fugen Bosatsu, 195 (Fig. 211)
Fujii Zensuke, *see* collectors and collections
fujimame, see wisteria bean
fujizuru, see wisteria vine
funny-face mask, 25 (fn), 46 (Fig. 43)

Gama (Toad) Sennin, 92 (Fig. 89), 178 (Fig. 178)
Gechu, 179 (Fig. 180)
Gedo mask, 91 (Fig. 87)
Gekkei Matsumura, 171
Genroku period, use of netsuke in, 60, 62, 69
Genryo, 139 (Fig. 133); *see* Minkoku
Gigaku dance, 24–25 (fn)
Gigaku masks, 24–25 (fn), 82 (Fig. 65), 90 (Fig. 84)
gisaku (copy), 215
glass *(garasu)* netsuke, 77
go (art name), 213
go (Japanese checkers), 85 (Fig. 73)
Go, Baron, *see* collectors and collections
gold *(kin)* netsuke, 76
gold bronze *(shakudo)* netsuke, 36 (Fig. 23), 76
gold lacquer *(makie)* netsuke, 131 (Fig. 119), 188 (Fig. 196)
Gonse, Louis *(L'Art Japonais)*, 203
good-luck doll *(amagatsu),* 104 (Fig. 114)
Goto Masayoshi, 96 (Fig. 98)
gourd *(hyotan)* netsuke, 44 (Fig. 37), 59, 60, 61, 77
Gravestone Annals of Famous Families of Naniwa, 208
Gyokkei, 143 (Fig. 140)
Gyokkin Iida, 77, 119, 122, 207
Gyokumin, 178 (Fig. 178)
Gyokusai, 143 (Fig. 141)
Gyokuso, 87 (Fig. 77), 146 (Fig. 148), 149 (Fig. 153), 195 (Fig. 211)

Gyokuyosai, 146 (Fig. 147)
Gyokuzan Asahi, 35 (Fig. 19), 110, 125, 126, 173
Gyuka Kamibayashi, 55 (Fig. 61), 124, 171

haiku (17-syllable poem), influence on netsuke, 170
Hakuryu, 123
Handaka Sonja, 89 (Fig. 82), 192 (Fig. 202)
hanko (stamped seal), see *in*
Hannya (female demon) mask, 24 (fn), 109
Haritsu, *see* Ritsuo
Harumitsu, 151 (Fig. 156)
Hashi-ichi, 115
Hayashi Razan *(Razan Bunshu)*, 60
Heita, 196 (Fig. 214)
Hida district, netsuke of, 129, 130
Hidari Issan, 130, 136 (Fig. 128)
Hidechika, 147 (Fig. 149)
Hidemasa, 147 (Fig. 150), 155 (Fig. 165)
himotoshi (cord holes), 121, 125, 160
hinoki, see cypress
hippopotamus tooth *(kaba no ha)* netsuke, 75
Hiradoyaki netsuke, 76, 92 (Fig. 89), 115
Historical Relics and Monuments of Osaka, 208
hitotsusage (single hanging article), 55
hiuchi-bukuro, see flint bag
hogan (honorary art title), 109, 118
Hohaku Shoju, 123
Ho-ichi, 85 (Fig. 72)
Hojitsu, 97 (Fig. 101), 103 (Fig. 112), 111, 125, 126, 180 (Fig. 182), 209
Hokufu, 130
Hokusai Katsushika *(Banshoku Zuko, Manga)*, 108, 125, 127, 171, 203
Hokusai's *Manga,* see Hokusai Katsushika
hokyo (honorary art title), 118
Hokyu Shoju, 123
Homin, 148 (Fig. 151)
Honcho Seiji Dangi (Discourses on Worldly Affairs), 60
honorary art titles, see *hogan, hokyo, tenka-ichi*
Horaku, 157 (Fig. 168)
Horeki period, use of netsuke in, 62, 113
horn *(tsuno)* netsuke, *see* rhinoceros horn, staghorn, water-buffalo horn
hornbill casque *(hoten),* 40 (Fig. 31), 78, 121, 158 (Fig. 170)

Masahiro, 176 (Fig. 173)
Masakatsu, 179 (Fig. 179)
Masakazu Sawaki, 91 (Fig. 88), 127, 132 (Fig. 120), 207
Masakiyo, 178 (Fig. 176)
Masamitsu, 130
Masanao (of Kyoto), 104 (Fig. 114), 123
Masanao (of Ise), 102 (Fig. 110), 110, 118, 128, 203
Masanao II (of Ise), 94 (Fig. 92)
Masatami, 176 (Fig. 174)
Masatoshi Sawaki, 127, 168, 207
Masatsugu, 44 (Fig. 39); see Kaigyokusai Masatsugu
Masayasu, 43 (Fig. 35)
Masayoshi, 130
Masayuki, 91 (Fig. 87), 180 (Fig. 183)
masks (men), 24, 24–25 (fn), 109; see also Buaku, funny-face, Gedo, Gigaku, Hyottoko, Jo, Kaminari, Kumasaka, Okame (Ofuku), Okina, Otoko, and tengu masks
Matauemon Kishu, 123
materials of netsuke, 73–78; see also specific materials
mei (artist's name), 214
Meibutsu Rokujo (Six Volumes of Noteworthy Objects), 55, 201
Meiji period, use of netsuke in, 164–65, 172
Meikeisai, see Hojitsu
men, see masks
menuki (hilt ornament), 31 (Fig. 9), 76; see also sword furnishings
metal netsuke, 36 (Figs. 21–23), 37 (Fig. 24), 43 (Fig. 35), 66 76, 80 (Fig. 63)
midake (Matsushima bamboo), 77; see also bamboo
Mikawaya Kozaburo, 166–67
Minko, 110, 111, 128, 134 (Fig. 124), 142 (Fig. 138), 170
Minkoku, 139 (Fig. 133), 182 (Fig. 185 and 186)
Mino district, netsuke produced in, 128
"Miraculous Teakettle," see "Bumbuku Chagama"
Mitsuaki, see Ishikawa Komei
Mitsuhiro, 30 (Fig. 6)
Mitsuhiro Ohara, 97 (Fig. 100), 100 (Fig. 106), 110, 119, 122, 204, 207, 208
Mitsumasa Kikuoka, 30 (Fig. 7)
Mitsunaga, 32 (Fig. 12)

Mitsuoki Otsuki, 114
Mitsusada, 183 (Fig. 187)
Mitsutoshi, 183 (Fig. 188)
Miwa, 28 (Fig. 3), 74, 83 (Fig. 68), 84 (Fig. 71), 125
Mokubei, 115
mokugyo, see Buddhist gong
Momoyama era, sculpture of, 24; use of netsuke in, 60–61
Mondo, see Ryukei Tanaka Mondo
monjin (pupil of), 118, 215
monkey doll (saru ningyo), 83 (Fig. 68)
mosha (facsimile signature), 214
Moso, 31 (Fig. 11)
mother-of-pearl (chogai) inlay, 74
Moto-ori Norinaga, 171
Murasada, 95 (Fig. 95)

na (given name), 214
Nagamitsu, 96 (Fig. 96)
Nagato inro, 59; see also inro
Nagato pipe case, 164
namban (southern barbarian), 186 (Fig. 193), 195 (Fig. 209)
nanako (fish-roe) ground, 30 (Fig. 7)
Naotsugu, 197 (Fig. 217)
Nara district, netsuke produced in, 123
Nara dolls (Nara ningyo), 39 (Fig. 29), 123, 129, 171
Nara era, sculpture of, 23–24, 25, 26
Nara ningyo, see Nara dolls
Narihira, 30 (Fig. 8)
narwhal tusk (ikkaku) netsuke, 64–65, 75
natsume, see jujube
Natsuo, 31 (Fig. 10)
negoro lacquer netsuke, 77, 159 (Fig. 172); see also lacquer netsuke
netsuke, artistic level of, 26, 62, 113, 115–16, 168, 172; carvers, 113–18, see also netsuke artists; carving styles, 74–77, 110, 122, 125–26, 129, 171; Chinese subjects and influences 62, 171, 201; classification of, 55–57; collectors and collections, 26, 165, 168, 174, 203–4; decline of, 164–65; designs and subjects, 55–57, 62, 70–71. 107–12, 115–16, 159–62, 169–72, 174; determining age of, 61, 162–63; distinguished from okimono, 159–60; export of, 162, 166–68, 172, 174; foreign interest in, 26, 165, 166–68, 172, 174, 203–4; ignored in Japan, 26,

yatate (writing-brush container) netsuke, 66, 80 (Fig. 62), 110
Yeisai, *see* Eisai
yellow pearl shell *(kigai)* inlay, 41 (Fig. 32), 78, 121
yew wood *(ichii)* netsuke, 74, 127, 129, 130
Yokoya, *see* Somin Yokoya
yomyo (childhood name), 214
Yoritomo period, use of netsuke in, 59
Yoritomo-style netsuke, 59
Yoshimasa, 187 (Fig. 194)

Yoshinaga, 102 (Fig. 109), 123, 200 (Fig. 224)
Yoshu Kotetsu, 94 (Fig. 93)
Yoyusai, 115
Yukoku, 82 (Fig. 66)
Yurin, 200 (Fig. 225)

Zelkova wood *(tsuki)* netsuke, 74
Zeshin, 115, 188 (Fig. 197)
Zokoku, 129
Zoroku, 115, 123